Metaversed

Luis Bravo Martins
Samantha G. Wolfe

WILEY

Published by John Wiley & Sons, Inc., Hoboken, New Jersey.
Published simultaneously in Canada and the United Kingdom.

ISBN: 978-1-119-88858-1
ISBN: 978-1-119-88859-8 (ebk.)
ISBN: 978-1-119-88860-4 (ebk.)

For general information on our other products and services or for technical support, please contact our Customer Care Department within the United States at (800) 762-2974, outside the United States at (317) 572-3993 or fax (317) 572-4002.

If you believe you've found a mistake in this book, please bring it to our attention by emailing our reader support team at wileysupport@wiley.com with the subject line "Possible Book Errata Submission."

Wiley also publishes its books in a variety of electronic formats. Some content that appears in print may not be available in electronic formats. For more information about Wiley products, visit our web site at www.wiley.com.

Library of Congress Control Number: 2022941854

Cover images: © Aliaksandr Marko/Adobe Stock Photos, © michalsanca/Adobe Stock Photos
Cover design: Wiley

SKY10040065_121522

To everyone I have worked with for years but never met physically—including my co-author.
To my masters in life, José Manuel Rodrigues da Silva, Catarina, and Miguel, who are always with me.
To Domingos, Munir, and Bruno for believing when belief was necessary.
To René Artois, cat extraordinaire and longtime companion of so many fights. Rest in peace, old friend.

— Luis

To Luis. You are amazing. Period. End of sentence.
To those who have supported and cheered me on every day, especially Maddy, Owen, and Katherine.
To Christy, Henry, Heidi, Michi, and the team at Climbing Wolf. Thanks for always being there.
To those who have been my mentors, supporters, speakers, contributors, and friends since the day I put on my first headset. You have meant more to me than you'll ever know.
To the innovative developers creating the metaverse. This is for you. Let's do this.

— Sam

About the Authors

Luis Bravo Martins is chief marketing officer at KIT-AR, a start-up enabling augmented workers in manufacturing companies. He started working on an e-commerce venture during the `dot.com` bubble and witnessed firsthand how the Internet's unknown forces could reshape human history. Fifteen+ years after, Luis realized we're now in for a much bigger change than the Internet. He writes, speaks, and creates awareness through communities like the VR/AR Association, Techstars, and XRSI.

Samantha G. Wolfe is the founder of PitchFWD, a strategic consultancy focused on accelerating the adoption of emerging technologies. An author, judge, presenter, and subject matter expert, Sam is known for her infectious enthusiasm, insightful talks and panels, incredible network, and inspirational mentorship. She is an adjunct professor at New York University's Steinhardt School teaching "The Business of Virtual Reality and Augmented Reality," "The Marketing of Innovation," and "Avatars and Virtual Humans," all courses she created and developed. Sam received her MBA at NYU's Stern

School of Business and a BA at Yale University. For more information, please visit samanthagwolfe.com or follow her on Twitter at @samanthagwolfe and LinkedIn at /samanthawolfe.

Contents

Acknowledgments

Major thanks to Nigel Wyatt for creating the opportunity, and to our team at Wiley—Jim Minatel, Melissa Burlock, Pete Gaughan, Patrick Walsh, and Barath Kumar Rajasekaran—for the trust and patience throughout this process.

Thanks to all the experts who took the time to contribute their unique insights to this book. Martina Welkhoff and Amy LaMeyer, for your preface and words of encouragement. Thanks to the inspiring members of our amazing metaverse ecosystem who contributed quotes to the book, namely (in alphabetical order): Alan Smithson, Alex Coulombe, Alina Kadblusky, Alon Grinshpoon, Amber Osbourne, Andres Leon-Geyer, Angeli Gianchandani, Anne Ahola Ward, Antonia Forester, Antony Vitillo, Ash Richter, Ben Erwin, Brandon Powers, Brendan Bradley, Carla Gannis, Christina Heller, Cortney Harding, Christy Seville, Chris Valentine, Danilo Castro, David Parisi, Elena Piech, Emily Olman, Gonçalo Prata, Henry Keyser, James Watson, Jan Pflueger, Jason Chung, Jason

McDowell, Jesse Alton, Jimmy Vainstein, Joanna Popper, Juliana Loh, Katie Hudson, Kavya Pearlman, Keisha Howard, Kiira Benzing, Linda Jacobson, Manuel Oliveira, Marco Magnano, Mariia Tintul, Marisa Borsboom, Mark Sage, Nuno Folhadela, Mike Pell, Rafael Pavon, Regine Gilbert, Richard Ward, Robin White Owen, Sammy Popat, Sarah Hill, Sonya Haskins, Susan Persky, Susanna Pollock, Tupac Martir, Valentino Megale, Veronica Costa Orvalho, Vince Kadlubek, and Unai Extremo.

Foreword

Like the authors of this book, we have been working in the space that is now called the metaverse long before that term was popularly used. The term was coined by Neal Stephenson back in the '90s, but only entered the common lexicon recently as it was adopted in corporate circles (one large tech company in particular) to describe a vision for the future of computing and our relationship with technology.

We were both drawn into the space not long after Facebook acquired Oculus and early consumer headsets started to enter the market. After first putting on a headset, we saw the potential for this infinite, immersive digital landscape to transform everything we knew about user experience. The opportunity for technical innovation was obvious, and we also saw an opportunity to innovate on the foundational culture and norms of the industry itself, which is why we started the WXR Fund to invest in women-led companies in the space.

Within hours of announcing our plans for WXR in 2017, we had hundreds of people from all over the industry sign on to support the effort. Talented executives, engineers, creators, and founders raised their hands to be mentors. Several industry luminaries ultimately committed as investors. Soon thereafter, we launched an accelerator program, from which 26 women-led companies graduated in 2018–2019. In late 2019, we began investing in start-ups, many of which are now squarely positioned to take advantage of the tailwinds the metaverse craze has created.

The metaverse is more than hype, yet not easy to explain. In this book, the authors skillfully define a term that is evolving and demonstrate how it is relevant to business professionals across all verticals. All major tech companies have products and R&D efforts in this area—from the newly renamed Meta to Tencent to Verizon. The book clearly details similarities and differences to the Internet age, including tips to apply this knowledge to a forward-thinking strategy.

These are pivotal times as we move into a world where digital and physical realities become more integrated, and 3-dimensional computing gives us skills that 2-dimensional computing could not. With technical advances in wearables, children born today will ask us why we used to use screens. *Metaversed* outlines the opportunities that exist today and the possibilities of the future across all sectors and then highlights specific areas of current adoption. The authors clarify how the metaverse is different from technologies commonly used today and give tangible examples of how to engage and grow.

The necessity to be physically distant due to the global pandemic has been a catalyst for growth in metaverse-related start-ups as people and businesses look for better ways to connect and do business virtually. Also, within the context of emerging technology, now is a rare opportunity to build a more inclusive foundation for the next wave of computing.

This book covers not only the opportunities of the metaverse, but also how to navigate the challenges faced by this new wave of computing. It encourages all of us to consider these factors as the uses for the metaverse continue to emerge.

As experts in the field, Sam Wolfe and Luis Martins are the perfect guides to make the metaverse accessible and relatable. They gracefully explain the different emerging technologies involved in realizing spatial computing, and how that can be applied across many sectors in a variety of ways.

Enjoy the read. If you see our avatars in the metaverse, say hello!

Martina Welkhoff and Amy LaMeyer

Managing Partners, WXR Fund

Part 1
Get Ready

Chapter 1
Predictions

[A]ll information looks like noise until you break the code.
—Neal Stephenson, Snow Crash

The metaverse. Do you know what it is? Can you describe it? If anyone tells you that they can, at least within the next few years, they don't really know. Well, they might throw in an educated guess, but they don't *know* know. They might be basing their answer on what they read online, the history of technology, maybe on references in books, movies, or TV shows. Some might have a deep awareness of what's possible now with emerging technologies and may offer a good guess as to what's ahead. But it will always fall short, as technological developments and ramifications are many, and we're still in the early days of exploring them.

Mark Zuckerberg mentioned the word *metaverse* over 80 times in his Facebook Connect introduction speech on October 28, 2021. That one talk sparked a frenzy of discussion by the financial press around the definition of the metaverse. For those working with emerging tech and blockchain communities, this public acknowledgment of the topic's importance felt like validation of their vision and years of work, ourselves included.

Mainstream excitement was (finally) building around this technological vision of the future. Even though the biggest tech companies—like Apple, Snap, Niantic, and Alphabet—had been investing billions in creating it, the sparkling hype generated by this speech created the sensation that the metaverse seemingly matured overnight and (finally) seemed within reach, even if many weren't thrilled about Facebook taking public ownership of the word *meta*.

Yet still, that moment marked only one inflection point in an uncharted, new path ahead. But that was just Meta's vision of the metaverse. Other companies joined in the conversation with their particular take on the next wave of computing. But how can businesses prepare for it if it isn't consensually defined? How can we understand the opportunities and threats we will face? Some say that hindsight is 20/20; it feels like we all need some 20/20 foresight during this time of transition.

Think of it like the Internet. Could you have explained it to a modern-day Rip Van Winkle (the fictional legend who slept for 20 years and awoke to find his world had changed)? It's hard to do in layman's terms, unless you start talking about how you would use it and how it could help in your day-to-day life. Maybe two decades ago, you'd start by describing the kind of access and benefits email and texting gives you, or all the information you were able to find in less than a second. That said, who could have predicted how it birthed smartphones? Game worlds where players are constantly connected and interacting? What about the cloud and social media? Or even the current debates around privacy and truth?

This lack of understanding of a game-shifting technology's impact isn't new. It's happened several times and looking back to the 1990s, it also happened with the Internet. The leading TV morning show in the United States during 1994 was *The Today Show*. On one of the episodes, Bryant Gumbel, one of the hosts, asked, "What is the Internet, anyway?" His cohost then requests from the off-camera producer, "Allison, can you explain what the Internet is?" The answer is bungled as they try to name the @ symbol, calling it "about" or "around," and talk about how it's a "massive computer network."[1] This TV moment has gone viral multiple times as some generations seem to laugh at people being awkward in front of new technology. It's almost an "OK, Boomer" meme in a TV clip.

The metaverse is a similar shift, only this time we're taking the Internet, bringing another dimension to it and setting it free in and on our physical world. Through several channels, we'll be living with digital and physical and sometimes hybrid elements simultaneously. It's almost impossible today to understand the full extent of this shift. We can start by identifying how technologies will interweave to create it. Also, now that we've witnessed the negative impact of social media, we need to determine how to mitigate the risks and challenges of bringing more technology to our businesses and to our lives.

For instance, if we want to go from digital screens to digital worlds that we are able to explore, then we'll need to consider moving from formats like text, images, and video into three-dimensional formats. It makes sense to use virtual reality (VR) and augmented reality (AR) technologies to view the metaverse, but not everyone is familiar with or comfortable using them yet. And what needs to happen with the current mobile Internet access so it grants users a metaverse experience?

It's not smooth sailing to begin any technology shift. Emerging technologies can make people uncomfortable, because any change causes discomfort. However, if users are convinced of the importance of the tech, they are willing to try to adapt. Just like on *The Today Show*, there was a similar verbal bungling of the description of metaverse right after Zuckerberg's speech at Facebook Connect. On CNBC's show *Squawk on the Street*, cohost and market pundit Jim Cramer attempted unsuccessfully to explain the metaverse. Note that Cramer's quote has been edited for clarity.

> [It's] the idea that . . . you can be in Oculus, whatever . . . It IS a hologram. . . . And . . . the typical way is to be able to sell something. Like what I said with . . . Unity, where you're looking at, what people are walking and you're looking at how people look and you're saying, you know what? I, and then you imagine yourself with it and you say, I went, you know, that's what size is that? And then . . . you press, you order . . . . There you go. Metaverse.[2]

As in 1994, a new technological shift is about to change everything yet again, but few are able to grasp the concept and even within the emerging tech industry, there isn't a consensus about what it is, its value, and how it will impact business and our personal lives, especially as the metaverse (or whatever we might call it in a couple years' time) is just being built. One thing we can all agree on is that no one who missed the last wave of computing wants to underestimate the upcoming's impact.

These are the challenges that we will address in this book. We will bring together the research, opinions of experts, numbers, and our own insights to get everyone as ready as we could ever be. We'll cover not only all the immediate opportunities, but also reflect on what's possible and on the needs and problems the metaverse can solve, as well as approach the concrete challenges ahead from a professional standpoint, as well as from a societal perspective.

Size Matters

First things first. How big will this metaverse be? Will it change your life and your business? Or is it just hype? It's believed that the metaverse can become bigger than the Internet, as theoretically it's a network that will connect every object, place, and person on the planet with almost all people, businesses, and organizations. . . eventually.

The continuous convergence of emerging technologies will bring additional utility and types of experiences that we can't yet fathom (the same way social media, messages, home banking, and so many other services keep on converging on our smartphone). The estimated size of the metaverse varies wildly, according to the reference we choose:

- $800 billion global market opportunity in 2024 (Bloomberg[3])
- Over $1 trillion in yearly revenues across "every sector" (JPMorgan[4])
- $8.3 trillion total U.S. consumer expenditure (Morgan Stanley[5])
- $8–$13 trillion total addressable market by 2030 (Citi[6])

So, it's more than fair to say the metaverse is greater than a trillion-dollar opportunity. That estimate alone puts it somewhere within the top 10 industries.[7] A market that is worth investing in and following, even if we can't quite define it unanimously. But don't worry, we will go into the specific business applications in a later chapter. For now, let's accept that the metaverse can become by itself a top 10 market and has the potential to impact every industry globally—maybe even more than the Internet and mobile computing transformed the way each of us does business around the world.

The Debate

There are many contradicting definitions of the metaverse. The simplest descriptions we found were "the next generation of the Internet" or "infinite worlds that connect the physical with the digital." Although seemingly easy to use in conversation, they are confusing to those who just have started to understand that technologies like AR and artificial intelligence (AI) are different in many more ways than one letter in their acronyms.

Other tech pundits use the term *Web3* to define the metaverse, focusing the discussion purely on the decentralized web and its model of governance, its blockchain, cryptocurrencies, and nonfungible tokens (NFTs). We'll get more into those in the following chapter, and how they are part of, but not all of, what we foresee as the metaverse. Still more people confuse it with Microsoft's term *mixed reality (MR)*, referring to a universe lying somewhere between VR and AR. Finally there's also those who mistakenly interchange the word with the Marvel Multiverse.

Although each definition of the metaverse has varying amounts of accuracy, none of them does justice to the promise of a new shared, 3D hybrid user experience that's so much more than the feeling of "presence" (which was probably the second most used term during Zuckerberg's October 28, 2021 keynote). Case in point, from his letter to investors after the rebrand: "The defining quality of the metaverse will be a feeling of presence, like you are right there with another person or in another place. Feeling truly present with another person is the ultimate dream of social technology. That is why we are focused on building this."

Working Definition

To the authors, the metaverse is the next stage of the Internet and results from the evolution of a wide variety of emerging, exponential technologies maturing simultaneously, converging and enabling a new interconnected relationship between physical and digital. This long list includes VR, AR, 5G, cloud computing, Internet of Things (IoT), haptics, cryptocurrencies, blockchain, AI, machine learning, object recognition, computer vision, and conversational AI. This wave of new technologies will enable a full digitalization of the physical universe and a seamless symbiosis with all things digital, creating a new interactive dimension merged with our physical one. Makes sense? It's OK if it doesn't for now.

The current standard 2D imagery will be joined by 3D interactive elements. Instead of just using a computer screen or tablet for interactions with the Internet (2D), we will browse digital objects and environments that appear three-dimensional (3D). This means your interaction commands won't be limited to taps on your smartphone's screen (2D) or voice commands. Through glasses or headsets that understand your physical surroundings and track your location, as well as your eye movement and hand gestures, you'll be able to walk around 3D digital elements that you will see overlaid on top of the real world and that can be seen by other users, if you choose to. From this, you could navigate to a virtual world, which would occlude your eyesight and immerse you in VR.

If this is still hard to imagine, let's use a movie reference. The goal is to enable everyone to have a version of Iron Man/Tony Stark's and Spiderman/Peter Parker's E.D.I.T.H. glasses, which will act like high-powered VR/AR glasses. The *Star Trek* holodeck and

Star Wars holochess are also good fictional references for immersive technologies—in each case, the characters unlocked a new graphical experience of the real world.

We'll start to move from a primarily heads-down (mobile phone) experience to a heads-up (glasses) one. We will move from a sit-down interaction to a walk-around one. We won't be relying on computers or tablets nearly as much, or at all. We will be increasingly wearing our metaverse access technology and it will increasingly become a seamless part of our everyday lives.

Forecasts and Theories

"For a long time now, the line between 'real' life and 'digital' life has been blurring," says Martina Welkhoff of the WXR Fund. "The metaverse is a further realization of that trend."[8] This foundational transformative shift due to technology innovation has been forecast for the past 5–10 years, although the individual technologies started their development way before that.

In 2016, the concept of the Fourth Industrial Revolution was introduced at the World Economic Forum (WEF) by Klaus Schwab, the executive director of the WEF at the time. He outlined how the current amount of technology would again shift our world, in the same way that the Third (the digital computer revolution), the Second (technological revolution with railroads and telegraphs), and the First (with the introduction of steam and water power) have.

Schwab shared a very powerful statement:

> We stand on the brink of a technological revolution that will fundamentally alter the way we live, work, and relate to one another. In its scale, scope, and complexity, the transformation will be unlike anything humankind has experienced before. We do not yet know just how it will unfold, but one thing is clear: the response to it must be integrated and comprehensive, involving all stakeholders of the global policy, from the public and private sectors to academia and civil society.[9]

This came to be known as Industry 4.0 and, as you can see, it calls for the involvement of all stakeholders to collectively respond to the expected social effects it could bring. This triggered a rise in corporate social responsibility and there was even a shared statement signed by 181 North American CEOs in 2019 committing to that mindset.[10]

Other theories explored this upcoming shift in business and its impacts on our life. The Sixth Wave of Innovation stated that companies needed sustainable business practices in order to survive and that the most likely way to accomplish this was through the use of technological processes such as digitalization, automation, and robotics.

Discussions of the coming metaverse often refer to speed and processing power of computers doubling every two years (Moore's Law) and the increase in power of networked elements (Metcalfe's Law). This is the law behind the term *network effects*, an oft-used buzzword in Silicon Valley that dictates a system's value increases based on the number of people using it. The metaverse offers the potential for a super-network effect, unlike what we have seen before.

This uber-network resembles the Internet of Everything (IoE), a research concept that aims to seamlessly interconnect a massive number of worldwide sensors, objects, animals, people, processes, and data through the Internet. Smaller items like doorknobs and tiles will share information about your house's inside and outside conditions; bracelets and other wearables will analyze the healthiest diet for that day. Satellites will not only map and survey geographical areas, but they'll be connected with city equipment and services, allowing citizens to sync with online services.

Trends

It's not only a technological evolution that is driving the creation of the metaverse. This transition is taking place against a backdrop featuring multiple and simultaneously developing, but fundamentally distinct, social trends:

Remote School and Work In the past few years, the pandemic accelerated the adoption of new remote work solutions.

Great swaths of people began to socialize in purely digital spaces. Work, learning, and entertainment experiences became remote. The force of circumstances led us to normalize a behavior that would otherwise take years to disseminate and be adopted. As Andy Liu of Unlock Venture Partners told GeekWire: "[The] worldwide pandemic has really changed and advanced people's perceptions on how work, study, commerce, and life in general can be done in a compelling digital/hybrid format."[11] This ongoing trend toward hybrid interactions began with the launch of the Internet, then email, and most recently, social media and smartphones.

Social Media Economy   Social media as we know it began in 1997 when the Six Degrees platform launched. It grew to almost one million users before it ceased operations, but not before convincing tech companies that there were business opportunities to be leveraged by connecting people on the Internet on public platforms. Next followed Friendster, LinkedIn, and Facebook. With advancements in server processing power, mobile message formats shifted from plain-text messages, to being illustrated by photos and videos, to becoming photos and videos. This led to the appearance of new platforms like Instagram, Pinterest, YouTube, and, afterward, Snapchat and TikTok. Entering our current decade, 3D formats are changing our digital interactions. Games like Minecraft, Roblox, and Fortnite are main stages, but social media filters are also decorating our faces during video calls. As 3D technology improves, our avatars and digital humans will also start playing a central role in social networks and on virtual and augmented reality platforms.

Creator Economy   In early 2022, "the creator economy" was all the rage. Like the gig economy, which had its momentum a decade before, the creator economy movement was essentially carved out of social media. At first, social media timelines were filled with cat videos and pictures of your meals. But as users spent more time and became more and more sophisticated, so did content creators, which started to attract millions of followers. That led to the rise of semi-professional and professional writers, artists, actors, or video producers and a whole generation that now considers being an *influencer* or a *YouTuber* a potential career path. In fact, in 2019, *Business Insider* found that U.S. and UK children ages 5–12 chose being a YouTuber as a top career choice, over being a musician, athlete, or astronaut.[12]

According to SignalFire, there were 50 million creators in 2021, among TikTokers, YouTube video producers, Instagram influencers, Twitch streamers, Spotify musicians, Teachable trainers, and GitHub-sponsored developers and podcasters who published their original content to their subscribers. There are also AR filter creators, 3D designers, and NFT artists are carving out their space as the creator economy grows toward the metaverse.

Decentralization   In recent years there has been a growing distrust of central governments, political parties, and corporate tech by millennials and Gen Z. Radical and populist political options started raking in an increasing number of followers searching for solutions to today's social, economic, and climate challenges. A movement started to create a new decentralized governance model for the web, reclaiming that all content done inside web platforms, namely the ones in Big Tech companies, should become decentralized. First we saw a financial decentralization with the rise of Bitcoin, other cryptocurrencies and other decentralized finance services; afterwards new decentralized business organizations like DAOs (decentralized autonomous organizations) appeared and Web3 communities—and enthusiast numbers keep on growing. We will see during the book how these trends play out in a bit more detail.

Characteristics

In spite of these glimpses and forecasts, we still need to find—or better yet, outline—a set of characteristics of the metaverse, so we can focus the discussion and planning.

It starts with a distinction between the benefits from each individual technology versus from their convergence. So it won't be just $1 + 1 = 3$. It will be an iterative $1 + 1 + 1 + 1$ and so on, as multiple layers of each technology bring in their own traits and features to weave into the mix. And that's why it's so hard to envision such a growingly complex ecosystem.

Some consistent characteristics are already present though, of which we selected the following ones that we see as unavoidable:

Phygital Interactivity   There's a belief there will be a digital twin of each person, place, and object and that these twins will be able to sync with the many digital worlds and layers available. This allows for an actual merge between everything physical and everything digital—an immense digital twin of the entire physical world assets allows these assets to prolong their existence and characteristics digitally and even to create hybrid elements, that are half-physical and half-digital. This reality continuity is what enables new, transformative services.

This creates a digital and physical connection (aka "phygital"), which is often discussed as one of the greatest values of the metaverse. (Yes, the name doesn't quite roll off the tongue.) Data and relevant information will be available on location according to your needs (for example, a construction worker and a historian likely would retrieve different details about a building). These digital twins of the world allow for elements to interchange between realities such as interactive digital people or creatures (like avatars or virtual assistants), fully digital places based on physical venues or objects (such as 3D graphically designed tools or art pieces). Activating equipment such as machines or cameras in the physical world could be done by pressing a button on a virtual one and the other way around too.

A Persistent Universe   The metaverse doesn't go away when you take off your headset. A digital twin of the world—along with a plethora of virtual ones—will be available to all of us whenever we want. Like the World Wide Web, these worlds will be persistently available and in motion even when a user is offline. However, that doesn't mean the metaverse won't stop working for users during that time. For example, your wearable's predictive algorithms will leverage your historical data and past behavior to create a balanced diet and exercise plan, in order to improve your day-to-day life.

Your closet will remind you of your upcoming meetings. Your car will know that you have a doctor's appointment and set your journey accordingly. Your glasses will remember the person whose name you always seem to forget. Your identity, your data, and your custom toolkit of personal and professional assets will be available to you 24/7, wherever you are. All there when you pick up your metaverse glasses again.

Interconnected and Interoperable   The vision of an open metaverse, similar to the World Wide Web, is one where users can easily move around without logging in and out and putting on new headsets or downloading new software. It's a place where you manage your digital currency and properties through a single channel, like the way a crypto wallet works. It is a vision shared by many experts, but not necessarily by Big Tech corporations, which nowadays base their businesses on gathering and analyzing external data present in platforms and content. They want to rule over as much of the metaverse as they can. But connecting all people, objects, and places is a daunting task. Even Big Tech companies publicly acknowledge that they can't do it alone. Elisa La Cava of Madrona Venture Group has analyzed the large number of companies and technologies involved in creating it: "No one company will be able to tackle everything by itself, and that gap is what creates opportunity for innovation and startups to excel and grow over time."[13]

Contextual   Allowing our avatars, digital and physical items, private and public services to become available across a possibly infinite number of worlds is a process we still don't know how will happen. And remember, we all want the user experience to be as intuitive as possible and that information changes according to the context we're in. We all should be able to share digital goods, experiences, and even your very own custom world with friends, family, or coworkers, and it could be customized for each relationship.

Decentralized   Blockchain is considered by several pundits to be one of the fundamental technologies that will enable the metaverse. Its promises of a new governance model enable a shared property of the metaverse by the users, where they can own stakes and establish contracts in a quicker and more transparent way. Again, no one believes that large corporations investing billions and national governments will just hand over the reins. Still, there are already levels of decentralization in place in several services and some decentralized market pockets showing that decentralized services are sought and can be a solution.

Community-Based Several visions of the metaverse foresee it as being driven by users, by all of us. Whether or not this proves to be true, the metaverse brings users more tools to connect among themselves and collect funds for causes and act on their behalf collectively. Indeed, these communities will empower their users to transcend their original role as they become owners, investors, and the drivers of the metaverse economy.

Gamified Online games are evolving into social spaces. Gamers are used to interacting online with a large number of users in real time, carefully selecting and customizing their avatars and selecting the best digital items and fashion that reflects their identity or in-game achievements. The metaverse allows for a similar experience to be extended to every digital world, as well as to the physical one, and play to earn and other gaming dynamics open new ways for consumers to engage with brands and volunteers to engage with causes.

Immediate Gone are the times of lengthy downloads. *Real time* will be the operative words, as there's almost no latency in the metaverse. 3D, data, and interactivity opportunities will be at your disposal right away when you need them. So, no technical delays or frustration can occur while billions jack into the metaverse simultaneously.

Plan Ahead

So yes, the metaverse does not exist yet. How can you understand the metaverse without experiencing it? For now, it's about learning about the vision and where we are today, as we are currently setting the stepping stones toward it. Add also the multiple technological building blocks, analyze their individual impacts, and then realize how leaders in the field have begun to set the infrastructure and integrate these technologies. You need to be aware of each of the 1s of the $1 + 1 + 1 + 1 + 1$, even if the collective sum of the metaverse will be more than its parts.

The metaverse won't be perfect, and, given the high expectations and degree of challenges, topics like safety, privacy, interoperability will need to be handled. According to CNET's Scott Stein, "Everyone's promising interoperability, but history suggests it will be multiplatform, semi-compatible and half- broken,"[14]

However, the fact that the metaverse is not built yet presents a unique opportunity. For the first time in history, we have a chance to discuss a massive game-changing technology and socially disrupting platform prior to the fact. No one asked us how social media, search engines, or the World Wide Web itself could be designed in the easiest, safest way—and truth be told, we never thought how much we needed that until things went wrong.

Now, within a relatively short period of time, we know the benefits and drawbacks that come with such a disruptive tech shift. That's one of the main reasons why it's so important to understand the metaverse and widen the discussion outside of just the tech industry. Together, we can create a more inclusive blueprint for the metaverse. Moreover, the challenges we're about to face will need a multidisciplinary effort. Business professionals from all areas, teachers, lawyers, scientists, historians, and sociologists, everyone can contribute with their experience and knowledge so we can start preparing for this tremendous shift.

We don't know yet whether this metaverse will change our lives over time or if it will happen overnight—and how much of an impact we will feel in our personal and professional lives. Will it be a disruption, an evolution, or a refoundation of the existing stage of the mobile Internet? No matter what, we'll need to learn how to live in this hybrid world and make the most out of it.

As you continue reading this book, we will attempt to pass on the awareness of what's coming and avoid falling behind. We won't teach you how to code, but you will be able to have a business meeting with metaverse specialists and make your decisions in a more informed way. So, in that Rip Van Winkle situation, you won't be a business owner dismissing the Internet and not investing in a company website. Instead, the following chapters will support you to know better what's at stake, the building blocks of the metaverse, envision opportunities for your company's growth and professional advancement. We'll also cut through the hype and lay out the challenges ahead in the clearest way possible. A transformation this size comes with a lot of responsibility and, because of that, we'll cover topics like safety, privacy, and, regulations—all of this to ensure that you, your business, your family, and yourself can take full advantage of this seismic shift.

Notes

1. "'What is internet?' Katie Couric, Bryant Gumbel are puzzled." *Today*, June 20, 2019. www.today.com/video/-what-is-internet-katie-couric-bryant-gumbel-are-puzzled-62308421624

2. CNBC, "Jim Cramer explains the 'metaverse' and what it means for Facebook." *Squawk on the Street*, July 29, 2021. www.cnbc.com/video/2021/07/29/jim-cramer-explains-the-metaverse-and-what-it-means-for-facebook.html

3. Matthew Kanterman and Nathan Naidu, "Metaverse may be $800 billion market, next tech platform." *Bloomberg Intelligence* (blog), *Bloomberg Professional Services*, December 1, 2021. www.bloomberg.com/professional/blog/metaverse-may-be-800-billion-market-next-tech-platform

4. Christine May and Adit Gadgil, *Opportunities in the metaverse*, (JPMorgan Chase, 2022). www.jpmorgan.com/content/dam/jpm/treasury-services/documents/opportunities-in-the-metaverse.pdf

5. Morgan Stanley Research, "Metaverse: more evolutionary than revolutionary?" *Morganstanley.com*, February 23, 2022. www.morganstanley.com/ideas/metaverse-investing

6. Kathleen Boyle, "Metaverse and money: Decrypting the future." *City GPS: Global Perspectives and Solutions*, March, 2022. https://ir.citi.com/gps/x5%2BFQJT3BoHXVu9MsqVRoMdiws3RhL4yhF6Fr8us8oHaOe1W9smOy1%2B8aaAgT3SPuQVtwC5B2%2Fc%3D

7. Trish Novicio, "5 biggest industries in the world." *Lists - News* (blog), *Insider Monkey*, March 24, 2021. www.insidermonkey.com/blog/5-biggest-industries-in-the-world-in-2021-925230/5

8. John Cook, "We asked seven venture capitalists if the metaverse is the next big thing or just a lot of hype." *GeekWire*, November 23, 2021. www.geekwire.com/2021/we-asked-seven-venture-capitalists-if-the-metaverse-is-the-next-big-thing-or-just-a-lot-of-hype

9. Klaus Schwab, "The Fourth Industrial Revolution: what it means, how to respond." *World Economic Forum Global Agenda*, January 14, 2016. www.weforum.org/agenda/2016/01/the-fourth-industrial-revolution-what-it-means-and-how-to-respond

10. Business Roundtable, "Business roundtable redefines the purpose of a corporation to promote 'an economy that serves all Americans.'" *Business Roundtable*, August 19, 2019. www.businessroundtable.org/business-roundtable-redefines-the-purpose-of-a-corporation-to-promote-an-economy-that-serves-all-americans

11. John Cook, "We asked seven venture capitalists if the metaverse is the next big thing or just a lot of hype." *GeekWire*, November 23, 2021. www.geekwire.com/2021/we-asked-seven-venture-capitalists-if-the-metaverse-is-the-next-big-thing-or-just-a-lot-of-hype

12. Paige Leskin, "American kids want to be famous on YouTube, and kids in China want to go to space: survey." *Business Insider*, July 17, 2019. www.businessinsider.com/american-kids-youtube-star-astronauts-survey-2019-7

13. John Cook, "We asked seven venture capitalists if the metaverse is the next big thing or just a lot of hype." *GeekWire*, November 23, 2021. www.geekwire.com/2021/we-asked-seven-venture-capitalists-if-the-metaverse-is-the-next-big-thing-or-just-a-lot-of-hype

14. Brian Cooley, "The metaverse isn't what you think it is, because we don't know what it is." *CNET*, January 2, 2022. www.cnet.com/tech/computing/the-metaverse-isnt-what-you-think-it-is-because-we-dont-know-what-it-is

Part 2

Understanding

Chapter 2
Technologies

Cyberspace. A consensual hallucination experienced daily by billions of legitimate operators, in every nation.
—William Gibson, Neuromancer

A large number of technologies are involved in creating the metaverse. Among the most important, consider technologies that allow seeing and mapping the world, the ones that calculate relative distances and adjust perspectives in real time, ones that integrate different services together, and others that manage real time data updates. These technologies are today coming together, connecting and converging to allow persistent and synchronous 3D virtual worlds for all of us. These are the building blocks of the metaverse.

When you're in the metaverse, you won't see any of these technologies the same way when you start up apps on your smartphone—you will just experience them.

Web3

To begin, let's set the basic concepts straight and separate Internet from web. These two are often confused. For the former, we're referring to the telecommunications infrastructure that connects computers in the biggest network of all time. It is all about connecting machines. The World Wide Web is much more about connecting humans and refers specifically to the largest information network available on the Internet. We can navigate it thanks to a novelty created in 1989 by scientist Tim Berners-Lee: the link. Suddenly, we could place a mouse cursor over a blue, underlined word or an image to be directed to another page of information.

Berners-Lee created the first web version when he decided to exchange information from his employer organization, CERN (stands for the European Organization for Nuclear Research), with other scientists and universities. He created the first web server in 1990, a computer that continuously connected to the Internet and enabled outside users to access its files, like the world's first website. That site is still live at info.cern.ch. By 1994 there were already 10,000 websites available, which ultimately became known as Web 1.0.[1]

This first version of the web was essentially read only. Sites on the information superhighway existed to convey just that— information—and users mainly interacted by sending out messages via email software clients or forms. Don't forget, we're talking about a network created by scientists and researchers, so it's only natural they also accounted for the largest number of web users at that time. There wasn't a social community as we know it in the 21st century in the same way, with e-commerce stores or online marketplaces. Of course, there were a few advertisement formats available, but they were in the very early stages of development.[2]

In 1999, the web started moving beyond this read-only version and the distinction became clear when the Web 2.0 concept appeared in 2004. Social media and search engines suddenly allowed us not only to read web content, but to become creators or curators as well. Everyone gained the power to push a button and publish texts, photos, videos, and what we today define as user-generated content (UGC) to an audience of millions, who could like, share, and comment on each post.[3]

This unparalleled reach at our fingertips brought in the advertising business as we know it today. Platforms were created around the opportunities to profile and communicate to the users of these services. Knowingly or not, we started sharing our own data in exchange for free use of services such as email, photo sharing, discussion groups, free hard drive space for backups, search engines, GPS services, or dating services. This data collection grew even more when smartphones allowed us to use these services wherever and whenever we wanted, collecting our location and travels, thus enabling ads to become more targeted and relevant.

At the same time, this brought a number of security issues and social problems, unforeseen by most. Free speech, privacy, and safety started being halved, as companies, countries, and hackers gained access to this data for their own personal gains. This prompted the current public discussions around this topic, led by organizations like the World Wide Web Consortium (W3C, w3.org), founded by Berners-Lee himself.

So, next comes Web 3.0. This is the web we're now building, also known as the intelligent web or semantic web. Berners-Lee, the original creator of the web, described it as "the Web [in which computers] become capable of analyzing all the data on the Web— the content, links, and transactions between people and computers, (. . .) [where] day-to-day mechanisms of trade, bureaucracy, and our daily lives will be handled by machines talking to machines. The 'intelligent agents' tech thought leaders have touted for ages will finally materialize."[4] It's a vision that elevates the concept of the web to a level where artificial intelligence can use the data to enable automated tasks and help us in our everyday lives, that fits with the vision of the metaverse. However, this version of the web doesn't necessarily include blockchain or cryptocurrencies.[5]

It's important for you to realize that Web 3.0 is separate from the term Web3, a difference that is not intuitive. Web3, along with the Spatial Web, are two alternative visions for our future web that have been rising in interest and that previewed several of the discussion topics brought in by the metaverse. When you say or write Web3, you're talking about a model for a *decentralized web*. Its concept was coined by Gavin Wood back in 2014 and is built around the idea that users can become co-owners of the web and free from corporate or government oversight to make the best version of the web. Most, if not all, of the interactions, would become peer-to-peer without gatekeepers in between to intermediate.

This decentralization rethinks how user data is gathered and handled. On Web3, every user has their own wallet that can identify them and enable payment across all services on the web; users can replace corporations and government in roles to make services on the web work; they can also own digital assets and digital currency without relying on notaries; they can own their data while navigating the web and performing transactions that are transparently available on the blockchain, for everyone to check.

As data is also decentralized, Web3's business principles are built around alternative means of monetization outside of using and selling personal data (which is the fuel for today's Internet advertising). Instead, it enables new business models that may contribute to the upcoming metaverse. Web3 then aims to create a more private, safer, and user-oriented version of the web based on blockchain.

Still, critics state Web3 isn't yet ready for primetime. Some refer to the need to massively transform the current infrastructure of the web to make Web3's final vision possible. Others say it depends too much on the processing power of servers to scale, since registering transactions on the blockchain is having an increasingly disconcerting ecological impact. Many highlight how wealthy users and venture capital investors, are slowly owning the ecosystem, subverting the cry for user participation and the decentralization principle of it all. Finally, others warn against the decentralization effect and how taking mediators and public officials out of the picture can create fertile ground for fraudsters and all kinds of crime. "(Decentralization) is a matter of culture over tech," explains Danilo Castro, Head of XR and Metaverse strategist at the Brazilian UOL Group. Regardless of all these issues, several online platforms and communities have announced themselves as being Web3 and are actively promoting its principles.

The Spatial Web

In 2019, Gabriel René and Dan Mapes published a book, *The Spatial Web,* outlining their vision for a third version of the web. In it, they discuss how the physical and digital are merging, and that this symbiosis will bring together the biological, digital, and physical sides of reality in a truly interoperable way. They envision a move from a text-and-image web into a full 3D explorable experience, where services and applications will be made available in physical spaces, be aware of each of these space's characteristics, and allow for seamless interactions with both digital and physical objects using gestures, voice, gaze, and our binocular vision the same way. Goodbye, mouse pointer and keyboard and other peripheral equipment. They state we are destined to interact more and more within the Spatial Web as we do biologically within the physical world.

Because it's such a foundational approach, René and Mapes propose a new system where:

- All web elements are available on top of a persistent digital twin of the world, available to every user via a new kind of spatial browser (web navigation software that is aware of the physical world).
- Every physical space, object, and person has a digital counterpart (digital twin) with its own ID, which can then be used for private or public purposes.
- Everything in the physical and digital world can interact seamlessly. This means a button pressed in virtual reality can turn on a machine in a physical showroom, and vice versa.
- New standards, rules, rights, and permissions will need to be set in order to interact spatially, namely by standards organizations like W3C.

Do these look familiar? By anchoring digital information to physical spaces and objects, the Spatial Web foresees us interacting with the world in a fully contextualized manner. For instance, if you're a parent entering the school of your children, you could have access to their schedules, their grades, their works for each one of their classes, and directions to their classroom. All of these could be seen hovering digitally where needed through your augmented reality glasses, headset, or plain old smartphone. However, if you are a member of the school's maintenance team and a pipe just blew up in the ceiling of the science lab, you'd be able to see a much different set of information overlaid, such as a digital representation of the pipe scheme over the walls and you'd find instructions available exactly where the problem is. This would be possible because the information on the Spatial Web and physical reality would be in sync, so you could recognize places, objects, and people anywhere.

As with Web3, there are critics of this model. The huge number of servers and processing power necessary to make it possible is a major problem, due to the toll it takes on the environment.

Both of these proposed alternative models of a future web (Web3 and the Spatial Web) were, as you saw, very influential in bringing together the concept of the metaverse and they are enabled by the same convergence of technologies and platforms.

Because there are several technological building blocks of the metaverse, it's worth going through them to help you understand in later chapters some of the new concepts and strategies we're sharing.

5G, IoT, and Edge Computing

For any of us to enjoy digital services, we first need to get connected and then stay connected to the Internet. This allows us to transfer data at the speeds necessary for our services (e.g., streaming apps) to run smoothly. An Internet connection is and will always be a bottleneck for digital services. Making sure the connection is available at all times and across a geography is as important as speed. The faster we move data from one place to another, the more waiting times are reduced for users needing it.

There is a big difference in the speeds available between cable access and mobile access. Depending on where you live and which services you have, cable networks can already deliver high-speed service for our computers and home appliances. However, throughout the day, many of us access the Internet through mobile devices like smartphones or tablets.

Let's start with a brief overview of the generations of mobile Internet access. That's actually what the "G" in 4G or 5G stands for: generation. Each one of these Gs is technically a new generation of mobile communications technology that provides better, faster connection performance. Also, each G is a standard, which means you should be able to use that kind of access the same way in any country that supports it.

1G began in 1970 and every G since has, one after another, lasted around a decade. 3G rolled out at the beginning of this century, as that was also the decade where GPS devices and smartphones hit the market. So, companies started to promote 3G as a distinguishing factor. The first 4G services came online around 2010, and those quickly became instrumental in the rise of the social media revolution. Services like Apple's Facetime, Uber, and TikTok appeared. This wouldn't be possible with the previous Gs' access speeds.

Transitioning from one generation to another does not work like a software update on your computer. Not only does infrastructure need to be replaced and sometimes rebuilt and tested, but new hardware and software also must be built, adapted, and distributed. This works the same for 5G and for the next generation that is called (you guessed it): 6G.

Since 2020, you might have noticed the millions of dollars of advertising and sponsorship at work touting 5G. The largest telecommunications companies are really trying to convince us to switch to this new Internet service. But what difference does it really make?

Indeed, it is a shift in how we experience mobile computing. It can supply up to 20 times the speed of a 4G connection, meaning that every app or platform you use can become much more powerful and many will be able to provide services in real time. Forget lengthy downloads and updates that overwhelm the memory in our devices and slow them down. You no longer need to worry at all about downloads. 5G is able to plug your mobile experience into the cloud and stream what you need directly to your device.

Minimal latency is another key benefit of 5G. We've all experienced latency, such as when you press play to see a movie on a streaming service and you have to wait an instant or two before it starts. 5G means immediate access and close to real-time information. Latency has also been an issue with Virtual Reality (VR) experiences, as they incorporate and use so much high-resolution external data. So, the switch to 5G is making VR developers very happy.

Edge computing boosts this opportunity for real-time information. In simplified terms, it draws the processing power closer to the source of the data, so that it reduces even more the time it takes to send, process, and receive it. This has a big impact on the Internet of Things (IoT) and its manufacturing version, the Industrial Internet of Things (IIoT). These are networks of objects and devices that have embedded sensors, from which data is gathered and then used for different applications. For example, IoT data allows families to know which devices are consuming more electrical power and need to be optimized, while IIoT data allows teams of engineers to keep track of the performance in a factory's production line.

5G is already rolled out in several countries, and the list of potentially disruptive services built on it is multiplying, which includes new home automation systems, autonomous cars, and new equipment in smart cities. So why are these Gs and mobile Internet so important to the metaverse?

It starts with the number of simultaneous connections. Today, the Internet connects more than 4.32 billion smartphones[6]; 13.1 billion IoT sensor-enabled devices, like alarms, thermostats, lights, or refrigerators[7]; and likely billions of computers. However, these numbers are not even remotely near the ones that will result from connecting all people, all objects, and all spaces in a continuously synced, hybrid, and symbiotic version of reality. The amount of data will be unlike what we've experienced before.

Every device will need to send and receive data continuously just to satisfy the minimum goals of the metaverse. Add on top of that all real-time interactions and transactions for every user, and you begin to understand the kind of infrastructure and connection speeds we'll need.

The next generation of mobile Internet, 6G, is aimed at connecting physical and digital at 100–1,000 times the speed of 5G. Although 6G standard specification is still undergoing heavy work and far from finished, it's generally assumed that it will be less latent and more ecological, enabling maritime and airspace Internet access as well. "The primary function of 5G (as was the case for all previous 'Gs') is communications," shared Walid Saad, a Virginia

Tech professor[8] and researcher in this field.[9] "6G, instead, will be able to deliver additional services to users, such as sensing, control, imaging/mapping, and localization. These functions will be needed to support autonomous systems."

Digital Twins

As the end goal of the metaverse is to synchronize digital and physical, then the prevalent digital format will most likely be 3D. Today, a large number of Internet services are already based on 3D formats. Games like Minecraft, Roblox, and Fortnite have onboarded hundreds of millions of users into 3D worlds. Social media filters are bringing masks, glasses, hats, and so many other 3D digital elements to our social sharing. We can even create 3D elements, using professional 3D editing software like Autodesk Maya, Pixologic ZBrush, SideFX Houdini, or online services like Sumo3D or SketchUp.

3D scanning apps and software are enabling handheld devices as common as smartphones and tablets to generate realistic 3D copies of physical objects. Apps like Laan Labs' 3D Scanner App or Qlone can generate on-the-fly simplified replicas of objects that can vary in size from a shoe to an armchair. Others, like Matterport, scan a physical room and generate a digital version of it that can be viewed in several ways, including through VR headsets.

People are also being scanned. Today, face scanning is in many of our smartphones and we use it to unlock our screens. Now this wouldn't be possible if your smartphone didn't already hold a digital scan of your face. But services like Didimo are taking it one step further and enabling users to scan their faces and bodies. It's also possible to scan and even create full-body 3D models of yourself in motion using volumetric and motion capture technologies.

All of these digital copies provide visual resemblance to the original ones, but they're not connected with the physical elements they represent. That's the main difference between a 3D model and a digital twin. The former is a copy. The latter holds updated information on the state of the original object, place, or person that it gets from sensors or that is just sent over the Internet. The number of digital twin applications sprawl through health, education, real estate, and retail, with the potential to impact an even wider variety of industries. Right now, digital twins are very visible in the enterprise and manufacturing fields, by connecting 3D models with IIoT systems and re-creating product manufacturing cycles from beginning to end. Hyundai and Unity Technologies offer a good example as they teamed up to create a digital twin of an entire car factory.[10] "Real-time digital twins will permanently change how we live, work, shop, and make a positive impact on our planet, representing a significant component of what is often referred to as the metaverse," shared John Riccitiello, CEO of Unity. "Hyundai's vision for the future, including the digital twin of factory operations, represents a significant technological step forward in manufacturing with unlimited potential in its efficiency."[11]

In Africa, digital twins also present an opportunity to leapfrog the physical absence of materials and equipment. "There are indeed a lot of opportunities," shares Gonçalo Pratas, Managing Partner of MGO Consulting, an XR developer studio based out of Cabo Verde. "From 3D asset design and 3D world building and even real-world digital twins, the opportunities exist for everyone in my region."[12]

With 6G, expect these technologies to operate at a much larger scale. For instance, we could see digital twins of cities with persistent holograms throughout. This will eventually lead us to grow several IoT systems into one big IoE (Internet of Everything),[13] that will gather people, processes, data, and things into one single, monumental network.

As you see, data is central to the metaverse. We collect it via mobile connections and through digital twins of, well, everything. But where's the computing power needed to process, organize, and save it? That's where cloud computing comes in.

Cloud Computing

If you work with technology—and at this point, nearly every person uses technology as part of their job—you probably have heard of the cloud. There's an ongoing debate about who should get credit for coining the term, but many believe the first public mention of cloud computing happened when Google's CEO Eric Schmidt referred to it in an industry conference on August 9, 2006:

> It starts with the premise that the data services and architecture should be on servers. We call it cloud computing—they should be in a 'cloud' somewhere. (. . .) it doesn't matter whether you have a PC or a Mac or a mobile phone or a BlackBerry or what have you—or new devices still to be developed—you can get access to the cloud.[14]

Although others contend it had already appeared in 1996 when Compaq Computer executives were discussing the future of the Internet.[15]

Cloud computing takes the data processing workload away from your computer and places it on other, remote computers, named cloud servers, that are far more potent and able to process increasing amounts of data. This allows our devices to not get bogged down while accessing complex platforms with denizens of integrated live feeds and other full-featured applications.

It has already impacted the gaming industry in a deep way. Besides being able to buy games online, gamers can now enjoy their titles being streamed directly to lightweight applications on mobile phones, consoles, or PCs, where they can interact with other gamers in multiplayer modes. They actually don't need to buy a game case from a physical store anymore. Instead, they just stream it into whatever platform is most convenient for them. Cloud computing allowed the gaming business to offer subscription-based services, and soon many others will follow.

The entertainment and music industries are already reaping its benefits. Streaming services have become the norm—Spotify and Netflix are two good examples. Spotify enables hundreds of millions of listeners to access podcasts and a music library of over 50 million tracks simultaneously.[16] Netflix has hundreds of millions of subscribers, from 190 countries, who access over 125 million hours of TV shows and movies.[17] Cloud computing is a key part of what enables these massive consumer-facing businesses to operate high-quality consumer experiences simultaneously around the world.

All data necessary for these services to exist is processed on the cloud, and the data needed for metaverse services will be also. Digital twins of physical spaces will sync with the actual physical spaces and enable augmented reality experiences to be available to everyone. The computing power necessary to make this happen will come from the augmented reality (AR) cloud. In the words of Ori Inbar, partner at Super Ventures and author of the concept, "The principle of AR Cloud is that all AR experiences should be persistent in the real [physical] world across Space, Time, and Devices."[18]

Cloud computing changes the game for AR experiences. We've seen hints of what's possible before. In 2012, the Chinese e-commerce grocer Yihaodian opened 1,000 AR stores near the entrance of their direct competitors' stores, showcasing the same products but with better prices.[19] Perhaps the aggressive moves that Starbucks took when they started expanding outside of Seattle in the 1990s will be re-created by them in the metaverse. An AR Starbucks on every corner of the metaverse, perhaps? But what would the Seattle coffee shop experience be in the metaverse? That is yet to be determined.

And Starbucks probably will need to, as this isn't in the far future. Some of the largest tech companies in the world, like Microsoft, Apple, and Niantic, are already setting up their own AR cloud services and tools that allow creators and organizations to share content, services and, of course, data. As the numbers grow bigger, more added-value services are bound to appear.

Headsets and Glasses

If 3D is going to become the metaverse's major format, then virtual reality (VR) and augmented reality (AR) likely will make up the majority of the metaverse's visible content and applications. Collectively they are known as XR (extended reality), a catchall term for all digitally created or enhanced realities.

For a quick definition of VR, think of it as replacing physical reality with a digital one. A VR headset immerses users into the sight and sounds of a coded world. With VR headsets and experiences, you are brought into a digital reality where your attention is focused on what you see and hear within that virtual space.

AR, on the other hand, overlays digital elements over physical objects and spaces that are seen by the computer vision via the cameras in your phone or on your tablet or computer. While VR is already experienced on headsets, at this time, AR experiences happen mostly through mobile devices. Consumer-level AR headsets are on their way as are XR headsets that toggle between two realities (VR and AR).

Antony Vitillo, a reference XR expert and blogger at Skarred Ghost.com, highlights that, "In 15, 20 years, we'll have consumer-level glasses with the shape we are all looking for. But in the meantime, we'll evolve in different ways and smart glasses connected to the smartphone will become relevant."[20] Also, contact lenses, like the ones being developed by Mojo Vision, are being built to enable AR without a headset, but instead directly on top of your eye. Their early prototype has already been worn by the CEO of the company, Drew Perkins, who stated, "Seeing the future literally put me at a loss for words. . . But to have optics, electronics, mechanical systems, and software all operating at the same time—and seeing it happen—was an historic achievement!"[21]

One of the main and most difficult purposes is to transition between VR and AR worlds and the physical world in a seamless way, similar to the way we already connect, socialize, and interact. XR headsets and glasses are equipped with microphones and motion- or gesture-detecting sensors so our voices and our bodies (beginning with our hands) play a bigger role in our interaction with digital elements in XR. We go from a handheld to a new, hands-free, spatial user experience (UX). The weight of the mobile phone or tablet is removed and the use of our voice and both hands expands our interaction with the spaces surrounding us, in a screenless experience. Mojo Vision likes to call their version of this "invisible computing."

This interface transformation does not stop there. Haptic gloves like those from HaptX and Ultrahaptics and full-body suits like Teslasuit's create opportunities for both enterprise and consumers to add more senses to XR experiences. Haptic interfaces are still in their early stages in fidelity or weight, but expect that to change. Even now, HaptX is used by car companies to test and feel their automotive designs in VR down to button-level precision.

There are also companies working to create smells that ultimately enhance the feeling of immersion. This is not an original idea, as the first examples could be seen in movie theaters in the 1950s and 60s: Smell-O-Rama (1953), AromaRama (1959), and Smell-O-Vision (1960). OVR Technology's CEO Aaron Wisniewski told *Fast Company*, "Smell has this profound effect over who we are, how we feel, what we do, what we buy, who we love." They are only one of a handful of companies focusing on scent.[22] Not to be outdone, there also are researchers and companies beginning to work on simulating taste as well and you can find some of their work shared through the Internet of Senses Institute.[23]

No matter the sense, the amount of data being generated by each interaction is quite large and then adding biometric feedback from wearables and information from gestures and voice commands adds even more to the amount of data being collected.

Artificial Intelligence and Machine Learning

Whenever the acronym AI is uttered, visions of a grand artificial brain making autonomous decisions over an army of robots fill our mind. You can thank blockbuster movies and premium TV shows for that.

Artificial intelligence (AI) is the result of simulating human intelligence in machines. By human intelligence, we're referring to activities like solving problems and learning or reasoning for a particular subject matter.

Still, activities like facial, gesture, and speech recognition, 3D scanning, eye-tracking are all based on AI's ability to learn to recognize elements. AI can generate data dashboards for digital twins, place them on the AR cloud, or filter and categorize IoT data at lightning speed. That's why it is so central in automation processes, and why it most certainly will be responsible for making sense of all data generated by the many converging technologies in the metaverse. Take Google, for instance, that has teased a prototype application that, in real time, translates what someone else is saying in a different language and presents users with captions for the conversation in augmented reality, visible through smart glasses.[24]

AI already is crucial in today's online services, including search engines, social networks, e-commerce sites, and, of course, advertising. Every personalized experience on the web uses AI to leverage personal data from our activities, interests, and preferences, for instance. And those personalization opportunities will continue to increase in number with the metaverse. On its Horizon Worlds platform, Meta already launched its Builder Bot,[25] a conversational AI that lets you describe with your voice exactly what you want to have in the virtual world you're building and then generates it for you. You can very literally speak a VR world into existence and that may well set a trend.

Machine learning (ML) is a type of AI that imitates how humans learn, gradually improving its accuracy. Some researchers believe that we'll see AI exceeding humans' collective capacity to learn, while others remain skeptical due to the diversity of senses and ways of learning available within the human learning experience.

AI optimizes and automates data computing needs as these technologies intertwine and exponentially grow, effectively allowing their convergence to happen. This automation guarantees each user will benefit from having their own personal experiences, or even their own custom worlds. Ultimately, it will enable a faster creation and maintenance of experiences in the metaverse.

Blockchain

In the beginning of this chapter and in the previous one, we already discussed how blockchain technology is making decentralization and Web3 possible. By maintaining a public registry of transactions on a public, distributed ledger visible to everyone, the system becomes more transparent, potentially owned by everyone and controlled by no one.

Whenever you register a transaction in the blockchain, you're setting up a contract between two unique crypto wallets, in simplified terms. Let's take cryptocurrency and NFT trades as examples. If you buy an amount of cryptocurrency, for instance, the contract will state one person is giving and another person is receiving cryptocurrency (like Bitcoin) under specific conditions and rules and the receiving user will get a number of tokens associated that indicate that he is the sole owner of that amount of cryptocurrency. If you buy digital art, the same will happen, only you'll be getting a non-fungible (which means one-of-a-kind) token (NFT) in your crypto wallet.

Even if you haven't heard of blockchain and somehow have stayed out of crypto discussions, you might have heard of NFTs. They were behind one of the biggest tech-hype rushes in this century. Digital art prices reached unbelievable heights, and, across several self-proclaimed metaverse platforms and on Twitter, NFTs collectibles started to be donned as profile pictures, worn as digital fashion by user's avatars or featured in galleries.

As with all hype fevers, it started to die down, although there are still many opportunities. NFTs are very useful, since they have the power to add interoperability and nimbleness to digital trading. However, when someone says they "own an NFT," that isn't technically correct. They own a digital or phygital good, and they can prove their ownership with an NFT, which is in fact a token.

In a moment where privacy, safety, and accountability are being heavily discussed, the promise of blockchain technology to govern data and users shines as an option for the upcoming metaverse. But we must understand how the pieces of the puzzle fit together.

Woven Together

What is particularly interesting and exciting about all these technologies is that they're all evolving and will continue to evolve within the same generation. How they'll fit and how this combination will happen, no one can say with certainty. But it is agreed that they will begin to weave together and ultimately converge into exponentially growing applications across the entire metaverse.

These technological building blocks of the metaverse will enable the connectivity, computing power, phygital synchronization, decentralization, hardware upgrades, automation, and optimization needed for the metaverse to bloom.

But we cannot forget that the underlying layer of them all is an immense amount of data. If you already heard that data is the new oil, brace yourself—it will be much more than that. Data is going to become the new oxygen.

Notes

1.   CERN, "A short history of the web." n.d. https://home.cern/science/computing/birth-web/short-history-web#

2.   Techopedia. "Web 1.0." techopedia.com, July 29, 2021. www.techopedia.com/definition/27960/web-10#

3.   Will Kenton, "Web 2.0." Investopedia, February 3, 2022. www.investopedia.com/terms/w/web-20.asp

4.   Tim Berners-Lee and Mark Fischetti, *Weaving the Web: The Original Design and Ultimate Destiny of the World Wide Web by Its Inventor* (HarperOne, 1999), Chapter 12.

5.   Laurence Van Elegem, "Web3 and Web 3.0 are NOT the same thing. Here's why." Nexxworks, April 28, 2022 (blog). www.nexxworks.com/blog/web3-and-web-3-0-are-not-the-same-thing-heres-why#

6.   L. Ceci, "Mobile Internet usage worldwide – statistics & facts." *Statistica*, February 22, 2022. www.statista.com/topics/779/mobile-Internet

7.   Lionel Sujay Vailshery, "Number of Internet of Things (IoT) connected devices worldwide from 2019 to 2030." *Statistica*, June 8, 2022, www.statista.com/statistics/1183457/iot-connected-devices-worldwide

8.   Kendra Chamberlain, "A glimpse into the future? Report predicts 6G features." *Fierce Wireless*, June 17, 2019. www.fiercewireless.com/tech/a-glimpse-into-future-report-predicts-6g-features

9. Walid Saad, Mehdi Bennis, and Mingzhe Chen, "A vision of 6G wireless systems: Applications, trends, technologies, and open research problems." *arXiv*, July 21, 2019. https://arxiv.org/pdf/1902.10265.pdf

10. Matthew Greenwood, "Hyundai and Unity team up to bring a car factory into the metaverse." Engineering.com, January 26, 2022. www.engineering.com/story/hyundai-and-unity-team-up-to-bring-a-car-factory-into-the-metaverse

11. Hyundai, "Hyundai Motor and Unity partner to build meta-factory accelerating intelligent manufacturing innovation." Hyundai press release, January 7, 2022. www.hyundai.news/eu/articles/press-releases/hyundai-and-unity-partner-to-build-meta-factory-accelerating-intelligent-manufacturing-innovation.html

12. Personal communication, August, 2022.

13. Viviane Cunha Farias da Costa, "Internet of Everything (IoE) taxonomies." *Scholarly Community Encyclopedia*, January 27, 2021. https://encyclopedia.pub/entry/6804

14. Eric Schmidt, "Conversation with Eric Schmidt hosted by Danny Sullivan." Interview at Search Engine Strategies Conference, August 9, 2006. www.google.com/press/podium/ses2006.html

15. www.technologyreview.com/2011/10/31/257406/who-coined-cloud-computing

16. Google, "Innovation at the speed of Spotify." Undated Google customer profile. https://cloud.google.com/customers/featured/spotify

17. Amazon Web Services (AWS), "Netflix on AWS." Undated customer profile. https://aws.amazon.com/solutions/case-studies/netflix

18. Pradeep Naik, "AR Cloud: The next generation of AR experiences." Undated Wipro white paper. www.wipro.com/content/dam/nexus/en/innovation/pdf/ar-cloud-the-next-generation-of-ar-experiences.pdf

19. Steven Millward, "China's Yihaodian plans 1,000 virtual AR supermarkets where you'll shop with your smartphone's camera." TechinAsia, October 15, 2012. www.techinasia.com/china-yihaodian-virtual-supermarkets-qr-codes

20. Personal communication, August, 2022.

21. www.mojo.vision/news/today-i-wore-mojo-lens

22. www.fastcompany.com/90744828/inside-the-smell-a-verse-meet-the-companies-trying-to-bring-smell-to-the-metaverse

23. https://Internetofsenses.com

24. Jessica Bursztynsky, "Google teases smart glasses prototype that translates languages in real time." CNBC, May 11, 2022. www.cnbc.com/2022/05/11/google-smart-glasses-prototype-translates-languages-in-real-time.html

25. Daniel Dominguez, "Meta AI Labs introduces BuilderBot, a voice control builder for virtual worlds." InfoQ, March 29, 2033. www.infoq.com/news/2022/03/meta-ai-labs-builderbot

Chapter 3
The Race Has Begun

You remember, it's the chance to build cathedrals, entire cities, things that never existed. Things that couldn't exist in the real world.
—*Dom Cobb in* Inception

O ne of the most exciting parts of working in emerging technologies is building a vision of the future. We might live and work with present technology, but each project takes us to what might be, what could be. It's all part of a bigger goal, and we can shape what's coming next. Those working in the emerging technology industry know that everyone in their company, everyone in their industry, is playing a part. Some companies may be huge successes, some might have made the wrong bets, but we're all needed pieces in the puzzle and the only constant in our roles is change.

No one knows this better than the biggest tech players: companies with billions of dollars at their disposal that can make bigger bets and make an increasingly bigger impact. So, when most of these behemoths get behind a similar vision, you know there is a massive social and economic change on the horizon.

But with the creation of any new markets and related platforms comes a turf war. Some companies have even started to name, to custom-brand, the next tech stage in a way that allows them to claim ownership. The most obvious is Facebook's switch to Meta. It caused a big stir, and many called out the company as they appropriated the prefix of the term for themselves.[1] It was almost like the company formerly known as Facebook was reverse engineering an eponym in order to assert their market dominance.

Years earlier, Magic Leap announced the launch of the Magicverse in its own company conference back in 2018. Niantic also wrote about how a "real-world metaverse"[2] was needed, NVIDIA on their site started promoting the Omniverse, HTC the Viveverse, and Apple, Microsoft, and Google have all been developing metaverse-related technology for quite some time, so it's only natural to think they're preparing their own claims. It's no wonder most people are getting confused with this whirlwind of terms.

Beyond naming it, companies are also claiming leadership of the pack by announcing product advancements and game-changing innovation. These announcements earn them a share of voice in the mind of the industry and can directly influence other organizations' decisions. However, most of the larger companies don't show their cards early in the game, keeping their strategies and future plans secret to try to guarantee competitive advantages. There are only glimpses of what they have planned during their developer meetings, their investor calls, and announcements. Their influence on the rest of the industry can be so great that often just a patent application can make news.

So, how is it possible to get a sense of a marketplace that is only beginning, based on media blips and on a concept that is not yet defined? How can you plan for the future of technology if the largest companies in the space are not that forthcoming with their plans? Well, you can make educated guesses based on the solutions already available and take into account how corporate players are nudging the market. Be mindful that, somewhere in the future, the metaverse will connect every service these organizations are developing separately, merged together in a single 3D, hybrid Internet. So, the following is an overview of the components of the metaverse being built and which companies are staking their claim. We will go through some of the pioneer stories in this area, then show

how gaming platforms are fundamental to the metaverse-to-be, as well as the already existing metaverse worlds. Finally, we will look at how these technology services fit together, defining what the groundwork of the metaverse will be.

Pioneers in Virtual Space

If you can believe it, the first 3D web projects launched 30–40 years ago. Labyrinth, Second Life, and the first gaming platforms showed us the benefits and challenges that await us in virtual worlds. Each supply us with a historical perspective and a sense of the trajectory being drawn into the future.

As an analogy to virtual worlds, the early versions of these pioneer projects will probably be seen to the metaverse the same way as brick phones were to the current mobile devices. Brick phones were launched in the 1980s, cost $4,000, weighed 2 pounds (almost a kilogram) and their full battery lasted 30 minutes when fully charged, but you still could make phone calls untethered to a phone line. Almost nothing like the smartphones of today, except for the fact that they are both phones.

The initial world platforms were slow and a bit clunky, but they allowed players' avatars to create new social interactions through games and experiences. These early virtual worlds were effectively early prototypes and their thousands of users prove that there is a human interest in interacting socially in 3D digital worlds. The following dives deeper into each to see what insights we can bring into the future.

Labyrinth

In 1994, the World Wide Web was still in its infancy. There was a call for presenters at the First International Conference on the World-Wide Web, and Mark Pesce flew to Geneva to showcase a 3D browser prototype called *Labyrinth*. (His research partner, Tony Parisi, stayed behind, as they didn't have enough money for both of them to travel.) Their browser enabled users to navigate through interconnected 3D worlds on the actual web using VRML (Virtual Reality Markup Language). To demonstrate the technical prowess of the solution, Pesce showcased a 3D model of a banana on a black background that, if clicked, opened the doors to a 3D web page right there on a browser.

Navigating 3D worlds over the web sounds exactly like a way to develop the future open, interoperable 3D metaverse we are looking for—still, this is a vision of 1994. Mark Pesce and Tony Parisi made an impact with their invention as, for the first time, they showed that a World Wide Web in 3D was possible, and tech companies in 1994 took notice. Through a partnership with Intel, for instance, VRML viewers were installed on 10 million computers but many other hurdles to their distribution ultimately led to their sunset.

"The software was much harder to deal with. People were excited about the VR possibilities, but there was no way economically it was going to get into consumers' hands at that point," says Tony Parisi.[3] This was part of the downturn of VR in the late 1990s. Of course, everyone who lived this moment became both excited and skeptical of this current rush of enthusiasm in immersive technologies. Twenty-five years later, 3D is slowly rising to become one of the main formats of information on the web, and navigating the metaverse might end up as an experience similar to the one demonstrated by Labyrinth.

Parisi is still part of the industry. He was heading XR efforts at game engine company Unity Technologies for almost six years and is now Chief Strategist of Lamina1, a company focused on enabling an open metaverse, one that bridges XR with the cryptoworld. He also used his knowledge and experience of VRML to co-create a new standard of 3D use called glTF.[4] Pesce is now an independent consultant who describes himself as a "Futurist, Inventor, Author, Educator and Broadcaster" (http://new.markpesce.com). He still writes his opinions about the metaverse and makes sure that people know that its "roots stretch back longer than Mark Zuckerberg has been alive."[5]

Second Life

In 1999, Philip Rosedale founded Linden Lab in pursuit of a child-hood dream of creating a virtual world. In the early 2000s, Linden Lab launched the first version of a privately owned digital world called Second Life. At the time, Rosedale proclaimed, "The 3D web will rapidly be the dominant thing and everyone will have an ava-tar."[6] He didn't make this claim just because users could easily cre-ate avatars and choose to walk or fly between public and private worlds, meeting people and sharing stories. He made this claim because this community was running, for the first time, a unique digital economy. Transactions were made with their own currency (Linden Dollars) and a LindeX exchange marketplace facilitated them. Digital artisans started, for the first time, to create and sell items in-world. And, most important, hype and enthusiasm brought in customers.[7]

In hindsight, the creation of a basic but autonomous digital economy was worth noticing, although it didn't receive enough traction as the available technology just wasn't sufficiently robust. Many people who established an early presence in Second Life left. In 2007, it was reported that 20 to 30 percent of users didn't return to Second Life after the first time.[8] Tom Boellstorff, who lived in Second Life for two years, said, "It's not often that going into a vir-tual world is sort of fulfilling a pre-existing need."[9]

In 2022, there were 70 million registered accounts in Second Life, and almost 30,000 regions within the platform, over half of them private. Buying and selling digital property that could afterward be leased was also a first on Second Life. Millions of digital goods were traded, and creators racked up around $80 million in 2021.

Second Life is also an interesting study subject due to the con-troversy it generated, especially as it relates to adult content. During its original launch Second Life opened up the platform to content creators of all kinds, without restriction. So a plethora of adult con-tent worlds appeared, with several flavors of legal and not-so-legal virtual sex venues. In these sex clubs, virtual experiences catered to a diversity of preferences and fetishes, where owners sold digital skins and accessories, much like their non-adult-content counterparts, but within the themes of their events. Second Life can be considered a pioneer of the business opportunities, as well as a case study for content moderation in virtual worlds. This is just one of the ways that Second Life was and still is a groundbreaker in most of the topics we'll be covering in this book.

Gaming-Verse

For gamers, this move to virtual worlds is hardly a change. Some of the most sophisticated games already have an ethos and deep backstories. The tabletop, role-playing phenomenon *Dungeons & Dragons (D&D)* has ushered in over 50 million people since its debut in 1974.[10] The *D&D* universe is experienced outside of a screen, as it is played on a table with dice, pencil, and paper. Players actually have to imagine the stories in their heads collectively, role-play their characters, and react to the plot twists another player (called the Game Master or Dungeon Master) creates and puts them through. No technology needed, just good storytelling and plenty of imagination. Making the move to avatars and 3D digital worlds was a breeze for these players.

These TTRPGs (tabletop role-playing games) still immerse players into their characters in a shared world that doesn't exist physically. Also, there's a sense of community among D&D players and they share the same set of rules and backstory. The world they play in, though, is only visible in the imagination of the people within a room, so it is no wonder these kinds of games moved online.

Effectively TTRPGs led to MMORPGs (massive multiplayer online role-playing games), revolutionizing habits of gamers and of people who are used to saying acronyms. Games like *Habitat* in 1986, developed by LucasArts, opened ways for 1991's *Neverwinter Nights*, the first MMORPG to allow 50 simultaneous players to have a graphical character and interact online. Mind you, each of these players had to pay $6 per hour, mostly to help cover the high costs of bandwidth at the time,[11] and most used a 56k dial-up modem to log in. We're talking about a connection 250,000 times slower than the standard 4G speeds. We wouldn't go so far as to call it massive, but it showed there were players with a genuine amount of will to play this game, in spite of the conditions.

The first game to effectively live up to the credit of "massive" was *Ultima Online*, launched in 1997, ultimately exceeding 250,000 subscribers and which is still available to play and receiving updates in 2022. *Ultima* marked a moment in online gaming when players started flocking to a platform not only to play a game, but to play with each other, team up, and trade items. New friendships created new social routines in-world between player characters, as in the physical world, with friends knowing each other's playing schedules. Suddenly, massive multiplayer online social games (MMOSGs) appeared, and gamers were not just playing, they were socializing through gameplay.

At the time of this writing, the largest gaming platforms accepted as MMOSGs are *World of Warcraft (WoW)* and *RuneScape*. *World of Warcraft* was released in 2004 and at its peak in 2010 had around 12 million subscribers. To give you a notion of the size of this market, these subscribers alone paid $180 million per month to play, which amounted to a revenue of $2.15 billion a year.[12] *RuneScape* is also a great example of a MMOSG but with free access. Players from over 150 countries learned community skills together, from combat to artisanship, harnessing an inventory they could trade and/or sell with others.

It's somewhat surprising that these MMOSGs seem to distance themselves from the early discussion of the metaverse. Their achievement of gathering millions of users who shared digital experiences daily and socialized both digitally and in the physical world sounds a lot like the gamified communities we believe will pop up around the metaverse. The concept of merging virtual worlds and social spaces is nothing new for the creators and the players. So perhaps to the gaming world, this talk of the metaverse is old news, and it sounds as if it is only focused on monetization and maybe that's why some hardcore gamers react negatively to the concept.[13]

Roblox

One of the companies that receives a lot of media attention for creating an online gaming platform is Roblox. The concept is built around real-world physics and a digital obsession with construction toys, combined with social networking tools and enabling every player to also become a creator.[14]

Roblox made the platform free-to-play from the very beginning, basing their revenue mainly on in-game purchases and partnerships. Since launching in September 2006, they've amassed over 10 million creators building on their platform who published over 24 million experiences to choose from. In 2020, it was reported that about half of all U.S. children were Roblox registered users.[15]

CEO David Baszucki shared that all of these players (67% are 16 and under) are already enjoying an early version of the metaverse with his company. "We're actually in the middle of it right now. There are over 200 million, roughly, monthly people on [our platform] every month. They do a lot of things. They have an identity; they have an avatar. They do stuff together. Sometimes when they can't be together in person, they'll go to a birthday party together or graduate from high school together."[16]

Network effects, especially between kids during quarantine, have been driving the growth of the platform. The Roblox team seems to know that the key to continued growth lies in enabling and supporting the community of professional and amateur developers who are creating more worlds and expanding the number of games on the platform. "Our job is simply to enable creators to pursue their vision," said Craig Donato, Chief Business Officer.[17]

The millions upon millions of Roblox games offer a lot of choices for players, but also a lot of opportunities for bad actors. Roblox uses 4,000 moderators, and its algorithm that reviews the platform for age-inappropriate content is responsible for the surprisingly few issues that have come to light given the massive number of games and users. Of course, no business is impervious to wrongdoing and, in December 2021, 15 years after the launch, a significant series of controversies arose. Discussions about how child labor laws would apply to younger game creators, how these players were accessible to pedophiles, and a black market for virtual goods were at the center of the storm.[18] These are not at all small issues for Roblox to address, and companies looking to engage children within their virtual worlds should take note of what can (and has) gone wrong to prepare for their own business and players. 4,000 people and an algorithm might seem like a lot, but it is small in comparison to tens of millions of players each day, their interactions, and all the data they generate.

Minecraft

To the unfamiliar and non-gamer crowd, *Minecraft* and Roblox might look similar, especially if you don't have kids in grade school. It is true that the aesthetics, avatar types, and some forms of interaction are similar, but that's where the comparisons stop.

Minecraft is focused on one kind of game, whereas Roblox is more of a gaming platform, with millions of different games associated with it. *Minecraft* is all about blocks. You "mine" and acquire new ones with your digital pickaxes to build every structure in the game with them. Roblox is not based on a singular standard game mechanic and your avatar can jump between games. *Minecraft* is the best-selling video game ever, and Roblox is free to play. *Minecraft*'s original development is based on the centralized quality standards of their team, unlike Roblox's army of external creators. *Minecraft* can easily be enjoyed as a solo experience, whereas Roblox social interactions are key to its experience. Have we convinced you how different they are yet?[19]

Minecraft was created by a Swedish programmer and designer nicknamed Notch (aka Markus Alexej Persson). He presented a tech demo of the Cave Game program in 2009, developed by his company Mojang Studios. Five years later, it was rumored that the company was acquired by Microsoft for $2.5 billion.[20] It's also estimated that, another five years post-acquisition, 100 million copies of the game were sold for almost $1.5 billion.[21]

Since then, its gameplay stayed focused on its blocks, which are the key element in everything we see, scattered into a landscape, with non-playing characters living in villages and mineshafts of monsters, spider enemies, and exploding blocks of TNT. The game updates include adding different biomes as well as different skins and offering new items to acquire.[22]

There was a venture into AR in 2019, where *Minecraft* launched an augmented reality application. Named Minecraft Earth, the app allowed users to create their own blocks in the physical world. It was downloaded 1.2 million times within the first week.[23] The effort to venture into AR was shut down in June the next year. Although 1 million seems like a large number for an indie game company, it just wasn't nearly large enough to be considered a success when compared to *Pokémon GO,* the app they most likely tried to emulate. That application hoarded 250 million installations in its first quarter and has a lifetime number of installations beyond a billion.[24] But even with that bump in the road, it's safe to say *Minecraft* is definitely one of the most important players in the gaming industry, with 238 million total copies of the game registered as sold in April 2021.[25]

So, what makes it so popular? One obvious reason is that *Minecraft* is appropriate and safe for kids of all ages. The way the building blocks enable players to do everything shows how digital worlds, avatars, skins, and digital items can be family friendly. It's been called "the most versatile game ever"[26] that offers "an infinite, blocky world of creativity."[27]Also, its educational tool, Minecraft Education edition, goes one step further in showing how 3D digital worlds can be available in classrooms.

Fortnite

In 2011, Epic Games hosted an internal event, where employees were challenged to create a new video game from scratch within a set, short period of time (aka, a game jam). One of the participating teams thought of combining a shooter and a construction game.[28] The early announcement described the gameplay like this:

"Imagine a world where you explore, you scavenge, you build and ultimately you survive."[29]

It was that concept that led to the 5–7+ year creation of the now multi-billion-dollar game *Fortnite*, which boasts over 400 million registered users[30] and generated $5.7 billion revenue in 2021 alone.[31] Even the game's most popular players became multimillionaires. Tyler "Ninja" Blevins was once reported to make $500,000 per month.[32] At this point, in the past few years, if you consider yourself to be a gamer, you must have played *Fortnite*.

For those non-gamers reading this, here are some quick insights into the game. Firstly, there are different *Fortnite* game modes. For instance, *Save the World* is a paid version created in 2017, while *Battle Royale* is free-to-play since 2019. Although the former was considered a success, it was *Battle Royale* that brought *Fortnite* into the collective consciousness. That mode hosts a 100-player fight until the last avatar stands. The currency used within *Fortnite* is the V-Buck, an abbreviation of Vindertech-Bucks, named after the (fictional) now deceased Dr. Vinderman, the founder of the (also fictional) weapons and vehicle manufacturing company Vindertech in Fortnite. So, now when you hear someone talking about Battle Royales and V-Bucks, you know they are discussing *Fortnite*.

In 2020, Epic Games took on probably its biggest non-fictional battle, a real-life legal battle with Apple. Epic believed that the App Store was retaining too much of the revenue of *Fortnite* (30 percent of all paid transactions), so it offered means for players to pay Epic directly. Apple wasn't happy and removed *Fortnite* from its platform (as did Google) and a legal battle ensued, as Epic decided to challenge the removal of *Fortnite* in the courts and in the press.[33] It caused many adults to watch the tech industry equivalents of King Kong and Godzilla face each other down legally and in public opinion. (Which one was CEO Tim Sweeney of Epic Games and which was Apple's CEO Tim Cook is up for debate.) The case is still ongoing as of this writing.

Epic Games trusted their players to be loyal enough to play on another platform and that left many school-age children very confused, especially as Gen Z and Alpha generations always assume they can get access to any video or game whenever they want. For the gaming generation, this was also the biggest practical example of how valuable interoperability is and of how important it became for games to be available on different platforms.

Beyond its dominant position in gaming since its launch, *Fortnite* has begun to establish itself as an entertainment platform. *Fortnite: Battle Royale* literally set the stage for some of the biggest 3D online concerts and music events ever, like the concert starring Travis Scott and his "Astronomical" tour that attracted more than 11 million attendees. Celebrities have even gotten in on the *Fortnite* fun, with special appearances by athletes LeBron James and Naomi Osaka, music releases by Marshmello and Ariana Grande,[34] and Dwayne "The Rock" Johnson,[35] all jumping in-world as avatars.

This is just the beginning, it seems. More than gaming, *Fortnite*'s vision of an entertainment world now spans beyond gaming consoles, mobile devices, and computers. "I do believe in this future of the world in which billions of people are wearing AR hardware, AR glasses are their everyday life and I believe that's the entertainment platform of the future," Sweeney stated recently. "And we're gonna be there."[36]

As you can see, the MMOSGs Roblox, *Minecraft*, and *Fortnite* each have many parallels to the vision of the metaverse. They have their own community, digital currency, and an economy based on a large number of digital skins, fashion apparel, and an increasing number of digital items that can be traded. To some level, they each allow 3D user-generated content (UGC) to be published. Roblox, for instance, leverages that power from the developer community it gathered. At the end of 2021, almost all of the games available on Roblox were created independent of the parent company. Although there are several shared characteristics, none of them is *the* metaverse we're addressing in this book, no matter what people might lead you to believe.

Also, through them, younger generations of users are already getting accustomed to playing and creating daily with 3D digital elements. 3D is going to be the next mainstream format of information and these platforms are making them at ease with three-dimensional digital spaces, objects, and representations of people, in advance of the metaverse actually being built. Twenty years ago, the main communication format on your phone was the voice call; then we started using text messages through SMS, WhatsApp, and Signal; then we started to share images through Pinterest and Instagram; share videos through platforms like YouTube and TikTok. Now this new generation of players is privileging the interaction within 3D environments because they're already doing it successfully and periodically, through online social gaming.

After voice, text, image, and videos, 3D interactions (via 2D screens) is now mainstream. It's the movement to bring 3D interactions in virtual and augmented worlds that will be the shift. "You absolutely can expect us to do things in gaming," explained Microsoft CEO Satya Nadella. "So, in some sense, they're 2D today, and the question is can you now take that to a full 3D world? We absolutely plan to do so."[37] John Riccitiello, CEO of Unity, has a similar view: "We believe the adoption of real-time 3D will change the way people interact with digital content and entertainment. . . . We expect more of the world's content to be 3D, real-time, and interactive. We believe this cycle will create an addressable market that presents us with decades of opportunity."[38]

Online Worlds for Sale

But gaming platforms are not the only ones leveraging 3D social networks and digital economies. More recently, games like The Sandbox, Somnium Space, SuperWorld, and Decentraland drew even closer to these creator communities by opening their very own digital worlds, all built on the blockchain. Decentraland is a social VR app and, as the name states, its governance is blockchain based and decentralized. This means the owners of their $LAND and cryptocurrency $MANA tokens will have a vote on all major decisions and investments the platform has to make. This world is run by a decentralized autonomous organization (DAO), meaning token owners are truly platform owners. The term "users" is no longer accurate. People that are a part of these platforms are creators, owners, and investors.

The same kind of decentralization happens inside The Sandbox. Although it started out in 2011 as a mobile game, it evolved into a full-blown blockchain-based UGC ecosystem with a market value that reached $3.88 billion. Sandbox owners (in this case, $SAND token owners) are also eligible to vote for major platform decisions, play games, attend shows, create and trade NFTs, as well as buy and sell digital land.

What makes digital properties valuable inside one of these platforms, besides their relative locations, is the quality of activities users look for when visiting or recommending them. So, yes, as with any other service platform, having good content, good experiences, good reasons for people to care about is, at the end of the day, what drives users anywhere. However, this value is directly dependent on how exclusive that content is.

Another very debatable topic driving digital land value up is digital scarcity. When a brand buys a digital property, it buys it because there is a small number of these available in that world to be bought. So if there is demand for these, their value will go up. If that platform's owner was to create as much digital land as you'd want, having digital property would become a commodity, similar to having a website and its value would go down accordingly.

Because of this artificial demand and scarcity, these platforms started gold rushes of their own and are now selling digital real estate, with property prices that soared above the one-million-dollar mark. Brands like Samsung and Adidas have bought and used their digital land to promote both physical and digital products.

Between past experiences, existing gaming platforms, and digital land up for grabs, there are already several 3D spaces that some pundits may point out as being "the metaverse" or multiple "metaverses" with little ems, as the journalist and author Charlie Fink puts it. Of course, this only helps to build up the confusion. You shouldn't say you're building your own metaverse the same way you don't say you're building your own Internet or your own World Wide Web.

The metaverse will be built of interconnected digital worlds, which will have lands, satellites, and their own characteristics.

There are still many unanswered questions, though. Are these the only kinds of metaverse platforms we're bound to encounter? What characteristics do they share? What components are required to interconnect worlds and make a metaverse that is useful and fair?

Infrastructure

Although it's tempting to assume so, the metaverse services actually will not be built just by publishing 3D interactive content. For real-time interactivity to happen, you'll need ultra-high-speed and a continuous, almost imperceptible, data transmission. Because, as you'll see, data is at the core of the metaverse-to-be.

First of all, telcos are the major players ensuring connectivity and high speeds. XR is an added value to business models for 5G and, in the future, 6G. So, it comes as no surprise that the two largest U.S. telecoms, AT&T and Verizon, have already declared publicly their commitment to the building of the metaverse. Deutsche Telekom in Germany and SK Telecom in South Korea have done the same. Yang Maeng-seog, head of SKT's metaverse business unit, even held a press conference in a virtual world just to announce it. "We have been receiving hundreds of partnership offers . . . we are aiming to expand our services beyond Korea and to the global audience."[39] More than a new set of services, telcos see the metaverse as a new and unexplored channel to expand their portfolio, where so much more data will flow.

But besides flowing, data and content need to be governed. Enabling blockchain applications as a way to deal with unforeseen shortcomings has a growing consensus as, at the very least, a booster of transaction transparency and safety in the metaverse. Although Bitcoin remains the most well-known cryptocurrency, Ethereum is a close second, sustaining digital contracts, NFT trading applications, and most of the remaining 9,000+ cryptocurrencies available on the market.

Other, more enterprise-minded blockchains like Quorum, Corda, and MultiChain are also enabling private organizations. They ease the creation of private blockchains, with improved safety traits which cater to more than 80 million crypto wallets already created in 2022.

Still, the infrastructure necessary for the metaverse includes services that still don't exist. To allow our navigation through the different worlds of the metaverse, we'll need our individual data, payment data, interaction data, and data governance to be persistently accessible by us. That requires services that can safeguard our identity, our private data, and our means of payment in every world we visit. Each must be built alongside and integrated within the infrastructure from day one.

Interface

The biggest companies within the space are building their own head-mounted display (HMD) headset or have partnered with others to build one, in order to own the entry point and potentially become the hardware provider for the greatest number of markets.

Corporate players producing VR headsets include Meta with their Quest glasses, along with HP, Pico, Varjo, and HTC, to name a few. The first AR headsets are being built by Microsoft (although they access what they call mixed reality), Jio, and Lenovo, and by start-ups like Nreal, Lynx, North (bought by Google), and Magic Leap.

But not everyone is betting on HMDs. Elon Musk created Neuralink, a company developing brain–computer interfaces to go beyond vision and create a totally new way for users to issue commands and see holograms through the power of brainwaves. Although not every company has implant technology on their development road map, the movement to what's next after glasses is already underway. How intrusive will it be? Well, that remains to be seen.

As tech launches go, the most exciting—and nerve-wracking— has been the to-be-launched new headset by Apple. It has been eagerly awaited by fans and pundits alike for years now, some antic-ipating similar around-the-block lines as with the iPod launch. In this day and age, people order products online, and so that kind of physical manifestation of excitement is highly unlikely. But, if it bring more mainstream attention to the topics of the metaverse and sparks creativity and visions of a potential future, Apple's device can be a tipping point.

Although you may see trade magazine headlines the day of Apple's glasses launch that say, "The metaverse is here!," don't believe the hype. First, because Apple probably isn't going to call what they are providing access to a "metaverse," and, second, it will surely be just another stepping stone toward a better technology. You likely don't even remember the (lack of) features on the earli-est smartphones and computers. The first iPhone didn't allow copy and paste between applications, and the Macintosh 128K lacked a built-in fan and sometimes overheated. Only when your friends and your friend's friends appear wearing AR glasses or when you receive them at work will the metaverse—or whatever we will be calling it then—have arrived.

But that will only be the beginning. It will be amplified when we touch, feel, grab, and drag these 3D elements with the help of haptic gloves or rings, for instance. And let's not forget the plethora of new devices connecting objects to places, to people, to other objects, and to the Internet.

Big Tech and 3D Content

Several key stakeholders are busy laying the 3D groundwork for the metaverse to come into existence. Due to their ambition and bud-gets, Big Tech companies are leading this effort. Each one of them is hoping to own a big chunk of the upcoming hybrid reality.

Microsoft Azure's Spatial Anchors, Apple's Location Anchors, and Google's Cloud Anchors are platforms that already allow users to participate in persistent 3D AR experiences on location. A corner may seem empty in physical reality, but it may hold an AR shoe store for one user or an AR bank for another. Niantic began to lay their claim with their worldwide phenomenon *Pokémon GO* and has ever since been building on its community and ability to scan the world. Cloud providers are not only doing their business of hosting files in their big data centers, they are also enabling creators with their own 3D creation tools. For instance, Amazon Web Services (AWS) owns both a technology to publish VR/AR experiences on the web named Sumerian and allows anyone to quickly deploy VR social meeting rooms through the open-source engine Mozilla Hubs (hubs.mozilla.com).

All these platforms need static and video content assets in 3D, which are being created and collected by the likes of Unity and Sketchfab (purchased by Epic Games in 2021). 3D fashion clothing is also being designed by fashion houses such as Gucci, Dolce & Gabbana, and Tommy Hilfiger or digital-fashion designer studios like The Fabricant.

Artificial intelligence is starting to automate and ultimately disrupt several processes. A good example can be seen on the AI-generated content being published daily by DALL-E or Midjourney. You can see it working at https://beta.openai.com/playground. Expect some 3D content to be AI-generated in the short term. UGC content in social media may well evolve into AI-generated content (AIGC) and that might very well be true for the metaverse.

Applications and Experiences

After 3D digital worlds become possible to access through headsets connected to the necessary infrastructure, we'll be able to finally build the applications that most of us will see every day. Epic and Unity's 3D animation engines will continue to breed new media, entertainment, and gaming markets from the ground up. Social media players like Meta, Snap, Twitter, and social VR platforms like Rec Room and VRChat will likely continue to empower creators and developers to build UGC content.

We will also see more enterprise solutions ranging from health, education, retail, and real estate to tourism, manufacturing, logistics, and advertising down the road. Of course, advertising will prove to be a very important piece of the puzzle, and its importance and size will vary immensely on the way data is governed inside the metaverse.

And let's not forget the need for a search engine or several that allow standard discovery of new services and content across worlds, regardless of where a user is. "The metaverse will only serve to enhance the search industry," shares Anne Ahola Ward, futurist and technical SEO expert. "People are always going to need a way to discover information or ask for help. If anything, the metaverse will help drive the future evolution of search as we know it."[40]

Conclusion

So, who will win and own the metaverse? That's a nearly impossible question to answer, but, hopefully, all of us. A true metaverse will need to be single, interoperable, and increasingly decentralized. It will grant us the opportunity to own our identity and the data we generate through our interactions across every world. Given the opportunities and social impacts, building an open structure where each of us partly owns the shared public space seems to take advantage of the new technologies, infrastructure, and creation process that the metaverse is bringing. Or maybe the best governance model is replicating the way the Internet is organized right now.

However, these visions are at odds with the well-established and deep-pocketed gatekeepers. It is expected that they will try to advance their own versions of the metaverse to avoid relinquishing control of their privileges.

Their effort is bringing many short-term benefits. They are investing in building up the first platforms and tools, while educating users on how to use them and create for them. To this effect, they actively sponsor the much-needed research and development that's improving all of the metaverse building blocks. Finally, we have to take into account the pioneer effect. It's anticipated that first logins into the metaverse will happen through existing platforms, as users feel safer with existing Big Tech brands than newcomers.

Odds are that we will start with a metaverse filled with links or portals integrating versions of these platforms together. Then, slowly, the structure of a single metaverse will mature and begin to solidify and the discussions of ownership will take the main stage.

Which companies will be the leaders in hardware, software, and the most popular applications and content is yet to be determined, although many companies want to declare some kind of victory. It's entirely possible that there will be new Big Tech brands appearing. But no matter what, we are at that moment in history where a new path is being defined.

Notes

1. Chris Stokel-Walker, "Why has Facebook changed its name to Meta and what is the metaverse?" *New Scientist*, October 29, 2021. www.news cientist.com/article/2295438-why-has-facebookchanged-its-name-to-meta-and-what-is-the-metaverse

2. https://techcrunch.com/2021/11/08/niantic-reveals-its-vision-for-a-real-world-metaverse-releases-lightship-ar-developer-kit

3. Matthew Terndrup, "Flashback: Tony Parisi on co-creating the virtual reality markup language." *UploadVR*, April 9, 2015. uploadvr.com/flashback-tony-parisi-on-co-creating-the-virtual-reality-markup-language-vrml-for-the-web-in-the-1990s

4. www.khronos.org/gltf

5. Mark Pesce, "Across the metaverse." *Cosmos*, August 27, 2021. http://cosmosmagazine.com/technology/across-the-metaverse

6. Andrew E. Chow, "6 lessons on the future of the metaverse from the creator of Second Life." *Time*, November 26, 2021. time.com/6123333/metaverse-second-life-lessons

7. Leslie Jamison, "The digital ruins of a forgotten future." *The Atlantic*, December 2017. www.theatlantic.com/magazine/archive/2017/12/second-life-leslie-jamison/544149

8. Parmy Olson, "Remember Second Life? That Could Be Facebook's Future." *Washington Post,* February 7, 2022. www.washingtonpost .com/business/remember-second-life-that-could-be-facebooks-future/2022/02/06/e30a928c-8755-11ec-838f-0cfdf69cce3c_story.html

9. Chow, "6 lessons," 2021.

10. Alexa Tanen, "7 Dungeons & Dragons statistics you should know about." *Dice Cove*, n.d. http://dicecove.com/dnd-statistics

11. Omer Altay, "The oldest MMORPGS in gaming history." *MMOS*, February 28, 2015. http://mmos.com/editorials/oldest-mmorpgs

12. Šerif Pilipović, "World of Warcraft statistics and facts 2022." *LEVVVEL*, March 8, 2022. http://levvvel.com/world-of-warcraft-statistics-and-facts

13. James Whatley, "The metaverse doesn't exist! You're talking about gaming." *The Drum*, May 17, 2022. www.thedrum.com/opinion/2022/05/17/the-metaverse-doesn-t-exist-you-re-talking-about-gaming

14. Rebecca O'Neill, "10 facts you didn't know about the making of Roblox." *The Gamer*, February 6, 2021. www.thegamer.com/the-making-of-roblox-history

15. Taylor Lyles, "Over half of US kids are playing Roblox, and it's about to host Fortnite-esque virtual parties too." *The Verge*, June 21, 2020. www .theverge.com/2020/7/21/21333431/roblox-over-half-of-us-kids-playing-virtual-parties-fortnite

16. https://finbold.com/roblox-ceo-says-were-in-the-middle-of-the-metaverse-right-now

17. Jordan McDonald, "Roblox's metaverse is already here, and it's wildly popular." *Emerging Tech Brew*, December 10, 2021. www .emergingtechbrew.com/stories/2021/12/10/roblox-s-metaverse-is-already-here-and-it-s-wildly-popular

18. Sean Murray, "Roblox is a cesspool of child abuse according to new report." *The Gamer*, December 13, 2021. www.thegamer.com/roblox-child-abuse-people-make-games-report

19. KidzToPros, "Minecraft vs Roblox: Which game is the best choice for your child?" *KidzToPros*, April 11, 2021 (blog). blog.kidztopros .com/blog/minecraft-vs-roblox-which-is-the-best-choice-for-your-child

20. David Curry, "Minecraft revenue and usage statistics (2022)." *Business of Apps*, May 4, 2022. www.businessofapps.com/data/minecraft-statistics

21. Genxee, "7 years later Minecraft $2.5B deal Microsoft's most successful acquisition?" *Influencive*, June 30, 2021. www.influencive.com/7-years-later-minecraft-2-5b-deal-microsofts-most-successful-acquisition

22. Andrew Galstian, "A complete history of Minecraft." *GAMERANT*, October 1, 2020. http://gamerant.com/minecraft-timeline-history

23. Mike Minotti, "Sensor Tower: Minecraft Earth dug up 1.2 million U.S. downloads in its first week." *VentureBeat*, November 21, 2019. http://venturebeat.com/2019/11/21/sensor-tower-minecraft-earth-dug-up-1-2-million-u-s-downloads-in-its-first-week

24. J. Clement, "Number of Pokémon GO app downloads worldwide from 3rd quarter 2016 to 4th quarter 2021." *Statista*, February 2, 2022, www.statista.com/statistics/641690/pokemon-go-number-of-downloads-worldwide

25. J. Clement, "Cumulative number of copies of Minecraft sold worldwide as of April 2021." *Statista*, May 6, 2022. www.statista.com/statistics/680124/minecraft-unit-sales-worldwide

26. Vasuda Bachchan, "5 reasons why Minecraft is the best-selling video game of all time." *Sportskeeda*, September 11, 2020. www.sportskeeda.com/esports/5-reasons-minecraft-best-selling-video-game-time

27. Max Eddy, "Minecraft (for PC) review." *PC*, January 25, 2016. www.pcmag.com/reviews/minecraft-for-pc

28. Rey Barreto, "History of Fortnite." *Sutori*, n.d. www.sutori.com/story/history-of-fortnite

29. Jimmy Donnellan, "The forgotten history of Fortnite." *Cultured Vultures*, March 26, 2021. culturedvultures.com/fortnite-history-development

30. Mansoor Iqbal, "Fortnite usage and revenue statistics (2022)." *Business of Apps*, June 30, 2022, www.businessofapps.com/data/fortnite-statistics

31. Donnellan, "The forgotten history," 2021.

32. Sam Gutelle, "After record-setting broadcast with Drake, Twitch streamer ninja says he makes $500,000 per month." *Tubefilter*, March 19, 2018. www.tubefilter.com/2018/03/19/tyler-blevins-ninja-twitch-subscribers

33. Malcolm Owen, "Epic Games vs Apple trial, verdict, and aftermath – all you need to know." *Apple Insider*, March 26, 2022. appleinsider.com/articles/20/08/23/apple-versus-epic-games-fortnite-app-store-saga----the-story-so-far

34. Mark Delaney and Joey Carr, "Fortnite: Every icon series skin so far." *Gamespot*, April 19, 2022. www.gamespot.com/articles/fortnite-every-icon-series-skin-so-far/1100-6495639

35. Rishabh Sabarwal, "3 celebrity cameos in Fortnite that failed terribly (and 3 that were a hit)." *Sportskeeda*, January 4, 2022. www.sportskeeda.com/fortnite/fortnite-celebrity-skins-popular-failed

36. Ian Hamilton, "Epic Games CEO Tim Sweeney on AR: 'we're going to need very strong privacy protections.'" *UploadVR*, March 26, 2019. http://uploadvr.com/tim-sweeney-ar

37. Dina Bass and Emily Chang, "Microsoft's own metaverse is coming, and it will have PowerPoint." *Bloomberg*, November 2, 2021. www.bloomberg.com/news/articles/2021-11-02/microsoft-s-own-metaverse-is-coming-and-it-will-have-powerpoint

38. Wall Street Reporter, "CEOs of Matterport, Liquid Avatar, Unity and ESE Entertainment targeting billion dollar market opportunities and explosive revenue growth in the metaverse and digital entertainment." *Yahoo!* February 9, 2022. www.yahoo.com/now/ceos-matterport-liquid-avatar-unity-150900108.html

39. Yoon So-Yeon, "SK Telecom talks new virtual world in its metaverse press conference." *Korea JoongAng Daily*, August 19, 2021. koreajoongangdaily.joins.com/2021/08/19/business/tech/metaverse-ifland-sk-telecom/20210819174100435.html

40. Personal communication, July, 2022.

Chapter 4
New Rules

We demand rigidly defined areas of doubt and uncertainty!
—Douglas Adams, The Hitchhiker's Guide to the Galaxy

Based on the collective lessons we've learned since the dawn of the Internet, we should all be happy to see more than *just* a few large companies involved in the creation of the metaverse. Governments and standards organizations worldwide, independent developers and creators, start-ups and universities are already stepping up to play their roles. Each is exercising a degree of influence on how every player acts and how this new hybrid dimension will work for us all.

Governments

When you talk about different business industries, sometimes you forget how fundamental governments are in defining the success of a marketplace. Besides their influence on health, education, security, and the entire monetary system, governments can subsidize industry growth or create tariffs on foreign competitive products to boost local production. On the flip side, new regulations, additional taxes, and fees can slow down marketplace growth.[1]

Around the world, governments are already setting up strategies to leverage the speed and size (and yes, the hype) of the future metaverse. Their motivations range from boosting their own digital economies, enriching their talent pool, and supporting job growth to testing new ways to compete, fighting new kinds of illiteracies within their countries, enabling effective public policy, regulation, and, well, taxes.

Cryptocurrencies

Cryptos are already influencing economic policy. Some 100 countries are exploring central bank digital currencies (CBDCs) in order to create a more transparent and standard approach.[2] Just a few examples: in September 2021, El Salvador adopted Bitcoin as an official CBDC, and one year before, in the Bahamas, the Sand Dollar started circulating. In China, the digital Renminbi boasts more than a hundred million individual users and billions of Yuan in transactions. Nigeria became the first country in Africa to introduce a digital currency, called eNaira, which facilitates diaspora remittances and social welfare disbursements to citizens.

This push is bound to bring cryptocurrency into the mainstream in some form, which will multiply the number of crypto wallets in use to an estimated 4.4 billion users by 2025,[3] exponentiating the number of global crypto-transactions. This is where taxes come into play. It's not just that the metaverse market value is estimated at a range from 1.5 trillion dollars[4] to 13 trillion dollars.[5] There's also a clear need to add transparency to every transaction and professional activity and bring all of them to the formal global economy.

In the United States, the IRS gives no specific guidance on digital property or NFT trading. Some existing tax rules can apply but these are still confusing for tax advisors. For instance, a direct crypto-to-crypto trade is seen as a sale and is therefore subject to capital gains tax. For example, when you swap Ethereum with other cryptocurrencies or sell NFTs. However, while NFTs can be considered collectibles and have a different tax rate, they're not *officially* defined as "collectibles" by the IRS. Just one of the many causes for the 2022 debate around crypto taxes.[6]

Other countries like Portugal or Hong Kong take more lenient views. "If digital assets are bought for long-term investment purposes, any profits from disposal would not be chargeable to profits tax,"[7] says Henri Arslanian, global crypto leader at PwC, highlighting how the Special Administrative Region of China does not tax cryptos owned by individuals, but only by businesses.

Other tax authorities, like the Inter-American Center of Tax Administrations (CIAT), even hope that part of the tax collection process itself becomes decentralized and automated on the blockchain.[8]

The hype around cryptocurrencies hit the apex in November 2021. Then the following May, TerraUSD, a stablecoin, and its crypto sister Luna both dropped in value and were delisted.[9] Next came Bitcoin, which lost 50 percent of its value, and Ethereum, the second most valuable cryptocurrency, was down by 60 percent. On one day, the entire market lost $200 billion. What was considered to be stable within the already volatile crypto industry suddenly was absolutely not. How did this happen? Many reasons were considered: inflation, interest rate hikes, reduction in the faith of crypto, the end of the financial impact of the pandemic, the war in Ukraine,[10] geopolitical instability, and the fall of the stock market.[11]

In June 2022, crypto had its first insider trading case. Although the loss of billions and illegal acts are terrible news, it didn't mean the end of the industry. According to the Gartner Hype Cycle[12], this happens just before that technology climbs the "slope of enlightenment" to reach the "plateau of productivity," while expediting regulations.[13] New technology always implicates the need to solve new sets of problems.

The attention being given to these issues and the fact that public authorities consider these strategies in their future plans shows how disruptive the metaverse could be and how seriously public officials are considering it.

Several kinds of public services are blossoming in virtual worlds. In late 2021, the Seoul Metropolitan government announced its 3.9 billion South Korean Won (KRW) ($3.3 million USD) plan to create a "Metaverse Seoul" over five years.[14] Although this amounted to a virtual version of the New Year's bell-ringing ceremony and other cultural events, 2023 is scheduled to see the launch of new services, including a public mayor's office capable of handling civil complaints and legal consultations, as well as business hubs, a start-up incubator, and a public investment organization. This is only part of the 223.7 billion KRW ($187 million USD) budget pledged by the South Korean ICT Ministry to develop their own metaverse ecosystem.[15] So it's fair to say there will be much more metaverse news in Korea in the next couple of years.

But other governments are also very active. Barbados established an actual embassy in the metaverse,[16] while Shanghai opened its holographic City Hall.[17] By developing virtual facilities and issuing meta-visas for their citizens, these countries and cities accelerate their citizens' onboarding on virtual worlds. Most of these government development plans include investments and incentive funding directly aimed at bringing in more entities to the mix; bridging efforts to accelerate research and development; instilling trust in this new ecosystem; connecting private and public interest; and bringing new services into the mainstream.

Developing official metaverse-related initiatives signals to both markets and professionals that governments are beginning to envision a future that needs to be built, which opens an avenue for new qualified jobs. Not just the ones hired to kick off and maintain public services in the metaverse, but an entire ecosystem of companies and talent. We don't know all of the new jobs that are coming, so we can only prepare for the future by getting ready for the jobs we know that are coming.

Considering that, in the current state of the mobile Internet, we are still fighting a digital divide, making sure everyone gets a fair chance in the metaverse is now fundamental. As the number of converging technologies evolving is so large, it makes this task even more complicated. Should you prioritize, budget, and then fund awareness and education on AI, AR, blockchain? All of them? Only some? Or should governments focus on the original divide and keep building from that point? It's still unclear, but basic access to the Internet and hardware is not equally available around the world and the metaverse can deepen that chasm. Take the warning of Elena Estavillo, former Commissioner of the Mexican Federal Telecommunications Institute (IFT): "Although [metaverse-related services] penetration has been growing in Mexico, not all people who have a cell phone have access to mobile data or may have a plan only to access basic services and not this new technology that will be very demanding in terms of data and connection."[18]

Public Standards Organizations

Governments are not the only ones to make the metaverse a more equitable and accessible system. One of the biggest hurdles for the metaverse to overcome is interoperability, granting each user access to every corner of the metaverse from anywhere else. Ensuring that in any integrated global system is nothing short of daunting. Now add a number of intersecting technologies and the vision of a hybrid world that we're not yet absolutely sure what it will look like, and you'll begin to realize how difficult this effort will be and how long it might take.

Those within the tech field understand that the metaverse will be the biggest, most complex endeavor in digital interoperability since the Internet. Any large shift takes time, effort, and funding. Choosing and possibly designing the right protocols and standards will be a necessary step for its growth into the mainstream, as well as to bring it into the creator economy. Standards are a shared set of rules that make sure that machines can communicate with each other efficiently. Take the World Wide Web, for instance. The largest network of content in the world uses HTTP (Hypertext Transfer Protocol) to make sure all web pages have the same basic structure and that a link can be operated in the same way.

Many experts believe that links can be the solution to interoperability, which means that the existing web is the best basis for a future single metaverse. Tony Parisi, co-creator of VRML, claims in his Metaverse Manifesto that "The Metaverse is the Internet." He says that we will use Web2 initially to create Web3 because there is "too much invested in the current infrastructure, and too high switching costs inherent in such a change, that it will simply never happen."[19]

This creates new challenges for using the web as the protocol of choice to navigate the metaverse. As Parisi states, "Where possible, legacy Internet and Web services will be subsumed into new paradigms, and novel methods of user access, content distribution, visual presentation, real-time communication and interaction developed as needed."[20]

WebXR standards are already being proposed by W3C to enable immersive experiences over the web. W3C's goal is to create "open standards to ensure the long-term growth of the Web."[21] To pursue that, it has created work groups like the Metaverse Interoperability Community Group, open to the community and specifically intended to ease up immersive content publishing and distribution over the web.[22]

Another influential standards organization is the Khronos Group, an open consortium of 170 industry-leading companies created in the year 2001 to maintain "royalty-free open standards for 3D graphics, Virtual and Augmented Reality, Parallel Computing, Machine Learning, and Vision Processing" as they announce on their home page. A widely used standard set by the Khronos Group is OpenXR, which streamlines XR experiences distribution and allows developers to be able to develop once and publish on different platforms. "We are gonna need an inordinate amount of interoperability, so for those of us that are active fostering collaboration through open source and open standards, we're gonna have a busy time over the next few years, as the metaverse comes together," shares Neil Trevett, president of the Khronos Group.[23] This was the main reason why many standards organizations and companies gathered around the tenet of an open metaverse and founded the Metaverse Standards Forum.[24]

But standard practices are not limited to technological software and hardware, as it's not only machines that need to find rules to speak to other machines. We humans also need to establish rules of communication when in new environments, and safety and privacy standards in virtual worlds are already visible in our digital lives. For instance, the XR Safety Initiative (XRSI) launched the XRSI Privacy and Safety Framework,[25] a set of tools to manage and mitigate safety and data risks these new worlds are bringing us. "Consumers have to be made aware, first, of the consequences, then second, of the control mechanisms that actually are being built so that people can be a little bit more in control of their data,"[26] shared Kavya Pearlman, founder and CEO of XRSI. (Full disclosure: Both authors of this book are on the advisory board of XRSI.)

No matter how many organizations and consortiums are created, the value of a tech standard is defined by its adoption. Only with the mainstream use of standards by developers is their value made tangible. This is especially challenging for a global metaverse standard while distrust between many nations is on the rise. Just think of how difficult it can be to have China, Russia, and the United States agree on shared data safety protocols. Or any protocol for that matter.

Creators and Communities

Although Big Tech might give the impression that they are filled with makers and creators, these companies technically are mainly hosting and enabling makers and creators. As with all versions of the Internet, the creative communities deliver the most value for users in the metaverse. (So you know, we're bundling all front-end and gaming developers, photo and video content producers and influencers as creators.) They hold the market's direction and choice of standards of the metaverse. As the saying used to go, "Content is King [and Queen]."

If you don't work in technology, you may not see the tremendous impact of developers and creators within the ecosystem.

Think of "hosting and enabling" like an iPhone. An iPhone is/was a tremendously innovative technology and set in motion one of the biggest economic and behavioral transformations we've seen. However, without applications, a consumer sees it mainly as an interactive screen with the ability to make calls (if you even do that anymore), schedule meetings, and do a couple of other things. The App Store turns the iPhone into a much more valuable and alluring experience. It gives you access to an ecosystem of games, tools, and experiences built by companies worldwide who compete for your time, attention, and engagement with their product. Each of them hopes that their app will become part of your daily (hourly?) ritual, like social media applications, which weren't even imagined at the launch of the Internet. They have become so widely distributed to audiences that new income streams, jobs, and an entire digital studio ecosystem was born from it.

For the Internet, the launch of Web 2.0 solidified the value of creators and developers of all ages, and the diversity of tools today enables virtually anyone to be a content creator. Could anyone have anticipated that Generation Alpha would birth a grade school social media influencer with 30 million+ followers?[27] What about a teenage girl dancer who found herself with over 100 million followers?[28] A true creator economy has been set in motion, where communities are not only spawning creators, but overall helping them to remain independent and relevant. Those who were once followers are now supporters, patrons, or fans.

With several new platforms available in the gaming industry and in the so-called Web3 businesses, new avenues for distributing digital products and content are being envisioned and built. Social blockchain tokens can be issued by brands, influencers, or creators, and reward programs are now integrating them.

"Web3 is starting to turn users and contributors into investors, and vice versa," shared Ian Lee, co-founder of the DAO software company Syndicate.[29] In mid-2022, one million DAOs were accounted for.[30] DAOs are model decentralized communities that organize themselves around a purpose without an actual CEO or CFO in place. They are similar to clubs or co-ops, where members acquire a minimum number of tokens that grant them power to vote on decisions, access to communication tools and other means that the DAO grants, besides the benefit of the community network and its potential profits and rewards, whatever form they may take. Members of DAOs are in this sense also similar to shareholders in many ways.

There are already many types of DAOs:

- Collector: *For group ownership of art*[31]
- Entertainment: *For voting rights over IP ownership*[32]
- Grant (aka Launchpad): *Enables groups to support projects*[33]
- Investor (aka Venture): *A distributed ownership of a company*[34]
- Media: *A way to support creation without advertising*[35]
- Operating: *Enables way to manage decision-making for a single organization*[36]
- Protocol (automatic market maker [AMM]): *Allows for group voting*[37]
- Service: *Supports and rewards talent hunting*[38]
- Social (aka Social Media): *Created to enable networking among owners*[39]

"DAOs are almost the purest manifestation of what Web3 and crypto are all about," says Ali Yahya of Andreessen Horowitz, one of the most active venture capitalists in this area.[40] One of the values of DAOs is that "with the click of a button" you can " . . . catalyze thousands or tens of thousands of people . . . eventually . . . millions of people . . . that all put together capital and put together ideas to work together for some common goal," he continued, regarding their investment in PleasrDAO.[41]

Effectively, the web is spawning a fresh new breed of fan-governed communities that are fundamentally shifting the balance of power inside the creator economy. More than users, fans are becoming drivers of the business world; it's now being driven not only by creators, investors, and businesses, but also by the communities themselves, that now include owners and investors. But they won't be the only ones.

Disruptors and Academia

Even with Big Tech's billions of investments in the metaverse, there is still the potential for a start-up, and likely many start-ups, to establish themselves within the new industry. Disruptive technologies generally aren't tested in the market by large organizations sitting on a steady business flow. They are built by innovators who can spot what is missing and are able to seize the opportunity in a timely manner.

There are a huge number of start-ups pushing forward the different technologies inside the metaverse building blocks. However, there are other key organizations that directly influence their outcomes.

Ever heard of Zynga, the makers of FarmVille? Oculus? Even Instagram? All of them were start-ups, disrupting their industries' business as usual. Even if you aren't in the start-up business, investments in new companies can give insights into the direction of industries. Or, at the very least, what people believe to be the trajectory of an industry and/or technology.

Open innovation and acceleration programs can also provide metaverse-related start-ups with investment opportunities, training, mentoring, and corporate leads for them to pilot their solutions with. Outlier Venture's Open Metaverse (http://outlierventures.io/base-camp) and The Sandbox Metaverse Accelerator Program (www.brinc.io/metaverse) are examples of metaverse acceleration efforts, bringing in millions of dollars or euros to support new start-ups in the field. And let's not forget Meta that, in addition to committing to 10,000 new jobs in the European Union, continues its push by setting up a FAIR accelerator in Germany and supporting several Metaverse grant programs.[42] Mainstream accelerators like Disney's, NVIDIA's, and Y Combinator have already invested in metaverse companies and new ones are going down the same path, like FOV Ventures[43], Krew,[44] and Seedify's DAO (http://seedify .fund).These, along with traditional investors, can definitely boost a start-up's chances of success.

An early 2022 report identified the biggest investors in the market at that time as being a16z, Galaxy (U.S.), Makers Fund, Animoca Brands, and Tencent (Asia), which portfolio of investments might shed a light on the priorities and vertical areas of start-up investment in this market.[45]

Many countries also support innovation directly and tech disruptors started their journey thanks to public research and development programs and their funding. Pillar II of the Horizon Europe program will fund €53 billion to "strengthen the impact of R&I in developing, supporting and implementing Union policies, and support the uptake of innovative solutions in industry, in particular in SMEs and start-ups, and society to address global challenges."[46] The Crown Prince of the UAE announced in July 2022 that his metaverse strategy would add 40,000 jobs and $4 billion to the economy. This should start by "fostering talent and investing in future capabilities by providing the necessary support in metaverse education aimed at developers, content creators and users of digital platforms in the metaverse community."[47]

The geography of these investments and acceleration initiatives is going to affect the concentration of start-ups, talent, and innovation in the physical world and directly influence which nations will be part of the first wave of metaverse users. Wherever there is investment, expect new companies, new jobs, and a new metaverse economy to pop up in the coming years.

Deep Tech Start-Ups

Innovation can come in all shapes and sizes and deep tech startups are becoming common in a space where transformation is so foundational. Deep tech (DT) is focused on creating value-added products from the most challenging research innovations. It's tech development before target market identification. These start-ups focus on the hardest technical challenges without having clear, pre-defined solutions. There are over 1,000 investors in deep tech across the world (although most non-exclusively).[48] Although more traditional investors and accelerators are realizing the impact of the metaverse, it's deep tech investors that are looking beyond the first few building blocks. They are betting on discoveries of the unforeseen applications, born out of the convergence of different technologies and how they will weave together, with patent development being of utmost importance.[49] Essentially, it's worth tracking deep tech developments to see what's coming next.[50]

Universities

Most of the deep tech insights that generate these start-ups stem from universities. These have their own accelerators and innovation ecosystems that support students wanting to build game-changing tech companies, while boosting new research opportunities and the number of internships available.

Recently, some universities have redefined what digital learning is, by setting up shop in the metaverse. University of Miami's XR Initiative[51] now includes three VR campuses where students can explore a wide array of topics in VR classrooms. Arizona State University's Narrative and Emerging Media program is being led by Nonny de la Peña, one of the most impactful VR storytellers.[52] The University of Pennsylvania's Wharton created a Cypher Accelerator for blockchain and crypto start-ups. The Tokyo-based public Chuo University has a VR-based class to teach students English.[53]

To boost innovation, many universities are preparing their own special metaverse efforts and have changed their curriculum. Manchester Metropolitan University in the United Kingdom and Lethbridge College in Canada have metaverse-related courses ongoing for years now and several other universities are following their example. Sammy Popat, interim director of the Mixed/Augmented/Virtual Reality Innovation Center (MAVRIC) at the University of Maryland shares that "The University of Maryland, College Park has launched the Immersive Media Design major, the only undergraduate program in the country that synthesizes art with computer science to develop immersive media. Students learn how to code, create and collaborate using digital tools and technologies."[54] Also, the University of Tokyo established a Todai Metaverse world where multiple metaverse-themed classes are taught.[55]

With investments or not, many of those who have grown up playing games and watching concerts in 2D virtual worlds will be entering the workforce. They already will know—and possibly expect—3D universes. And those trained at universities in metaverse-related technologies will have an even greater advantage and opportunity to transform what's ahead. In fact, the next Mark Zuckerberg could be coding a game-changing program from their dorm room or remote classroom right now.

Notes

1. Mary Hall, "Governments' influence on markets." *Investopedia*, May 6, 2022. www.investopedia.com/articles/economics/11/how-governments-influence-markets.asp

2. CBC Radio, "Government-issued digital currency could be the coin of the future." *CBC Radio Spark*, January 14, 2022. www.cbc.ca/radio/spark/if-we-build-the-metaverse-will-anybody-come-1.6312339/government-issued-digital-currency-could-be-the-coin-of-the-future-1.6312460

3. Juniper Research, "Digital wallet users to exceed 4.4 billion by 2025, as mobile drives digital payments' revolution." Juniper Research press release, March 16, 2021. www.juniperresearch.com/press/digital-wallet-users-to-exceed-4-4-billion-by-2025

4. PwC Global, "Seeing is believing: How VR and AR will transform business and the economy." November 19, 2012. www.pwc.com/seeingisbelieving

5. Jack Denton, "Metaverse may be worth $13 trillion, Citi says. What's behind the bullish take on Web3." *Barrons*, March 21, 2022. www.barrons.com/articles/metaverse-web3-Internet-virtual-reality-gaming-nvidia-51648744930

6. Greg Iacurci, "Make a killing on NFTs and crypto? The IRS may tax them differently." *CNBC*, January 11, 2022. www.cnbc.com/2022/01/11/make-a-killing-on-nfts-and-crypto-the-irs-may-tax-them-differently.html

7. Adriana Hamacher and Stephen Graves, "11 countries that don't tax Bitcoin gains." *Decrypt*, (2021). http://decrypt.co/43513/countries-that-dont-tax-bitcoin-gains

8. Alfredo Collosa, "Taxation in the metaverse: Some preliminary considerations." *CIAT*, March 9, 2022. www.ciat.org/ciatblog-blockchain-para-mejorar-la-recaudacion-del-iva-parte-1/?lang=en

9. Marco Quiroz-Gutierrez and Taylor Locke, "A 'stable' coin lost its peg over the weekend and pledged $1.5 billion in Bitcoin trying to stabilize. Here's how the algorithmic stablecoin was supposed to work—and didn't." *Fortune*, May 10, 2022. http://fortune.com/2022/05/10/what-is-algorithmic-stablecoin-terrausd-bitcoin-crash

10. Lion Shirdan, "Top 4 reasons the cryptocurrency market is crashing." *Entrepreneur*, July 1, 2022. www.entrepreneur.com/article/429047

11. Marco Quiroz-Gutierrez, "Why is crypto crashing? Analysts list the key reasons behind this week's implosion." *Fortune*, May 13, 2022. http://fortune.com/2022/05/13/why-is-crypto-crashing-bitcoin-ethereum-tech-stocks

12. One of the most well-known foresight tools, the Gartner Hype Cycle methodology previews how a technology or application will evolve throughout the years, usually obeying the same stages. www.gartner.com/en/research/methodologies/gartner-hype-cycle

13. Ashley Capoot, "Former Coinbase manager and two others charged in crypto insider trading scheme." *CNBC*, July 21, 2022. www.cnbc.com/2022/07/21/former-coinbase-manager-and-two-others-charged-in-insider-trading-plot.html

14. Aaron Chow, "Seoul will be the first city government to establish a metaverse platform." *Hypebeast*, November 9, 2021. hypebeast.com/2021/11/seoul-will-be-the-first-city-government-to-establish-a-metaverse-platform

    Robert Drage and Kyle Baird, "South Korean government investing $186 million into metaverse platform." *Beincrypto*, February 28, 2022. beincrypto.com/south-korean-government-investing-186-million-into-metaverse-platform

15. Jim Wyss, "Barbados is opening a diplomatic embassy in the metaverse." *Bloomberg*, December 14, 2021. www.bloomberg.com/news/articles/2021-12-14/barbados-tries-digital-diplomacy-with-planned-metaverse-embassy

16. One of the most well-known foresight tools, the Gartner Hype Cycle methodology previews how a technology or application will evolve throughout the years, usually obeying the same stages. www.gartner.com/en/research/methodologies/gartner-hype-cycle

17. Arnold Kirimi, "Shanghai includes metaverse in its development plan." *Cointelegraph*, December 21, 2021. http://cointelegraph.com/news/shanghai-includes-metaverse-in-its-development-plan

18. Ethan Rana, "How the digital divide in Mexico will affect the metaverse." *Bullfrag*, January 25, 2022. www.bullfrag.com/how-the-digital-divide-in-mexico-will-affect-the-metaverse

19. Tony Parisi, "The seven rules of the metaverse." *Metaverses*, October 22, 2021. medium.com/meta-verses/the-seven-rules-of-the-metaverse-7d4e06fa864c

20. Tony Parisi, 2021.

21. www.w3.org

22. Metaverse Interoperability Community Group, www.w3.org/community/metaverse-interop

23. Neil Trevett, Ruth Suehle and David Morin, "Open standards governance." *Building the Open Metaverse,* podcast, October 27, 2021. http://cesium.com/open-metaverse-podcast/open-standards-governance

24. https://metaverse-standards.org

25. XRSI, "The XRSI Privacy and Safety Framework." XRSI, n.d. http://xrsi.org

26. Kavya Pearlman, April 20, 2021 in *"The Data Diva" Talks Privacy*, produced by Debbie Reynolds, podcast, www.debbiereynoldsconsulting.com/podcast/e24-kavya-pearlman.

27. It's Ryan Kaji with his YouTube show, Ryan's World.

28. Charli D'Amelio on TikTok.

29. Miles Kruppa and Hannah Murphy, "Crypto assets inspire new brand of collectivism beyond finance." *Financial Times*, December 27, 2021. www.ft.com/content/c4b6d38d-e6c8-491f-b70c-7b5cf8f0cea6

30. Sharmeen Shehabuddin, "DAOs: Where are you going, where have you been?" *Consensys*, September 24, 2021. http://consensys.net/blog/blockchain-explained/daos-where-are-you-going-where-have-you-been

31. Christian Heidorn, "The top list of DAOs you should know in 2022." Tokenized, n.d. http://tokenizedhq.com/list-of-daos

32. Cointelegraph, "Types of DAOs and how to create a decentralized autonomous organization." *Cointelegraph*, n.d. http://cointelegraph.com/decentralized-automated-organizations-daos-guide-for-beginners/types-of-daos-and-how-to-create-a-decentralized-autonomous-organization

33. Christian Heidorn, n.d.

34. Christian Heidorn, n.d.

35. Christian Heidorn, n.d.

36. Cointelegraph, n.d.

37. Christian Heidorn, n.d.

38. Cointelegraph, n.d.

39. Christian Heidorn, n.d.

40. Lucas Matney, "Andreessen Horowitz backs NFT investor group behind rare Wu-Tang Clan album purchase." *Techcrunch+*, December 14, 2021. http://techcrunch.com/2021/12/14/andreessen-horowitz-backs-nft-investor-group-behind-one-of-a-kind-wu-tang-clan-album-purchase

41. Lucas Matney, 2021.

42. Nick Clegg and Javier Olivan, "Investing in European talent to help build the metaverse." Meta, October 17, 2021, http://about.fb.com/news/2021/10/creating-jobs-europe-metaverse

43. Cindy Tan, "Former director of HTC's global accelerator Vive X launches €25M fund for metaverse investments." *NFTGATORS*, March 11, 2022. www.nftgators.com/former-director-of-htcs-global-accelerator-vive-x-launches-e25m-fund-for-metaverse-investments

44. IshanOnTech, "How the Krew accelerator program will support blockchain start-ups in Web3." *HackerNoon*, June 23, 2022. hackernoon.com/how-the-krew-accelerator-program-will-support-blockchain-start-ups-in-web3

45. Elihay Vidal, "Mapping the Israeli metaverse start-up landscape." *ParlayMe*, January 24. www.parlayme.com/post/mapping-the-israeli-metaverse-start-up-landscape.

46. European Commission, Directorate-General for Research and Innovation, *Horizon Europe, pillar II - Global challenges and European industrial competitiveness*. Publications Office, 2021. `data.europa.eu/doi/10.2777/886065`

47. Marco Quiroz-Gutierrez, "The crown prince of Dubai says he has a 'metaverse strategy' that will add 40,000 jobs and $4 billion to the economy in 5 years." *Fortune*, July 19, 2022. `http://fortune.com/2022/07/19/dubai-metaverse-strategy-crypto-emerging-tech-web3`

48. Hello Tomorrow, "Deep tech investors mapping." Hello Tomorrow, n.d. `http://docs.google.com/spreadsheets/d/1BqNO714kXRhjG5jcB89FwR1huRKBwBKtV7ZHwwLjPhk/htmlview#`

49. `https://technation.io/news/what-does-it-take-to-scale-a-deeptech-company`

50. Hello Tomorrow, "Deep tech investors"

51. Janette Neuwahl Tannen, "University community leaps into the 'metaverse.'" News@TheU, January 20, 2022. `http://news.miami.edu/stories/2022/01/university-community-leaps-into-the-metaverse.html`

52. Darragh Dandurand, "Arizona State launching new VR/AR classes, Nonny De La Peña to helm." *VRSCOUT*, March 28, 2022. `http://vrscout.com/news/arizona-state-launching-new-vr-ar-classes-nonny-de-la-pena-to-helm`

53. Immerse, "Chuo University students launch VR English conversation classes to advance metaverse language learning research." *Immerse* (blog), February 1, 2022. `www.immerse.online/blog/chuo-university-students-launch-vr-english-conversation-classes-to-advance-metaverse-language-learning-research`

54. Personal communication, July 15, 2022.

55. Zen Khurana, "The University of Tokyo gears up to offer courses on metaverse." *AFKGAMING*, July 25, 2022. `http://afkgaming.com/blockchaingames/news/the-university-of-tokyo-gears-up-to-offer-courses-on-metaverse`

Part 3

Opportunities

Chapter 5

A Great Reset

How puzzling all these changes are! I'm never sure what I'm going to
be, from one minute to another.
　　　　—Lewis Carroll, Alice in Alice's Adventures in Wonderland

In June 2020, the annual meeting of the World Economic Forum (WEF), also known as the Davos summit, was held under the ethos of a "Great Reset" for the global economy. The WEF's founder and executive chairman, Klaus Schwab, announced how the COVID-19 crisis had demonstrated just how broken our socio-economic system is and how climate and social change demands that we improve our relationships with one another and with our climate. The UK's now King Charles, during that same event, stressed this message: "We have a golden opportunity to seize something good from this crisis. Its unprecedented shockwaves may well make people more receptive to big visions of change."[1]

That Davos summit highlighted the fact that with the pandemic raging, the climate crisis, and the economy at a crossroads of pressures and uncertainties, new models of work were changing our ability to connect and work remotely. In record time, teams of scientists worldwide developed vaccines, and global distribution systems ensured its timely distribution; real-time statistics kept us on track as to how we were taming the beast; and our smartphones became gatekeepers of health certificates and apps that determined our freedom of moving, traveling, and entering public buildings.

At the same time, this Great Reset taught us how to communicate and interact primarily with screens rather than in person with people. Pew Research in October 2020 reported that 71 percent of people worked from home, most of whom had never worked remotely before.[2] By May 2022, we had adjusted to remote work and were comfortable with video calls. Not only had team collaboration become hybrid by default, but events and physical experiences changed. An integrated digital and physical environment became more of an expected reality with the integration of "virtual event tech." We got used to interacting with digital representations of people and recognizing others on screen. This is part of a shift in personal and social behavior that has been happening for quite some time but that accelerated during the pandemic. But no matter the global sentiment, technological innovation and convergence continuously offer new, sometimes unexpected lifestyle options— from the personal sphere to interpersonal relations, to more widespread social and global impacts.

Personal Impact

The potential impact of the metaverse cannot be understated. Let us first start with our individual daily lives. In our future hybrid reality, when we tell someone that we are going for a morning walk, we might have to explain if it's in a physical or a digital world, almost like a future version of walking outside or inside on a treadmill. But the number of possibilities will increase dramatically: If we walk outside wearing our AR glasses, we may be joined by a personal avatar guide, or we could be running side by side with a digital replica of our favorite sports star. If we have a usual racetrack, we could choose to customize our surroundings with our favorite movie elements or enter a gamified experience and earn points by running faster and going farther distances.

This simple example demonstrates just one of the shifts we'll see in our personal interactions with the world, as it's much more than a walk with digital graphics and virtual coaches. Potentially our whole definition of real changes. If we spend a significant amount of time in a virtual environment, does that make it as real to us as a physical one? It's the same with the everyday objects in our lives; if we see a digital artwork in our living room through augmented reality (AR), does that make it real? Perhaps our future job only exists within the digital metaverse. Will that be a real-world job?

"I see a metaverse as being more of a way to extend and expand our reality and identity," shares Amber Osborne, Senior Marketing Manager at Mozilla Hubs, an open, private VR spaces platform. "Allowing people the ability and freedom to create their 'world' as they want and be who they want. The sky isn't the limit in a metaverse, the sky doesn't have to exist at all."[3]

Individualized perceptions of the same experiences will become common, as each one of us will be able to witness a moment with the presence of different digital elements. Curtis Hickman, co-founder of The VOID, the critically acclaimed immersive entertainment company, shared his craving for "a pair of magic glasses that allow me to look into a million realities. Realities that are stacked on top of each other one after the other like layers. I could then use my glasses to switch between layers of reality, like flipping channels—looking into different parts of the Metaverse. Then, as John Gaeta has often talked about, many of these realities would be dialable—allowing me to tune the amount of visual immersion I desire. A scale from just a hint of AR to full VR, and everything in between."

Our workplace habits have already begun to change. We can choose to join meetings in person or via web conference, while some organizations let us meet and work with our colleagues in private virtual worlds, powered by platforms like Virbela. As AR glasses become more readily available, we might have coworkers attending physically, standing next to holographic projections of other team members who will be seen in the same room but will be remotely connected, although their avatars will have matching gestures, expressions, voice, and gaze. Everyone will be able to see everybody else in the workplace, but the channels we use to do so will be different.

And this brings us to a tough question: If we all witness events through different filters, in different realities with different elements, which point of view is the true one? Our memories of the same experience will be different for each person. How will this affect our tolerance to understand one another's arguments in a discussion? How will the metaverse change the way we interact? We have yet to determine the answers to these questions, especially at the scale we're talking about.

Interpersonal Impact

If you are of a certain age, you might remember the launch of music "in-ear headphones" (as earbuds were called at the time). People were walking down the street seemingly talking to themselves, as we no longer saw people holding their mobile phones next to their ears. If we noticed someone talking out loud to apparently no one, it took a second to understand what was happening, and that they were actually having a phone conversation. Through habit and increasing social acceptance, we learned to accept a different behavior that technology brought in.

Human interaction changed again when we started to look down at small rectangular screens to exchange messages. If we ride a train or subway, we no longer look around or talk that much to each other. Instead, many of us are maintaining discussions on the mobile device in our hands.

New, different behavioral changes will come with a hybrid reality. Not only will the people on the street and on the subway see digital elements which are invisible to us, they will be staring and gesturing at them. We will be doing the same as well with several kinds of augmented reality elements. Expect some confused looks until everyone has had their own AR experience and understands that these arm and hand movements have meaning—pretty much the same way you don't question what is happening if you see someone walking down the street having one half of a conversation.

VR also has begun to change how we interact with each other. Initially VR was created as a solo experience. Virtual worlds now can house hundreds, sometimes thousands of simultaneous users, much like online social media platforms. With our headset on, we feel transported to a new virtual place. Other users around us can recognize our 3D avatars, since we're both sharing the same virtual space. Marvin Minsky, at the suggestion of his friend Patrick Gunkel, used the term telepresence to describe the feeling of "being there." It reflects the "importance of high-quality sensory feedback and suggests future instruments that will feel and work so much like our own hands that we won't notice any significant difference."[4]

There are mirrors in VR worlds. If we look in one of those mirrors, we'll be able to see ourselves as being the avatar, the character thar represents us. Our body understands and adjusts. We "embody" our digital avatar. According to authors Yasuyuki Inoue and Michiteru Kitazaki, who explore embodiment in virtual worlds: "We can see parts of our body in the first-person perspective as an ego-centric view, while the mirror proves us an allocentric view of our body."[5] This third-party perspective on ourselves builds our connection to our virtual presence, because of three specific senses:[6]

- A sense of body ownership in VR, and you can witness this every time we duck when something is thrown at us in VR;
- A sense of agency, where we feel able to control actions of an avatar the same way as with the physical body;
- A sense of self-location, where we perceive being where the avatar is, inside a VR world.

If someone else joins us in virtual reality through spatial audio and body tracking, we feel that they are next to us. It's technically known as "social presence."[7] We turn our head to where they are, and we see their body movements and gestures. This is the main reason why so many VR users will tell you that you won't understand the in-world experience.

Most avatars are still cartoon-like, but there are several companies delivering more realistic avatars, some even generating versions that are close to digital clones of ourselves. But hyper-realism is not needed for us to understand and accept other avatars as a presence of fellow humans. When it comes to avatar faces, our brain wants to perceive and interpret expressions. It's called *facial pareidolia*. It's what happens when you see a face in the clouds or think the front of a car has a personality.[8] So the avatars can be cartoonish, but we're still able to recognize our friends or colleagues in a virtual world.

However, not all humanoid beings in digital realities will have a human being remotely connected. AI-based virtual beings will bring in another factor within digital experiences. Alongside avatars, we'll be able to speak and interact with these beings that can resemble public personalities, sports mascots or just like, well, avatars.

These AI-based, digital graphic beings will become more ubiquitous, and we will interact with them the same way we do with avatars. We will talk to and hear from them and this has already been predicted in movies like Steven Spielberg's *AI* or Denis Villeneuve's *Blade Runner 2049*. How this changes our behavior in in our home, work, or social interaction has yet to be understood and the same with being able to separate them in the social interactions we have.

As a whole, one of the key balances we'll need to determine in the metaverse is how to identify and separate the physical from the digital and the artificial from the human, as these will blur into a persistent, hybrid world.

SDGs and the Metaverse

The metaverse will have impacts both personally and socially. There will be societal changes, and central and local officials will need to follow and address these shifts, even as we are just beginning to understand them.

City profiles will be continuously transformed with the introduction of many different vehicles and devices in our lives. The social usage of these devices will generate different kinds of spaces. For instance, the same way radio and TV earned a place in our living room, new equipment to access the metaverse may earn a place in that same living room—or maybe that will justify the appearance of new holorooms in our houses.

However, the biggest underlying change will be the data made available from sensors in potentially every single object, place, and person. This data will be able to feed AI services, create truly smart cities, and automate many of the services that we know today. Mike Pell, "Envisioneer" and Director at The Microsoft Garage, foresees this impact: "Not only is the Metaverse significantly advancing the state-of-the-art in dimensional data visualization, it also allows us to see measures and analytics in a new light. This combination of new technologies and immersive approach unlocks a level of insightful explorations that we couldn't get close to before—being in the presence of recognizable data coupled with the ability to directly examine and manipulate it in real-time is true game changer."[9]

Also, public spaces will be filled not only with physical elements, but also AR ones, which means municipalities will need to make decisions on what should be allowed to appear in this new hybrid space. An AR pop-up store could be opened on a street but shouldn't be opened over a cemetery or church. But where can they become persistently available? Our houses should not be sprayed with AR graffiti. But how may art be showcased in public places? Several kinds of regulations will need to be considered, in order to safeguard these public spaces.

There are even larger issues within the world that cannot be ignored when talking about the metaverse's impacts, especially human and environmental. In 2015, the United Nations created a *2030 Agenda for Sustainable Development* (https://sdgs.un.org/2030agenda) that establishes goals for the sustainable development of our planet. These can provide the crosshairs to where the dramatic shift in technology potentially can address inequality and poverty, improve health and education, spur economic growth, and still maintain a sustainable approach.

Jimmy Vainstein is manager of the Metaverse4Good Program at the World Bank and shared with us a vision of "a metaverse that can support the work that is currently being done in sustainable development. Decision makers could be virtually transported to visualize development challenges in 360 or 3D spaces and would be able to see how others are living in poverty. Metaverse environment could be taken these experiences further and allow valuable interactions with stakeholder and even with some of the people affected by development challenges. The World Bank VR program has amassed a large amount of immersive content which could be adapted into these interconnected worlds (360 images, 3D renders) and put to use for decision making or create awareness."[10]

There are 17 Sustainable Development Goals (SDGs) in the *2030 Agenda,* which include No Poverty, Zero Hunger, Good Health and Well-Being, Quality Education, Gender Equality, and Reduced Inequalities. None of these goals is new to those concerned with the state of the world today. But how is it that the metaverse can impact any of them?

We can already see some examples of how these goals are affected for the better:

- Climate Action: When people, places, and objects turn digital and their usage becomes mainstream, there will be less unnecessary travel, less unnecessary materials consumption, and, overall, less waste and pollution.
- Decent Work and Economic Growth: New remote work models will allow workers in developing countries to access a more global job marketplace and welcome more skilled workers into their ecosystem, who will still be working for organizations in their country of origin.
- Good Health and Well-Being: Surgeries and more sophisticated telemedicine services can be expanded, as well as health tracking devices that can improve the effectiveness of health service providers.
- Gender Equality: As avatars begin to be used more often, gender will start to play a lesser role. An avatar does not have to have

a gender, and increasingly users' digital representations will become more widely accepted.

- Industry, Innovation, and Infrastructure: The greater use and sophistication of collaboration tools will enable more worldwide sharing of knowledge between experts, increasing the number of R&D projects, events, training, and new tools globally. Open source solutions like Vircadia[11] or Ethereal Engine[12] will be able to accelerate the presence of private and public services in the metaverse for any country.
- Partnerships for the Goals: Connecting and working with other professionals across the world will create relationships and personal bonds, which will make the pain, suffering, and sustainability issues of local regions feel closer and more in need of support.
- Peace, Justice, and Strong Institutions: Augmented signs, announcements, and living information for cities will allow for more intimate relationships between citizens and municipalities. Also, a new kind of journalism may appear. "Fields such as politics, crime news, daily report, and similar areas need speed, and they usually deal with small production budgets. Conversely, 'slow' storytelling and location-based news will be the first sectors to benefit from this," shares Marco Magnano, journalist and co-founder of the XR Safety Initiative (XRSI).
- Quality Education: The access to quality education can increase for remote locations. VR and AR glasses allow users to see, hear, and interact with remote participants face to face. Classes, educational tools and resources and even teachers could be available in digital formats, enabling classrooms that do not have the necessary physical means.
- Reduced Inequalities: As a new hybrid dimension is brought to life with the metaverse, the same services could be available on location in any country. This means that AR pop-up stores and international organization offices could serve customers the same way, regardless of their geography. Again, this effect can be boosted by the number of open source solutions available in the ecosystem.

- Responsible Consumption and Production: More accurate and readily available virtual "try-ons" can reduce waste in retail. As gestures and voice commands improve, there will be less need for peripheral hardware production, with a positive impact on land and atmospheric pollution.

In addition to these benefits related to the UN goals, the metaverse might be able to help in other key development areas:

- Decreased Corruption: Decentralization and transparency enabled by the use of blockchain technologies could create an opportunity for increased transparency and undermine corruption efforts.
- More Foreign Investment: Cryptocurrencies and digital contracts can boost direct foreign investment by individuals in a developing market's economy.

At the same time, several challenges also arise from the metaverse that could hinder all of us in achieving our SDGs:

- 3D Black Hats: Realistic avatars, full-body scans, and biomarkers could create an opportunity for black hat actors. Without regulations in place to stop such things from happening, people or AI-driven digital beings could present themselves as fake citizens and perform all sorts of wrongdoing.
- Cyber-Avatar ("Cybertar") Pirates: They may hunt for first-timers in the metaverse and try to swindle them, creating an unsafe environment and high level of distrust.
- Deepening Digital Divisions: Metaverse technology and sustaining infrastructure may be less available in developing countries, deepening the digital and educational divide. From his experience at the World Bank, Jimmy Vainstein agrees with us and shares that "The digital divide must be seriously considered as the metaverse starts to take hold. We must acknowledge that nearly 3 billion people remain offline and almost half of the world is not using mobile internet. Great progress in the birth of

the metaverse can potentially expand these gaps and continue to leave people behind. As we implemented some of our first metaverse pilots in education and other environments, we have seen first-hand as bandwidth limitations and lack of proper hardware are real obstacles that have limited the number of people that would attend a virtual class or event in the metaverse. Not everyone has access to computers with microphones or even audio speakers, nor strong processors to be able to properly load complex 3D environments. Let alone VR headsets."

- Increased Energy Consumption: Every system in the metaverse, hardware and software, consumes energy, which in itself might be a hindrance (as it cannot be used where electricity is not available) and a sustainability hurdle to making its usage universal.
- Multidimensional Spamming: More visual and auditory pollution can affect how new services are rolled out and educational tools are put in place.
- New Scamming Opportunities: Fraud and scams will appear even more real (yes, an avatar of a known politician or a "Nigerian prince" might actually start talking to you). Or an evil digital twin of yourself.
- Privacy Issues: As biometric and behavioral data is collected, unwanted access to it may result in increased privacy trouble, behavior conditioning, and criminal activity (i.e., blackmail).
- Worsening Mental Health: More time spent in-world can have an impact on our physical and mental health, which may have even bigger consequences in areas where health monitoring and overall services are not that robust.

With the metaverse, change will happen at all levels, starting from our individual selves and climbing up to the very notion of what is real. Data will be collected all the time. The impact will be felt across the board, and all stakeholders will be called in to leverage the benefits and tackle the challenges. Failing to do that might have consequences of cataclysmic proportions because, as we just have begun to see, the stakes could not be higher.

Notes

1. Phillip Inman, "Pandemic is chance to reset global economy, says Prince Charles." *The Guardian*, June 3, 2020. www.theguardian.com/uk-news/2020/jun/03/pandemic-is-chance-to-reset-global-economy-says-prince-charles

2. Kim Parker, Juliana Menasce Horowitz, and Rachel Minkin, "How the coronavirus outbreak has—and hasn't—changed the way Americans work." Pew Research Center, December 9, 2020. www.pewresearch.org/social-trends/2020/12/09/how-the-coronavirus-outbreak-has-and-hasnt-changed-the-way-americans-work

3. Personal communication, 2022.

4. Marvin Minsky, "Telepresence." *Omni*, June, 1980. http://web.media.mit.edu/~minsky/papers/Telepresence.html#:~:text=Telepresence%20emphasizes%20the%20importance%20of,Telepresence%20is%20not%20science%20fiction

5. Yasuyuki Inoue and Michiteru Kitazaki, "Virtual mirror and beyond: The psychological basis for avatar embodiment via a mirror." *Journal of Robotics and Mechatronics*, 2021. www.jstage.jst.go.jp/article/jrobomech/33/5/33_1004/_pdf

6. Daniel Roth, "Intrapersonal, interpersonal, and hybrid interactions in virtual reality." Unpublished doctoral dissertation, January 2020. www.researchgate.net/figure/Three-components-of-embodiment-self-location-body-ownership-and-agency-Left_fig2_339128557

7. Bavo Van Kerrebroeck, Guisy Caruso, and Pieter Jan Maes, "A methodological framework for assessing social presence in music interactions in virtual reality." *Frontiers in Psychology*, June 11, 2021. www.frontiersin.org/articles/10.3389/fpsyg.2021.663725/full

8. Jennifer Ouellette, "Our brains 'read' expressions of illusory faces in things just like real faces." *Ars Technica*, July 13, 2021. http://arstechnica.com/science/2021/07/our-brains-read-expressions-of-illusory-faces-in-things-just-like-real-faces

9. Personal communication, 2022.

10. Personal communication, 2022.

11. http://vircadia.com

12. www.etherealengine.org

Chapter 6

Doing Business in the Metaverse

Things are only impossible until they're not!
—Captain Jean-Luc Picard in Star Trek: Picard

Along with the metaverse, a powerful new economy is brewing. It features interoperable monetary systems, tracking and management of transactions, and new kinds of jobs. Some of these changes have already occurred, but soon they will be ubiquitous. This shift opens up new business opportunities and models.

When will this happen? It's hard to say–you could say it's already happening. This economic change will happen over time, but we can identify its key transformation drivers.

Decentralization is one of the most impactful shifts, as it empowers individuals and communities both socially and economically. We cease to play the single role of users of tech platforms as we did on Web 2.0. By the means of cryptocurrency, NFTs, and other blockchain tokens, we can become owners, investors, and much more involved in the digital side of our lives. More of us will take up additional roles in the web beyond being just users. So, more data, money, and decisions will flow, increasing the level of transactions in the metaverse.

Although this might sound like a fairly simple movement toward deeper participation in businesses, gaining public buy-in to this shift is no simple feat. It can happen only if we are able to trust in the metaverse and trust each other in it.

As many new headlines make very clear, Big Tech isn't known for being trustworthy. Their data collection and surveillance techniques have often resulted in privacy and safety problems, fake news, and several kinds of fraud. So, building a trustful tech landscape is key for business in the metaverse.

Data safety and security is paramount. But at the same time, to ensure that trustful ecosystem, we will need to use specific data in order to do business or interact professionally in every digital world we visit: We'll need to prove our identity to other stakeholders and in some way present our credentials; we'll need to make sure there are secure ways of payment accepted across worlds, so that business can be done in a more seamless and timely manner; finally, a registry of our property ownership will become essential, so users can trade or prove ownership of their purchases within the metaverse. We already are on our way to making this possible. Today we find Web3 platforms identifying their users, enabling payments, and allowing digital ownership through crypto wallets, that solve all these challenges in a decentralized way.

Even though it's not yet proven that crypto wallets are the best way to satisfy the mentioned needs, it deserves our attention as it's the first live example of a system that ensures this level of persistence and interoperability.

Persistent Wallets

A few years ago, many of us began to tap our phone, instead of taking out a plastic card to pay at a register. These digital payments made through our smartphones demonstrated to the world the promise of digital wallets. Apple Pay, Google Pay, Alipay, and PayPal are four of the most popular digital wallets, although many other companies have joined in the competition. Estimates point to almost 5 billion digital wallets being active in 2025.[1] So while these might seem like they're a future technology, they're actually a current one.

Crypto wallets are another kind of wallet that hold a major difference–they're not installed in Big Tech computers, but are decentralized across the blockchain and, as such, these wallets enable us to manage our crypto tokens. A crypto wallet is unique, as it has a private key, which is held by the sole identifier. Because of this, cryptocurrency is transferable across every crypto wallet, even those created through different services like Coinbase, Mycelium, or MetaMask, as each wallet has a unique address in the whole system. This is unlike trying to do direct transfers between your PayPal and Apple Pay digital wallets, for example.

A crypto wallet can hold up to an infinite sum of tokens of more than 10,000 cryptocurrencies (although about 20 of them hold 90 percent of the total market value). Cryptocurrency is digital money that does not depend on any financial institution to exist. Now most of you would think, "Okay, so where does the value of that money come from?" Well, if that cryptocurrency is in someone's wallet, that someone had to exchange it with either other cryptocurrencies or with government-backed currency or fiat currency. Cryptocurrency exchanges are declared in the public blockchain and help establish a value, which is subsequently altered given the supply and demand dynamics in the market—or speculative activity, if you prefer. Of course, as it's decentralized, there is no oversight entity in place. So, these valuations may quickly become volatile and fall prey to the actions of big whale investors and to more fraudulent schemes. That's why it's so important to analyze all details available if you ever decide on investing in one. CoinMarketCap, CoinGecko, or Messari are three popular sources for users seeking updates, information, and analysis on the topic.

Cryptocurrencies offer several benefits to companies and professionals: global access, quicker transfer speeds with low transaction costs on a globally accepted currency, which given value is internationally recognized. So, it can be a good help for any company developing international commerce of goods (both digital and physical) and services.

Also, cryptocurrencies are often seen by users not just as a means of payment, but also as an investment asset. Other, more complex financial applications can also be broken down and traded as tokens. Bhairav Patel is CEO at Defactor, a decentralized finance startup linking traditional investments with the Web3 decentralized way. His point of view is very optimistic: "DeFi has evolved a lot over a short time and what we are seeing is a desire from investors to obtain more stable and secure yields. There are still those out there that love volatility, but we are now being approached more and more by businesses that want to access funds for cash flow and investors that want to put their funds to work in less risky asset classes. For us, is the desire for returns on real-world assets that is in big demand in the DeFi space at the moment—whether that is funding real art, inventory, invoices, or even real estate."

When discussing blockchain and crypto, the conversation often includes NFTs. NFTs are non-fungible tokens that are able to assign ownership rights to a unique asset (be it digital or physical) by means of what is essentially a digital contract. For instance, you can quickly generate an NFT on OpenSea or Rarible and start selling your digital art or essays associated with that NFT, in the conditions you declare in the NFT. It's important you understand that the NFT is just the contract, not the art piece itself. An NFT can only validate your ownership, not guarantee or safeguard it.

The process of creating an NFT is called *minting*. So, when you're minting your NFT, you're actually writing an underlying smart contract on the blockchain. This is similar to writing a physical contract that is going to be signed by the parties involved; it is like having a notary stamp and file the contract on a public ledger to make it official—except the notary does not exist, as it's all up on the blockchain. After the contract is set and the NFT minted, that contract can be traded as a token, in a much nimbler way than traditional ones. This tokenization simplifies processes with digital items like artworks, digital fashion, tickets, and community items but also with physical ones. Take the example of Tangible (www.tangible.store), a platform where NFTs represent ownership of a range of physical products, from wine bottles and watches to real estate properties and gold bars.

Crypto wallets have then this power to enable digital identity, digital payments, and digital ownership across several realities, including the physical one. This happens through tokens like NFTs and cryptocurrencies, which fulfill different goals. NFTs are non-fungible, which means each one is unique and can obey a custom set of rules. Cryptocurrencies can be swapped or exchanged mutually, which means they are fungible and can be accepted as a means of payment in increasing cases, including when you're buying an NFT.

Are You Tokenized?

Not only can objects and spaces become tokenized in the sense that they can be identified through a single token that represents them, but our digital representation can be too. Although it might seem far-fetched at the moment, think about how each of us currently uses profile pictures in our social media lives: a professional photo for LinkedIn, a relaxed picture for Twitter, a graphic for TikTok, or maybe a family photo for Facebook.

When the metaverse emerges, our digital identities will evolve into more advanced representations and likely become more important in our lives. Instead of the flat images we use on social media, we will have 3D, interactive avatars of ourselves. Complicating matters is that each of us might have multiple avatars. We might want a realistic one for the office, a playful one for hanging out with friends, another type with family, and so on.

With those multiple 3D representations comes the need for personal ownership and safeguards. Now some people use a paragraph of legal text on social media as protection, but that won't be nearly enough in the metaverse. We will want to own our avatars and validate the identities of those around us. We will need to prove that it is, in fact, our own digital representation, that no one has stolen our avatar identity and is acting like the avatar equivalent of an

Internet catfish. Digital tokens could be used for that authentication. We could hold all of them in our digital wallets, almost like our current IDs (e.g., driver's license, passport) for the metaverse. In addition, each of us may want to outfit our avatars with distinctive digital fashion, accessories, and even mementos, similarly to how we choose clothes for ourselves. This actually is what fashion houses are betting on and that may bring about a more sophisticated knock-off marketplace. We each will want proof that we have acquired an authentic piece of digital clothing, that token of proof likely within our wallets.

Eventually, technology may advance enough that we will have AI-powered beings and robots supporting us in our daily lives. Besides being able to help us with professional processes and automate some of our tasks, we may use AI assistants. For example, the same way we use "out of office" notices, we may have a digital being that manages certain office tasks while we are on vacation, such as letting people know we are unavailable for a call and scheduling a new one. But we will need a token of proof that they are our representatives, since bad agents could take advantage of this, especially as we would interact with them through voice, gesture, eye tracking, and other biometric support interactions. Eventually, if there are no signs that identify a virtual being, we even may forget we're actually talking to an AI.

This tokenization of digital people, places, and things might appear more in the real world as well. For example, we could use tokens for personal use, such as enabling each of us to have control of our medical records. We could control who receives our records and under what circumstances. Then, our future crypto wallets also would hold our metaverse identification, proof of ownership of our AI assistants, and our personal preferences. Richard Ward, Metaverse Senior Manager at McKinsey, believes that "companies will pop up offering Insurance, Medical, Dating, etc. services for things where Web2 didn't capture the physical person. Will the magical Web3 save us all with its ideas of decentralization and individual control of data? Maybe. You can definitely build a good enough Metaverse without Web3. So, it needs to earn its seat at the table. Yelling 'this is theoretically better!' isn't enough. Personally, I find the slide with Web1 lots of passwords, a Web2 signin with Google/Facebook/etc. then a Web3 connect wallet, compelling. Because we already have 'independent password vaults' as alternatives to log in with Google. But is the Web3 tech and hassles. . .worth it? To be seen."[2]

In 2022, Vitalik Buterin, co-founder of Ethereum, announced a new method to define a user's digital identity in Web3 called Soulbound Tokens (SBTs). These can't be transferred or sold. They're directly connected to a user and can only be revoked by the issuer. Given these characteristics, SBTs can offer a great opportunity to certify ID credentials, academic degree certificates, and to sort out some of the aforementioned challenges. This technology is expected for release in 2024.

Again, it's not guaranteed that crypto wallets are going to become the standard for persistent and interoperable digital identity, payment, and ownership across the metaverse, as there are layers of privacy and safety to be dealt with. However, we will need one. "From a business perspective, it is about common standards and interoperability. Investing in new pipelines, workflows, and changing processes is a cost and time-intensive endeavor and there is always an ROI as a measurement for success behind it," shares Jan Pflueger, responsible for XR method development at AUDI AG. "A second challenge is to overcome the encapsulated thinking of creating 'the' Metaverse platform which can never exist—it has to be an open space, otherwise, it is just another proprietary platform not delivering the benefits a connected ecosystem could do."[3]

Because of the potential implications, these technologies offer opportunities to create new kinds of services, new types of businesses, along with multiple opportunities for misuse.

Business Models

The metaverse adds another dimension to our life. The ability to create, own, trade, share, or even remove digital objects, places, and people in this digital world won't operate separately and apart from our physical one. It will be woven within it. Starting with the behavioral changes we observed in the past chapter, we'll get used to seeing people interacting with elements that are invisible to others. We'll summon digital beings and objects into our presence and see, hear, and, with haptics, touch them. Some of these may be attached to physical objects, like maintenance instructions and warranties on each and every domestic appliance we own. Others might be fed data from sensors from buildings and equipment in the physical world. The synergy will grow bigger and bigger as we grow into a hybrid reality.

"We already live our lives in digital. If I was to try to explain to my granny what I do for [a] living, she would most likely conclude that I am playing [on the] computer all day. We live in digital: try to take away the phone from people, some would not be able to last even one day without it," shared Mariia Tintul, Managing Director of Wise Guys XR, a startup accelerator dedicated to immersive technologies. "I think what the metaverse brings in this regard is a better place to be digitally. I don't think it can replace real life experiences, but it can definitely prolong the time we spend up in our head consuming digital. By better means of exploring information and communication, we will definitely create more and more opportunities for businesses in this area. So, business models and generally new businesses are inevitable."[4]

The metaverse will create business opportunities similar to the way the Internet and mobile computing have done. New companies can grow out of persistent digital items and services available 24/7, either on-demand (an always-available digital human) or spatialized (in virtual or augmented locations). Organizations, creators, or even other users will be able to buy, sell, trade, or earn rewards that are valuable to specific communities and collectors. This opens up the potential for new kinds of business, some of them built around the token market dynamics.

But never forget that Big Tech has built their companies around one thing: data. Marco Magnano, co-founder of the XR Safety Initiative, expressed his concern on this matter: "Every immersive experience we build relies on an unprecedented amount of information on the person and the environment to be enacted. However, we still don't fully understand what data is needed and what can be optional. To ensure that the Metaverse will be a safe environment, we need to study and classify data and foster the adoption of updated data regulation laws that can offer safety by design."

Leveraging the massive increase in data being generated is surely a big priority for the likes of the future FAANG collective.[5] We're not talking just about data coming from a form and search pattern recognition. This data from the physical world will be able to be retrieved through smart glasses and from your biometric inputs like gestures, voice commands, or body movements. This can amount to a constant tracking of user behaviors, which almost unavoidably leads to privacy and safety issues, and the potential for user backlash on the metaverse and loss of interest. Data management and protection in the metaverse industry must be a top priority.

From the very beginning, all interactions with clients or consumers will be spread across virtual, augmented, and physical worlds, and that will mean a significant change to tracking and maintaining customer relationships through that diversity of worlds, as well as a significant change in the data-gathering mechanisms. Susan Persky, Director of the Immersive Simulation Program at the National Human Genome Research Institute, told us about the potential in these products. "When people use tracked, immersive technologies to interface with aspects of the metaverse frequently and over long periods of time, they can generate a staggering amount of data as we move through space and interact with our surroundings and each other. Data related to these body movements are already, today, able to predict who may be exhibiting symptoms of health problems such as cognitive impairment, attention deficits, or movement disorders." She added that there are also challenges ahead. "If these data were processed and transmitted to one's healthcare provider, they could be a treasure trove—allowing us to identify disease at an early stage or track recovery through daily activities. If these data were processed and transmitted to less trusted parties, however, they may reveal private health information without our awareness."[6]

Decentralization also can impact businesses, beyond expanding our individual roles as investors and owners. It's all about organization. DAOs (decentralized autonomous organizations) are cooperative groups owned by their members that exist to fulfill a common need. This can be utilized for something as simple as reducing prices through collective buying to getting access to otherwise unreachable markets, items, or audiences.

Some current examples as of this writing are LexDAO, which develops legal software solutions, and Mirror DAO, which enables writers to promote and sell their articles and post them directly as NFTs for sale in a decentralized marketplace.

DAOs also can be a new way to test the interest of a business mission, build a community, and even fundraise. With a DAO, some decisions must be made by the community inside it. It's a new collective approach to business creation and growth.

Hybrid Experience Economy

In the beginning of the 1990s, a new "experience" economy was identified, an evolution of the service economy.[7] As explained in a *Harvard Business Review* article at the time, a bakery is a service to outsource baking, whereas a carnival is a service to outsource events, such as a birthday party. Location-based entertainment (LBE) companies, like Disney Parks and high-end hotels with casinos have always sold experiences, but now all types of businesses are embracing them. Stores are more than just places to display merchandise, brands have begun staging pop-up locations in the middle of shopping mall corridors, and food and kitchen appliance brands have held cooking demonstrations and classes. Capital One banks created coffee shops in their lobbies. All of these were built with the goal of immersing a potential customer in an experience to build loyalty and more sales.

By being able to flow along the virtuality continuum and between virtual, augmented, and physical worlds, the metaverse opens up a huge potential number for new, custom experiences. Alex Kreger, a user experience design expert, shared with us that "in the experience economy, people don't just buy and sell products, services or features. They also want the experiences and emotions behind them. In the metaverse, I think this paradigm will become mainstream. People will pay large sums for intangible items that provide social meaning and offer relevant experiences."[8]

Retailers who were quick to tap into physical experiences should consider integrating digital ones as well. "Retailers of the future should deploy an experience-first model where they embrace the experience culture and deliver richer and more meaningful engagement with their customers," states Richard Lim, CEO of Retail Economics.[9] Interconnected digital and physical goods and services can be built to create new kinds of memorable, spatialized experiences, available at the touch of a real or a virtual button.

Sales, rental, licenses, and subscriptions need not happen in the traditional setting of a store. They can take place throughout an experience that is lived in one or several of the realities available to users. Parks, streets, events, and stadiums might hold impossible buildings, art pieces, and other unique moments to be had. Gamifying wine-tasting sessions or historical tours might be not just a way to create an experience and drive people to specific physical locations; it can also enable the same physical location to be reinvented over and over again, with some levels unlocked only if you have experienced the previous one. This way, the same physical location might be enjoyed in different ways by the same users throughout time, thanks to this new dimension.

Transforming our perception and merging digital and physical creates new opportunities for businesses. New product placement or merchandising techniques can be used. Digital versions of a product can be shown in 3D throughout these augmented or virtual worlds. The products themselves have the potential to become hybrid. Books may come with exclusive AR author lectures or NFTs to be part of a larger movement. For example, we could create volumetric captured avatars of ourselves that are unlocked when you buy the physical book. If we wanted to create a virtual Metaversed University, we could offer an NFT—a M(etaversed)FT—that could be bought or sold to get access to classes, in-person events, lectures, discounts, etc.

New Jobs in the Metaverse

All of these trends will bring about new kinds of workplaces, jobs, and responsibilities. For instance, in the metaverse, new employees can enter a digital copy of a physical workplace first to make onboarding easier. The office watercooler corner can be replicated and visited both physically and in virtual reality. Work socialization, policies, and etiquette will likely evolve as well. We likely will interact with our colleagues in person, sometimes with their avatars, and sometimes with their AI-based virtual beings. The creation and management of the latter will require the expansion of IT responsibilities or a new Avatar Maintenance role.

Accounts payable and receivable are evolving. Some workers are looking to receive part of their salaries in cryptocurrency. "If you're working for a project in the crypto sphere, the odds are that you are already getting part or all of your salary in some form of crypto, whether that be stablecoin or the project's own token," shares Bhairav Patel, "As a company, we are paid our invoices from crypto projects in USDC and I think that as crypto becomes easier to convert into fiat, many companies and individuals will want to be paid in it as transfers happen instantly and oftentimes the fees are less than accepting fiat currency."[10] CFOs may need to hire Crypto Payment Accountants.

As professional upskilling was needed to deal with the Internet, a huge number of new metaverse-related skills will be brought in by this new economy. Some might be based on entirely new activities, while others will be enhancing the current physical job requirements. According to the World Manufacturing Institute,[11] in 2025, we'll have 2 million unfilled job openings in the manufacturing sector alone due to an increasing shortage of skilled labor.

Metaverse technologies can mitigate potential losses by enhancing workers digitally, getting them trained faster and more effectively, and by giving them tools to reduce errors and waste in their jobs. A Metaverse Trainer role or a Robot Manager position might be needed. Schools and universities are starting to see the gap and filling it. Courses—like coauthor Sam Wolfe's "Business of Virtual Reality and Augmented Reality" and "Marketing of Emerging Tech" courses at New York University's Steinhardt School—focus on the nontechnical skills necessary to understand part of the growing metaverse economy. Several other courses at Lethbridge College, Oxford University, and other universities cover one or more of the building blocks we referred to, but not the whole interconnected lot, in its unavoidable complexity and potential. We eventually may be taught by an AI Professor Twin or an AI Teaching Assistant, trained by the actual professor leading the class.

The diversity of impact and new roles is potentially too great to study in just one course. The metaverse experience economy will need great storytellers, virtual world creators, and digital game designers, as well as responsible managers. Storytellers will need to know the intricacies of setting up experiences in specific places, the tools available to do it in the best possible way, and at the same time be able to tell a story that is coherent cross-world and drives the user toward the proposed goal. Or each of those could become new jobs such as Meta-Storytellers, Hybrid Technologists. Architects will need to consider the physical and virtual worlds. This might mean teams of Physical Architects, Virtual Architects, and perhaps Hybrid Architects that can connect both. There will be more layers for everything in the physical world. There could be jobs for people who define and manage physical and virtual policies, regulations, and building experiences for those living and working within them. A Cross-Reality Experience Designer may soon exist. Executive roles may shift and open up the opportunity for Chief Metaverse Officers. Their job would focus on the virtual and real-world interactions from proof-of-concept to pilot to deployment. Their role would include identification of market opportunities, building use and business cases; influencing engineering roadmaps; and establishing key performance indicators. These might be supported by NFT Strategists ready to activate play-to-earn strategies who know exactly how to engage users with meaningful experiences inside a specific market.

Marketing professionals also will need to adjust and adapt. Marketing departments may have to hire employees solely focused on hybrid experiences, like the Digital Marketers of the past. They would be responsible for understanding the consumer journey from building trust during the first contact with a customer, through onboarding, identifying ways to improve and cross-sell physical and virtual experiences, as well as build loyalty and referral. Maybe they launch, then monitor and support NFTs owners as well as any customer DAOs run by the business.

Finally, we'll see jobs associated with maintaining privacy and safety within the virtual space. Metaverse Safety Officer could be their title. Besides the digital controls that platforms release, they will require regulatory oversight and making sure the heavy complexity and the number of moving parts in this new digital world harm neither us nor our trust in it. At the beginning, each of these jobs will require some knowledge of the technological building blocks, but, with time, the development of them won't require specialists or coders. Just like websites were initially used by technical experts, and now almost anyone can set up a site and it's part of many departments to manage its requirements (e.g., marketing, advertising, IT, accounts receivable). Metaverse technologies will evolve as will user interfaces and AI to make it easier for anyone to create and manage the technologies associated with them. One of the potentially most impactful changes may be digital humans and avatars, the focus of the next chapter.

Notes

1. Boku, Inc., "More than half of the world's population will use mobile wallets by 2025." Globenewswire, July 8, 2021. www.globenewswire.com/en/news-release/2021/07/08/2259605/0/en/Study-More-than-half-of-the-world-s-population-will-use-mobile-wallets-by-2025.html

2. Personal communication, 2022.

3. Personal communication, 2022.

4. Personal communication, 2022.

5. They represent 5 of the best performing stocks in Big Tech, namely Facebook, Apple, Amazon, Netflix, and Alphabet's Google.

6. Personal communication, 2022.

7. B. Joseph Pine II and James H. Gilmore, "The Experience Economy." *Harvard Business Review Press,* 1999.

8. Alex Kreger, "Preparing your company for the metaverse." *Forbes Business Council post,* February 25, 2022. www.forbes.com/sites/forbes businesscouncil/2022/02/25/preparing-your-company-for-the-metaverse/?sh=4ed5bdac72b6

9. Retail Economics, "The retail experience economy." *Retail Economics* video, October 25, 2019. www.retaileconomics.co.uk/video-library/the-retail-experience-economy

10. Government-backed currency. Personal communication, 2022.

11. The Manufacturing Institute, "Manufacturing industry faces unprecedented employment shortfall: 2.4 million skilled jobs projected to go unfilled according to Deloitte and the Manufacturing Institute." The Manufacturing Industry press release, November 14, 2018. www.the manufacturinginstitute.org/press-releases/manufacturing-industry-faces-unprecedented-employment-shortfall-2-4-million-skilled-jobs-projected-to-go-unfilled-according-to-deloitte-and-the-manufacturing-institute

Chapter 7
Digitalizing Humans

You don't choose your Avatar. . .your Avatar chooses you.
—Jake Sully, Avatar

"Alexa, what's the weather today?" "Siri, what's today's date?" In 2018, these requests became part of the daily lives of smart speaker owners. These software agents became personified in our minds, as if we were interacting with real people. It was like we were talking to a small being living within a piece of hardware or a friendly colleague on a speakerphone. Although their usage has been declining slightly,[1] these voice assistants marked a turn in how almost 200 million of us[2] moved from tapping a screen to simply speaking our wants and needs to a piece of hardware.

This isn't the first time in recent years that new innovations have changed the way we interact with technology. With smart screens with computer vision, we began to gesture toward a piece of hardware to establish what we want. With mobile phones, we started to trigger an action through our gaze to a small handheld rectangle object made up of mostly metal, glass, and plastic. There is, in fact, an entire field of research established in the 1980s that is focused on "human–computer interaction."[3]

This also isn't the first time that human–computer interaction has been transformed by giving technology human-like characteristics. In 2003, with a small yellow circle.[4] Emojis (named after the Japanese terms for "picture" and "character") were created to communicate feelings much more quickly and efficiently than ordinary text. According to Emojipedia,[5] as of September 2021, there were 3,633 standard emojis; 47 of those emojis demonstrate emotional states.[6] Compare that to the 21 emotions that can be registered on a human face.[7] Based on those statistics, you could argue that we are better at nonverbal communication via emoji than in person.

After the birth of the emoji, human interaction changed again with Snapchat. In 2015, the social media company used the smartphone camera lens to create the first AR lens. It was an evolution of graphic communication from within our screens onto our faces. We didn't just use text and icons to communicate graphically, but now we could overlay graphics onto images and video. It created an alternative to voicemail and text messages. Only a year later, a study showed that 75 percent of millennials would rather lose the ability to talk on their smartphone instead of messaging, because of the convenience and the fact that messages could be sent on their own schedule.[8]

Digital communication changed yet again in 2020, as we found ourselves in the biggest remote work and learning shift in the history of humankind. Many of us, along with most businesses and schools, had to learn how to use visual conference tools like Zoom. We each quickly discovered their benefits and drawbacks. Our countless hours staring at stacks of rectangles was emotionally depleting. Founder of the Stanford Virtual Human Interaction Lab, Jeremy Bailenson, defined why it was so exhausting in a February 2022 article published in *Technology, Mind, and Behavior*. The research found that the following criteria caused our fatigue: excessive eye contact, viewing of ourselves for extended periods of time, lack of physical mobility, and excessive "cognitive load" (i.e., it's really difficult to monitor nonverbal communication clues).[9]

We all seemed to crave an easier way to communicate remotely, something that didn't overwhelm our brains. 3D digital worlds, virtual reality, and augmented reality may be the next step in emerging technology communications. Initially we will lose some of the facial cues. With the visual technologies of the metaverse, we can start to add in body movement cues, although they will still be quite rudimentary. It's as if we are moving closer to real-world interactions as the metaverse comes closer. Our own 3D avatars may advance our communication abilities to heights we never even imagined. And AI-based digital beings may change the way we accept and interact with computers once again.

Definitions

So, if we are evolving toward a world of avatars, digital humans, and virtual beings, what are they really? Each of them is a slight variation on the same thing: a digital representation of a person, animal, or being (e.g., anything you could imagine, from an alien to a zebra). Some are representations of real people, like you and me, and others represent brands or services.

Simply put, an avatar is a digital representation of ourselves (or a fellow person) in a digital world. This representation can be hyper-realistic, highly cartoonish, or somewhere in between. Avatars are what we choose to look like while roaming VR worlds and video games. Eventually, each of us will own several avatars in the metaverse. You may have one for work, one for your friends, another for family. We choose what they look like, how they dress, what digital objects they own. Already there is an avatar fashion market that is expected to hit $55 billion in 2030.[10]

On the other hand, virtual beings and digital humans don't exist in physical reality. They are autonomous or semi-autonomous, meaning they are run entirely by AI or they are managed by one or more people embodying the virtual being. Digital humans are a specific kind of virtual being, as they have humanoid form. Chatbots, although they don't have digital bodies, are within this category, as well as personal or enterprise robots.

Facts

Avatars already have broad usage on several platforms. Gaming is the most apparent use as it has been a part of the industry since the beginning. Initially we represented ourselves in games with low-resolution graphics, but that has evolved all the way to highly realistic graphics of our own faces. "You've already played with avatars. Sometimes they represent you. Sometimes you use them to represent a vision of yourself or to test out new personality traits," says Veronica Orvalho, CEO at Didimo, a user-generated avatar and digital human creation platform. "But those avatars are going to become a lot more realistic. Not only are they becoming three-dimensional like computing is, and more than look kind of like you, they are now starting to really represent you, with your emotional nuances, personality, and even your own voice, recreated."

The virtual beings market is still in its early days, but there is a large potential market for them. The first generation of these technologies are chatbots, which are often implemented on websites for on-demand customer service. The numbers are already quite impressive:

- The global chatbot market is expected to be $1.25 billion by 2025 (Interactions).[11]
- Most brand–customer communications are expected to be via AI, primarily bots, until 2025 (Servion Global).[12]
- 41.3 percent of online buyers use conversational bots during the purchase process.[13]
- Finally, chatbots are expected to save businesses 2.5 billion hours by 2023.[14]

Virtual beings are moving beyond automatic text conversations on websites and there are a number of opportunities to develop more lifelike and personified versions. This includes improvements on their graphics, but also the movements of the body and the sophistication and speed of person–computer conversations.[15]

However, their usefulness, efficiency, and efficacy can be disputed by other statistics. According to Gartner, 40 percent of the chatbots launched in 2018 are no longer used.[16] There is even a term—"the spiral of misery"—that applies to when a chatbot doesn't understand the verbal request over and over.[17] There were also some epic failures of chatbots in the recent past, exposing the existing shortcomings of these assistants, like their limited pre-definitions or the bias of their human creators. For instance, Yandex's Alice chatbot,[18] while providing support, wasn't able to correctly filter users' words and ended up promoting pro-Stalin views, as well as wife-beating and child abuse–condoning speech. That said, an article in the March 2022 issue of the *New York Times* was subtitled, "Customer service chatbots may finally become more intelligent, more conversational and more helpful." Aya Soffer, Vice President of AI Technologies at IBM Research identified the key to improvement is "to define the intent of the human during the interaction."

Creation

So how does one create digital beings? In a recent article,[19] this process was broken down into a few simple steps:

- Building and Texturing: *Creating the shape, size, and looks of your digital human*
- Animating: *Establishing the range of movements and gestures available*
- Giving Intelligence: *Embedding the digital being with AI*

There are many fascinating companies within the market. MetaHuman Creator from Unreal Engine (www.unrealengine.com/en-US/metahuman) has developed graphics which seem almost indistinguishable from humans. There are also companies like Replika (http://replika.com), Didimo (http://didimo.co), Virbe (http://virbe.ai) or Soul Machines (http://soulmachines.com), each with their own approach to generating digital humans on demand.

Avatar or virtual beings can take many kinds of graphical forms. Different looks and animation types allow us to best represent ourselves differently in different worlds. For instance, if we're talking about a disco party in a VR club, you might choose to show up as an anthropomorphic animal. Whereas for a professional training session, you may choose a fully animated avatar of yourself that might be more appropriate for work. Or your organization could encourage the use of fantastical creatures for avatars to encourage diversity and inclusion, as everyone's gender, race, sexual orientation, age, or religion will be much less apparent and more likely to reduce bias between coworkers.

One of the most awkward aspects of the current avatars is the fact that they are mostly half-bodied avatars. They are all torso, arms with hands, and heads. They float in space, leg-less, while eyes and lips are synced with the users' expressions. In 2022, most VR headsets are unable to continuously detect our leg movements and height but new versions of this hardware are expected from 2023 onward and our level of embodiment with avatars is bound to be greatly impacted.

Embodiment, Presence, and Identity

If you have ever used an avatar, you begin to feel like that avatar is an extension of yourself. You and the avatar are one. This is referred to as a feeling of embodiment and it can be a mind-expanding experience. In a virtual world and through an avatar, any user can feel the presence of both other avatars and virtual beings.[20] If you have ever tried multiplayer VR, you may remember how you felt when there were other people in the virtual room with you. You could survey the room and see the discussions, gestures, and interactions taking place nearby. If you recognize a voice, you may move over to their avatar and interact with them as if you were in the same physical space, even if their graphic representation is quite simple. Surely, a very different experience than conference-call rectangles.

Bailenson and other researchers have shown that authenticity can happen using similar tricks from the real world, but now created in code,[21] such as mimicking body movements and eye tracking (but not *too* much). Then apply what cartoonists know such as physical nuances that bring out emotion like the larger eyes you find on Disney's Anna and Elsa.[22] These make you feel that even autonomous digital beings are relatable and authentic, even human.

The applications of digital beings don't need to stick just to digital worlds. They can and will translate into physical beings, aka robots. For instance, Hyundai[23] presented their Metaverse Factory, during CES 2022. One of its most remarkable features was the ability for operators to sync their movements remotely with physical robots on the factory's shop floor, allowing for manual work at a distance. So, in a way, these users will have some sense of embodiment (SoE) through a remote physical robot, especially if there are high-quality haptics involved. This could lead to us working side by side with colleagues both in avatar and in robotic form.

How these avatars, virtual beings, and robots will represent ourselves then comes into question. First, it's a much more dynamic experience than what we get from email, chat messaging, or even a 2D video call. It's much closer to being in person, even if you are interacting with a fantastic creature. They are representing a fellow human (if an avatar or remotely operated robot) and something that was created by a human/s (if a virtual being or AI-based robot). In the former, it becomes a direct reflection of how we represent ourselves.

In January 2022, a study[24] showed 52 percent of gamers believe their avatars are better reflections of themselves than their actual physical identity. This number climbs to 65 percent when talking about Gen Z, and 60 percent when talking about millennial gamers. It's fair to say several generations already consider avatars to better express their personal values and beliefs, and the metaverse is bound to create even more options for them to expand and enrich their freedom of expression.

Things will begin to (or continue to?) be creepy as we get closer and closer to something that seems human but isn't. This feeling is often referred to as "the uncanny valley." It's when something digital or robotic begins to resemble the human form, but your mind somehow knows there's something wrong and untrustworthy about it. It is believed to have been used first in Japanese by

Professor Masahiro Mori in 1978 to describe robots that appear so human-like[25] to the point that they become unlikeable.[26] Luckily for our stomachs, a lot of the creepiness factor around avatars and virtual beings usually lies mostly at the cutting edge of technology (e.g., a lot of humanoid robots), or bad creative choices by Hollywood studios (see Tom Hanks in *The Polar Express* or the entire cast of the 2019 film *Cats*).

The Real Influence of Virtual Influencers

Throughout this century, digital beings have been a part of our lives, even if you haven't paid too much attention to the phenomenon. Remember Gorillaz? After winning a Grammy, they keep on filling stadiums and having collaborations with artists like Snoop Dogg. They were and still are digital. Although they stem from Damon Albarn's music and Jamie Hewlett's art, we still relate to the digital band characters and maybe some of us won't be able to recognize the actual human performers. The same happened with ABBA and their Voyage 2022 music experience, where the band members decided to present themselves to their fans as realistic avatars that resembled their 1970s versions. You'll find many other music artists performing in Roblox, Fortnite, and other virtual worlds.

The impact of these digital beings or digital representations is felt across platforms and shows how eager, or at least accepting, we are of relating directly with them. This is also seen on social media, where some of these artificial, humanoid beings have millions of followers, even though everyone understands that their design, backstory, interests, social media posts, and so on are not posted by a human being, but by a team of creators. Although these virtual influencers do not exist physically, their followers relate with the lifestyle they showcase and with the brands and products they promote.

On April 23, 2016, Brud Agency posted their first Lil Miquela image on Instagram. Although it was first unclear whether or not she was a human being, quickly the buzz around her picked up, as she started taking pictures and interacting with real celebrities on her social media accounts. By June 2018, the fictional character of Miquela Sousa was named as one of the most influential people on the Internet by *Time* magazine. You read it right-influential people. But just two years before, in 2016, there was no way Trevor McFedries and Sara DeCou, co-founders of Brud and of Lil Miquela, could have predicted the number of luxury fashion campaigns with brands like Prada, a Coachella interview, and a growing popularity of their virtual influencer's original songs.[27]

Lil Miquela's popularity is just one example of the size of the virtual influencers market, but she is not the only one making waves. Instagram has already verified many virtual influencers, and some of the most renowned digital humans in the world include:

- Hatsune Miku (http://piapro.net/intl/en.html): *This 16-year-old with blue hair is one of the most well-known digital humans. Birthed in Japan, Miku's popularity allowed her to move beyond social media and, like Gorillaz, to feature in concerts on stage, through a rear cast projection on a specially coated glass screen.*
- Imma Gram: *The first Japanese virtual influencer, Imma ("now" in Japanese) is the same as any other model and she features in photographs not only of online events, but of physical ones as well. She's worked with some of the top designers in the world including Valentino, Dior, mainstream designers like Puma and Nike, and consumer brands like IKEA and Amazon.*[28]
- Knox Frost: *Although inactive or discontinued at the moment, Knox is/was a different kind of digital human, as he took pride in being a robot. His social media was all about his efforts to try to fit in a society filled with humans who most of the time don't understand him.*
- Lu Do Magalu: *She is the face of Magazine Luiza, a retailer founded in the mid-20th century in Brazil. Lu is the most popular virtual social influencer in 2022 with over 31.2 million followers across social platforms.*[29]

Brands took notice and started to develop their own virtual influencers as brand ambassadors. KFC created the parody virtual being "The Colonel" to take over their social media and it eventually collaborated with TurboTax, Old Spice, and Dr. Pepper brands.[30] From "her" social media accounts, Barbie does what most fashion models do and interacts with followers. She also collaborated in the creation of the first official Barbie-like avatars.[31] Even in the perfume industry, where new campaigns are usually fronted by well-known models, we see a change. To lead their campaign for their new perfume, "Candy," L'Oréal and Prada created a digital human with the same name, that they felt connected better with Gen Z and TikTok natives.[32]

If you don't have an Instagram account, it might seem like this could be a future trend, but the impact of virtual beings is already pretty pervasive. Hype Authority reported that virtual influencers are more engaged with their audience than human influencers.[33] Perhaps this may be due to the fact that humans make mistakes, change their perspectives, decide to opt out altogether, this seems vague, or simply move on to do something else. A virtual influencer is likely more stable, takes no holiday, does not feel the need to renegotiate contracts. It totally reflects the input of many executives who can then manage and run the business without the emotions or feelings of a growing celebrity getting in the way. Users like emotional responses, but they prefer their media outlets to be reliable, and brands, at the end of the day, want to communicate their message in the most effective way. This of course can mean a huge disruption in celebrities' role in brand sponsorship.

Some of you Gen X and Boomers may think these influencers appear inauthentic and toy-like, but to the generations growing up on video games and social media, they are anything but. According to The Influencer Marketing Factory, 70 percent of North American consumers aged between 18 and 44 follow at least one virtual influencer and 40 percent have already bought products or services promoted by virtual influencers.[34]

Industry Applications

"Humans have an inborn need to connect with others. I fundamentally believe digital humans will become the next interaction model," announces Veronica Orvalho, CEO of Didimo. Digital humans won't live just in the consumer market. They are set to become the new interfaces with most of the services in the metaverse, replacing expanding menus, scrolling pages, and push buttons. Instead we can interact with a virtual being in a nice conversation, where we'll just state what we want and point where we want it.

This will of course affect the whole industry of User Interface / User Experience Design in ways that we can only begin to understand.

And the disruption will not end there. The movie industry, for instance, has already been using digital characters for a long time and, more recently, has even started to use digitally re-created versions of deceased actors to co-star alongside physical celebrities. From Carrie Fisher in *Rogue One: A Star Wars Story* to Paul Walker in the last *Fast & Furious* movies, we're getting used to seeing already deceased actors play story-defining roles in movies. Sometimes they even appear on stage: Amy Winehouse and Tupac Shakur holograms recently performed on stage.[35] Will actors scan themselves to preserve their 3D digital replicas and keep themselves young on screens for eternity? What will image rights mean in the metaverse? James Earl Jones' agreement to stay as an AI voice of Darth Vader[36] seems to say there is a chance that actors and actresses may live as long as there is an audience for them.

We'll see, but there are more traditional consumer industries looking into this, including:

- Banking: *New Zealand's Bank ABC is already integrating digital humans into their customer service, in an effort to support younger customers.*[37]

- Customer Care and Contact Centers: *The opportunity to create custom-made assistants for each user that are mindful of the user's needs and wants will impact this industry and grow its size and dimension.* The California DMV's chatbot only saw 6% of its 2.3 million interactions escalate to talk with live agents.[38]
- Retailers: *As digital humans have been shown to make people comfortable, stores have "employed" them for customer service jobs.*[39] *In social media and in messaging applications like Discord or WhatsApp, chatbots are picking up tasks like web searching, payment processing, moderation, delivering notifications, and scheduling events by themselves.*
- Travel and Tourism: *AskDISHA is a great example of a chatbot operating in this market: It allows all Indian railway customers to book or cancel tickets, ask for refunds and clarify all doubts about a train trip by using voice commands and without need for a password.*[40]

Leadership Training   Neuroscience studies have shown that digital humans can teach leadership skills as effectively as human coaches or more so.[41]

Mental Therapy   Patients with PTSD, anxiety, and depression have had more success being treated by digital humans, precisely because they're not human.[42]

Social Companionship   Digital humans and virtual beings can be great allies in enabling continuous support to anyone who gets lonely or becomes socially isolated. However, these relationships pose several risks, as the human counterparts in them are highly fragile and therefore suggestible.

Human Resources   If empathy-like behavior and company policy can be coded into a digital being, future employees will be speaking to a digital HR representative to resolve some of their issues and take care of daily needs.[43]

There also could be many benefits to using digital humans, beyond those immediately affected by the interactions.

Autonomous Work Although virtual beings' interaction is primarily conversational, there is a movement that aims to surround workers in their workplace by virtual beings that are indeed created to support and augment real workers. The concept is that real humans are better at creative problem-solving. Soul Machines' co-founder Greg Cross believes, "At some point in the future, you might be able to create a digital version of yourself or multiple versions of yourself, and they can go out and do stuff, make money for you, make money for your company, while you're doing something else that's a whole lot more fun."[44]

Digital Twins Although the term has primarily referred to a physical location up to now, there are multiple applications for digital human copies in industries like the medical field. For example, if you had a digital twin of yourself within your digital wallet, it could be used to run simulations of treatments and surgery, besides enabling a number of business models.

Work Distribution In the same way that the Internet transformed the workforce, with some jobs becoming obsolete and other new jobs being created, a similar impact is expected with virtual beings. Clerical work tasks are becoming managed digitally, and real humans would take on the higher-value operations.[45]

As technology evolves and conversational AI enables much more seamless support, we'll start seeing that some of the challenges will also grow in size.

The Issues

Increasingly, avatars will become part of our digital identity and digital beings will create value through the work they'll automate. As AI, machine learning, and robotics evolve, graphics become more detailed and textured, and as Internet connection speeds increase exponentially, digital humans will be more than lifelike—they will seem real and maybe even become real Things are starting to get a little complicated, not just code-wise, but also ethically and morally.

In the immediate future, we'd like to highlight our two main concerns: overreliance/over-delegation and coding bias.

Bias As for bias, studies have established that tech developers are primarily men, usually white or Asian.[46] This means that there will be blind spots in the code, intentional or unintentional, that might come across as sexist or racist. Even more, futurists like Sinead Bovell are alert to the fact that digital humans like Shudu, an artificial model depicted as a Black female, is in fact managed and maintained by its white male creator. "The future is heading in a direction where people can create and control identities outside of their own ethnic groups," Sinead shared. "This creates ample opportunity for exploitation of already marginalized communities, and if we aren't careful, this can become a massive societal problem."[47]

Overreliance Our increasing dependence on tech agents brings comfort to our lives, solves several problems, but it creates new ones as well. At the worst, blindly following technology can have disastrous impacts (see GPS fails), or, at the very least, embarrassing and meme-able results. We know that it's possible to become sedentary and rely on tech to do all our work. We need rules and tools to create balance, which is key for a sustainable and responsible usage of technology. Gerd Leonhard, author and futurist, defined this term as "Digital obesity, in which data, information, media and generic digital connectivity are consumed to a point they have a negative effect on health and well-being, happiness and life in general."[48]

But in the longer term, we find more defining topics that need to be addressed by us, namely:

Ownership Although it might seem straightforward, ownership of one's digital humans is anything but. For example, could you lose your rights to use your avatar if the platform you created it in so decides? Are you giving it away when you accept the terms and conditions of its service? As your avatar becomes part of your identity, you'll likely want to own it and then decide where and how it is used.

James Watson, Chief Marketing Officer at The Glimpse Group, thinks identity will be one of the biggest challenges ahead, "because when you interact with someone in the metaverse you need to be sure they are who they say they are. SSI (self-sovereign identity) is the most important acronym you've probably never heard of, but in the near future it will be key to establishing identity in the metaverse."[49]

We also will have the potential to keep our avatars "alive" with AI after our deaths. Should they be? Who will inherit these when you're gone?

Rights   Not only will we need to establish ownership of our own avatars while we operate within them, as avatars become more autonomous, we will need to determine responsible parties when things go wrong. We will need to establish the personal rights and liabilities of the company who built it versus the government in the country in which you live. Is an owner responsible for a digital human's actions? Or is it the company that built its machine learning algorithm?

Misuse   There is also the potential for misuse of one's personal 3D image, voice, and movements. There is a multiplicative potential for hyper-realistic deep-fake videos for political gain, bribery, or revenge porn. Hopefully, we'll see a rise in services that identify these kinds of fakes and clones. Still, there will be a clear need for companies to self-regulate and industry legal frameworks.

Control   Sci-fi books and movies have warned us countless times about computer intelligence apocalypse: Stanley Kubrick's *2001: A Space Odyssey* had HAL, who scared almost everybody with quotes like "I'm sorry . . . but . . . the computer must assume control . . . I must, therefore, override your authority now since you are not in any condition to intelligently exercise it." This isn't just a fictional warning. Even Elon Musk has said that increasing the abilities of AI is like "summoning [a] demon."[50] The world will resemble a much nicer concept of computer code coming to life than most dystopian tales, but we all need to be concerned about what will be possible when AI becomes more sentient.

Whether or not you believe that AI will ultimately trigger the end of humanity, we still need to define what it really means, being human, as there are already conflicting definitions from philosophical, psychological, religious, and evolutionary standpoints. The topic of the humanity of virtual beings is tied into defining the theory of mind, if you believe humans have a soul, when life begins and when it ends. To say these are somewhat tricky concepts to discuss is an understatement. Luckily, we have some time, as natural language processing (NLP) is still coping with colloquialisms, slang, sarcasm, and some accents.[51] Also, the costs of creating the most natural digital humans are still quite high and involve a lot of maintenance.[52] But it's a matter of time until this debate becomes inevitable.

Be that as it may, digital beings will probably become a standard interface to every service and organization in the metaverse and maybe each of us will own at least one of them and an avatar as tokens in our wallets. They will have an impact on each of us and on the way we interact socially and at work, as the metaverse holds the power to affect pretty much every industry.

Notes

1. Eric Hal Schwartz, "Alexa faces uphill battle to hold user interest as smart speaker sales slow." *Voicebot.ai*, December 22, 2021. http://voicebot.ai/2021/12/22/alexa-faces-uphill-battle-to-hold-user-interest-as-smart-speaker-sales-slow-report

2. Federica Laricchia, "Smart speakers—statistics & facts." *Statistica*, March 20, 2022. www.statista.com/topics/4748/smart-speakers

3. www.interaction-design.org/literature/book/the-encyclopedia-of-human-computer-interaction-2nd-ed/human-computer-interaction-brief-intro#

4. https://emojitimeline.com

5. http://emojipedia.org/stats

6. www.nature.com/articles/s41598-021-04357-7

7. https://time.com/43758/human-faces-can-express-at-least-21-distinct-emotions/#

8. Jack Loechner, "Text vs. talk gets millennials' attention." *MediaPost*, May 13, 2016. www.mediapost.com/publications/article/275332/text-vs-talk-gets-millennials-attention.html

9. https://news.stanford.edu/2021/02/23/four-causes-zoom-fatigue-solutions

10. Tugba Sabanoglu, "Fashion in the metaverse—statistics and facts." *Statistica*, June 1, 2022. www.statista.com/topics/9013/fashion-retail-in-the-metaverse/#dossierKeyfigures

11. Jim Freeze, "Why the human touch is crucial to AI-powered virtual assistants." *Interactions*, February 27, 2019. www.interactions.com/blog/virtual-assistants/ai-needs-humans-to-succeed

12. Uneeq, "Chatbots." *Digitalhumans.com* (undated). http://digitalhumans.com/chatbots

13. Mark Kilens, "2020 State of conversational marketing." *Drift*, September 14, 2020. www.drift.com/blog/state-of-conversational-marketing

14. Juniper Research, "Chatbots to deliver $11bn in annual cost savings for retail, banking & healthcare sectors by 2023." *Juniper Research*, July 3, 2018. www.juniperresearch.com/press/chatbots-to-deliver-11bn-cost-savings-2023

15. Joe Murphy, "Virtual humans: the video evolution for metaverse-bound voice assistants, brand ambassadors, and media personalities." *Voicebot.ai*, March 28, 2022. http://voicebot.ai/2022/03/28/virtual-humans-the-video-evolution-for-metaverse-bound-voice-assistants-brand-ambassadors-and-media-personalities-heading-to-the-metaverse

16. Jim Freeze, 2019.

17. www.nytimes.com/2022/03/03/technology/ai-chatbot.html

18. Natasha Lomas, "Another AI chatbot shown spouting offensive views." *TechCrunch+*, October 24, 2017. http://techcrunch.com/2017/10/24/another-ai-chatbot-shown-spouting-offensive-views

19. Toni Witt, "What are digital avatars and why do they matter?" *Acceleration Economy Network*, March 28, 2022. http://accelerationeconomy.com/metaverse/what-are-digital-avatars-and-why-do-they-matter

20. Gonzalo Suárez, Sungchul Jung, and Robert W. Lindeman, "Evaluating virtual human role-players for the practice and development of leadership skills." *Frontiers in Virtual Reality*, April 12, 2021. www.frontiersin.org/articles/10.3389/frvir.2021.658561/full

21. Gonzalo Suárez et al., 2021.

22. Bret Kinsella, "Voicebot podcast on Soul Machines and the rise of virtual humans" (Interview with Greg Cross), *The Voicebot Podcast,* October 21, 2021. www.soulmachines.com/2021/10/voicebot-podcast-on-soul-machines-and-the-rise-of-virtual-humans

23. Alan Truly, "Hyundai wants to build a metaverse that uses real robots." *Screenrant,* January 6, 2022. http://screenrant.com/hyundai-robot-metaverse-project

24. Dentsu Gaming, "The rise of gaming: Consumer sentiment study." *Navigator,* January 2022. http://assets-eu-01.kc-usercontent.com/27bd3334-62dd-01a3-d049-720ae980f906/b559283d-16c8-40fd-86c7-e78cb9b06125/Dentsu%20Navigator%20Rise%20of%20Gaming%20January%202022.pdf

25. Masahiro Mori, "The Uncanny Valley." *Energy*, 1970. Translation 2012 by Karl F. MacDorman and Norri Kageki. https://spectrum.ieee.org/the-uncanny-valley

26. Cambridge University, "Scientists identify possible source of the 'Uncanny Valley' in the brain." *Research*, July 1, 2019. www.cam.ac.uk/research/news/scientists-identify-possible-source-of-the-uncanny-valley-in-the-brain#

27. Eric Dahan, "Can virtual influencers have real influence?" *Virtual Humans*, July 29, 2020. www.virtualhumans.org/article/can-virtual-influencers-have-real-influence

28. www.virtualhumans.org/human/imma-gram

29. www.lbbonline.com/news/how-lu-from-magalu-became-the-biggest-virtual-influencer-in-the-world

30. Eric Dahan, 2020.

31. Karen Surian, "Balmain x Barbie & beyond: A look into Barbie's first digital fashion collaboration." *Journal of Business & Intellectual Property Law*, April 21, 2022. http://ipjournal.law.wfu.edu/2022/04/balmain-x-barbie-beyond-a-look-into-barbies-first-digital-fashion-collaboration

32. Cosmetics Business, "Prada's virtual influencer is the new 'face' of Candy perfumes." *Cosmetics Business*, October 22, 2021. http://cosmeticsbusiness.com/news/article_page/Pradas_virtual_influencer_is_the_new_face_of_Candy_perfumes/180103

33. Eric Dahan, 2020.

34. The Influencer Marketing Factory, "Virtual influencers survey + info-graphic." *Influencer Marketing*, March 29, 2022. theinfluencermar ketingfactory.com/virtual-influencers-survey-infographic

35. www.vox.com/the-goods/2018/10/23/18010274/amy-winehouse-hologram-tour-controversy-technology

36. https://mashable.com/article/james-earl-jones-gives-rights-to-darth-vader-ai

37. Bank ABC, "Bank ABC's AI-powered digital employee 'Fatema' is the world's first digital DNA™ human." *Bank ABC*, September 11, 2019. www.bank-abc.com/En/AboutABC/Media/Press/Pages/Digital-Employee.aspx

38. Benjamin Palacio, "Commentary: Speaking of chatbots, how is DMV's Miles doing?" *GovTech Industry Insider*, December 8, 2021.

39. Bret Kinsella, 2021.

40. www.zeebiz.com/indian-railways/news-irctc-train-ticket-booking-no-more-password-required-just-ask-disha-20-to-book-your-berth-how-it-works-201727

41. Bryan Robinson, "Virtual humans outperform real people teaching career leadership skills, study finds." *Forbes*, April 19, 2021. www.forbes.com/sites/bryanrobinson/2021/04/19/virtual-humans-outperform-real-people-teaching-career-leadership-skills-study-finds/?sh=92f80f29b9e0

42. Bryan Robinson, 2021.

43. Bret Kinsella, 2021.

44. Alexis Ong, "This company is making digital humans to serve the metaverse." *The Verge*, October 27, 2021. www.theverge.com/2021/10/27/22746679/soul-machines-metaverse-digital-humans-labor

45. Bret Kinsella, 2021.

46. Galen Gruman, "IT snapshot: Ethnic diversity in the tech industry." *Computerworld*, July 16, 2020. www.computerworld.com/article/3567095/it-snapshot-ethnic-diversity-in-the-tech-industry.html

47. https://youtu.be/RtId9uJzHfg

48. *Technology vs. Humanity*. Leonhard, G., Fast Future Publishing, 2016

49. Personal communication, July 2022.

50. Stella Lincoln, "Find what Elon Musk said about real world AI." *European Business Review*, April 22, 2021. www.europeanbusinessreview.com/find-what-elon-musk-said-about-real-world-ai.

51. Jim Freeze, 2019.

52. Eric Dahan, 2020.

Chapter 8
Metaversed Markets

I know that the future is scary at times.
But there's just no escaping it.

—*Ernest Cline, Armada*

At this time, it is highly unlikely for anyone to grasp the full impact of the metaverse. "We're on the verge of being disrupted by more than two dozen technologies . . . 'a tsunami' of emerging technologies," says Raja Rajamannar, Mastercard's Chief Marketing and Communications Officer.[1] We're talking about an absolutely new dimension in our lives, a new ecosystem where new behaviors will breed new ways to work, do business and to live.

In order to present you with a vision of the major transformations ahead, we'll first take a look at what is being done already inside the metaverse building blocks. If you come across someone who is just learning about the metaverse, they tend to believe that its impact will be felt only on gaming platforms or social networks; or some may add Web3 platforms into the mix. But the transformation about to occur will happen across every industry.

Our goal with this chapter is to expand the general understanding of the impact of metaverse. We will look across vertical markets and offer insights on their current and upcoming transformations. There is no doubt that you are the expert when it comes to your job or business, and you will be tempted to skip ahead to your particular industry. But, in doing so, you will miss out on how other use cases could apply to your own. Sometimes, innovation happens when you take something from one industry and apply it to another.

Please be patient with this (very long) chapter and bring an open mind. Many of the metaverse building blocks are already in place. Work this information inside your company's transformation strategy, so you can keep ahead of the curve and ready for the future metaverse opportunities and challenges!

Industry Applications

The following is a list of many different industries that are already being impacted by the metaverse. Each is outlined in detail in the following sections.

- Art and performance
- Advertising, PR, marketing
- Retail
- Gaming
- Entertainment
- Sports and fitness
- Automotive, aviation, aerospace
- Military
- Healthcare
- Hospitality and tourism
- Architecture and real estate
- Manufacturing
- Training and education

Art and Performance

Many emerging technologies achieve a bigger market awareness with the help of pioneering creative minds. Artists, actors, dancers, and creators are seldom the ones willing to play with unfamiliar tools and bring their visions to life. Experimenting with and using new tools is a natural part of the creative process. Artists are often comfortable not knowing the outcome at the beginning of a project, as they are ready to take chances and do whatever it takes to showcase their vision.

The National Endowment for the Arts (NEA) studied this phenomenon in a recent two-year study. Ann Eilers, NEA acting chairman, stated that "Tech-centered artists can be invaluable partners for leaders in the arts and non-arts sectors alike . . . [as they present] complex ideas through a creative and accessible lens."[2] The NEA realizes that creators who take risks in their process can offer valuable insights into how to (or how not to) build new technological applications and services.

The metaverse offers tremendous opportunities for the art world:

Access   Many galleries and museums have begun to create digital twins of their exhibitions and art pieces that can be visited both on screens and in VR. These new virtual spaces act as digital extensions of the physical exhibition floor.

Archive   Models of physical and hybrid artifacts and monuments can be scanned in great precision over time. This can monitor any changes and, more importantly, archive their existence so it makes sure we never lose them entirely—at least, not a digital version of them.

Creation Tools   Artists have now the power to create full digital worlds. They can re-create the physical world and bend it to their will, using VR or AR formats or use AI tools or IoT sensors to make something unexpected, impactful, or thought-provoking. Indeed, generative AI tools are allowing creators to produce their art much more quickly and diversely. They also develop hybrid art rising from combining both the digital and the physical worlds and by creating new objects, where digital actions can trigger physical effects and vice versa.

Display   Web3 and Metaverse-related worlds offer new locations for artists to showcase work that are less or not bound to a physical structure.

Educate   Exact digital replicas of the same digital art pieces–or even digital copies of physical artworks of any size—can be exhibited in any classroom, on-demand. Teachers also can use metaverse spaces to instruct their students.

Promote   Artists and creators have gained recognition and connected to communities in a much more meaningful way that drives more awareness and demand.

Sell   Using NFTs enables artists to sell original or licensed copies of their artwork without intermediaries and with royalties paid directly for each sale.

Subscribe   Artists' work might be available not only through ticketing or sales of the art itself, but through a membership model like Patreon, where patrons pay for access to premium content and events.

Who are the artists that are opening our minds to new possibilities? There are actually way too many worthy people to mention. Instead, the following are a few examples of artists who have inspired us personally to see the possibilities of this market.

AR House LA

Many heard about Lucas Rizzotto for the first time when he invented a "personal time machine" by wearing 360° cameras on his face for one full year. He published the recordings and allowed us to peek into his life through his YouTube channel. Besides his many hilarious and insightful social media posts, Rizzotto created the concept of the AR House, a place in Los Angeles that offers a home and creative space for AR artists. It's evolved into a membership community, a 4-week long program for cohorts of creators, and an immersive events venue. The collective prototyping and the opportunity to see artists mash-up work have been inspiring to anyone who follows their journey.

Beeple

Mike Winkelmann decided in May 2007 that he was going to create and post a new graphical work of art each and every day.

Once he was done with the 5,000th one, he stitched them all together in a colorful, myriad digital canvas and went on to make history. His work has been described as "pixels on screens depicting bizarre, hilarious, disturbing, and sometimes grotesque images."[3] But it was when *Everydays: The First 5000 Days* was sold for $69.3 million at Christie's, that people took notice. Winkelmann's success marked the rise of the NFT market and inspired many other creators and collectors to jump on the bandwagon. Although he isn't even comfortable with calling himself an artist, stating he is "just making whatever the hell I want and hoping people will want to buy it,"[4] his relevance goes well beyond that job description.

Kiira Benzing

Kiira Benzing is an award-winning creator. It is her integration of new technologies and storytelling techniques that makes us fans. She found ways to jump around and dance in VR with the largest group of volumetrically captured dancers (at the time) in *Runnin'* (2019). In her piece *Loveseat*, featured at the 2019 Venice Film Festival, the topic was a reality show, where physical and digital merged in ways that hadn't yet been imagined. Actors simultaneously performed both in real life and in a VR world and audiences could join in either. Her next work won a Lion at the 2020 Venice Film Festival. *Finding Pandora X* was an immersive theatrical piece bringing the audience into the story as a Greek Chorus where they interacted live with Broadway-level actors in VR. We are excited to see the impact of Benzing's *Skits & Giggles*, the first VR variety show.

Nancy Baker Cahill

Nancy Baker Cahill is another creator who operates on the cutting edge of technology. She distributes her work and supports other artists through her 4th Wall app, created to "to challenge traditional conventions of public art and introduce a participatory, immersive art experience."[5] It's that vision of setting pieces in nontraditional locations that opened our eyes to how previously unused physical spaces and places can become art galleries. Any location can be redefined as an art show. At the 2022 Tribeca Film Festival, for instance, Cahill inaugurated her AR piece *Mushroom Cloud NYC / RISE* just over the Hudson River. The piece also was minted as an NFT on the blockchain.[6]

Carla Gannis

The artist and NYU professor Carla Gannis is hard to miss. She is often clad in unitards with bright blue hair or traveling through her digital artwork via her avatar C.A.R.L.A. G.A.N.. which stands for Cross-platform Avatar for Recursive Life Action Generative Adversarial Network. That isn't what puts her on this list, though—it's her interest in bringing classic painters to life using a new artistic toolset that includes technologies like photogrammetry. Often known for her 2013 version of Hieronymus Bosch's *The Garden of Earthly Delights*, which was filled with emojis, Gannis continues to innovate and often takes classic artists like Pieter Bruegel the Elder and spins them into the future, making something entirely new.

Krista Kim

Krista Kim is best known for selling the first NFT house project for a whopping $500,000[7] and for preaching Techism, a movement connecting emerging technology with the emergence of new art. In its manifesto, she states:

> Art is no longer limited to a frame on a wall. Art is becoming ever more an interactive practice. Collaboration has always enabled art's creation. Collaboration materializes consciousness. Art is consciousness. Techism is an appeal and return to that consciousness, the consciousness of art as shared, as thing, as idea and as experience . . . it sees art and technology as companions meeting the next wave of human expression—digital humanism.[8]

Jeff Koons

We know that listing this prolific artist as an inspiration might lead to an eye roll, but the reason he's included might not be what you'd expect. In 2017, Snapchat featured an AR version of Jeff Koons's balloon animal in Central Park. Not everyone appreciated it and almost immediately after, graffiti artist Sebastian Errazuriz hijacked the project and covered it in virtual graffiti. He shared socially that, "It all seems fun, but I believe it is imperative we start questioning how much of our virtual public space we are willing to give to companies."[9] A similar hijacking of art took place in 2018 when guerrilla artists created a MoMAR app that used artworks within the New York's MoMA as triggers for their own work.[10] Both episodes make us realize that public spaces in the metaverse bring on new potential challenges and not just creative opportunities.

Tupac Martir

Spanning the fields of lighting, projection, video, sound design, music, composition, choreography, costume design, and even puppetry and stop-motion animation, Tupac merges these with digital lighting, cutting-edge animation techniques, and Mexican culture. The award-winning immersive live show *Cosmos Within Us* showcased on stage the experience of a member of the public immersed in a story about a memory. *Unique* was the first live immersive performance to integrate AI algorithms to produce live shows customized for each attendee.

A Lot More to Explore

There is so much creativity being explored with the different metaverse technologies. You can do your own digital art browsing at Spatial, Museum of Other Realities, Acute Art, Serpentine Gallery, Movers and Shakers NYC, HOFA, and throughout Decentraland and Somnium Space. There are also location-based art experiences that incorporate AR, like Artechouse and Arcadia Earth. Artists are constantly experimenting, so expect many more to come along with the advancement of these technologies. Enjoy the art, but also ask yourself what new approaches can make sense for your business.

Advertising, PR, Marketing

After artists have taken risks and experimented with new formats, creative advertising teams and marketers are usually the next to be inspired and test new grounds. There is no doubt these industries can benefit immensely from the metaverse, as the vast amount of data being collected can bring in and generate new, more effective formats for brands to promote themselves.

In 2018, one of the authors of this book, Sam, wrote a chapter specifically about advertising and AR that continues to apply. At the time, she identified the following opportunities. Each are briefly described here:

Amplify   Add more information to a location or product.
Filter   Overlay data and graphics on top of spaces, products, and consumers.
Gamify   Promote ways for potential customers to play with the brand.
Personalize   Show a product on you or within a custom environment.
Visualize   Create always-available digital versions of a product.
Wayfind   Help customers find their way in spaces to your product, service, or event.[11]

But now phygital spaces create a new, greater, more impactful way to interact with audiences. There is the potential for brand marketers to dive even deeper into customer journeys. Here are some opportunities for metaverse advertising strategy and tactics:

Behavioral Insights   Not only will you have the opportunity to identify users, but continuous recognition of physical objects, spaces, and people enable more targeted ads and experiences. Additional data from sensors, robots, and IoT can expand these insights even further to something resembling more of a persistent marketing research tool.
Community Building   Create groups of like-minded customers by providing social gatherings within metaverse platforms. This offers the chance to build loyalty, and potentially allows for product and campaign testing.

Display Advertising   Find new locations to showcase phygital advertisements, not bound by any physical frontier and available across digital and physical experiences. Even better if it moves beyond just "display" and creates a valuable interaction experience.

Gamification   Social tokens and AR mechanics enable more opportunities to increase and lengthen time of engagement, besides leveraging different game-like activities.

Hybridization   Include a new class of digital and hybrid assets to add meaning to one's experience, enable digital ownership and enhance target market's experiences over time.

Product Placement   Integrate products and services more seamlessly. Louis Rosenberg, CEO of Unanimous AI and a pioneer of VR and AR, defines VPP (virtual product placement) as "a simulated product, service, or activity injected into an immersive world (virtual or augmented) on behalf of a paying sponsor such that it appears to the user as an integrated element of the ambient environment."[12] Remember these products or experiences don't have to be realistic or follow the physics of the real world, and maybe shouldn't, to take full advantage of the technologies.

Spatialization and Branching Narratives   Keep the customer journey in mind, but now shift to 3D interactive experiences and elements. Some can be explored openly and some with choose-your-own-adventure story-led decisions

Virtual Beings   Take your brand personality and turn it into a virtual being that can embody the brand values of your company. These don't have to necessarily sell a product or service as they are building trust and a relationship with your customers. They also could be interactive, 3D visual versions of your current chatbot technologies.

World Building   Create virtual and augmented spaces that enable branded experiences anywhere relevant and useful to your company and your customers. Decide whether that space should re-create reality or would your customer be more engaged in something that is on brand, but not possible in the real world.

There are many considerations as we enter the world of metaverse advertising, marketing, and communications. One that we have touched on before in a broader context is interoperability. Advertising is easier to distribute with standardizations. The Interactive Advertising Bureau (IAB) has begun that task already, but it will continue to evolve along with the technology.

The Media Rating Council, IAB Experience Center, and IAB Tech Lab launched the *Intrinsic In-Game (IIG) Measurement Guidelines*, which include new standards for ads appearing inside gameplay and 3D platforms. In the words of George Ivie, CEO at the Media Rating Council, "we can now have greater consistency versus having vendors create their own rules for their measurements, which enables publisher and buyer trust as the industry works together to create a non-intrusive ad experience."[13]

These new amounts of data and ways to advertise and market to target audiences bring with it not just creative opportunities, but a need for industry-wide change and evolution. As there are new types of experiences being created, advertising rules of engagement need to be updated as well:

Ad Restrictions Restrictions on advertising locations (for example, schools, places of worship) need to be considered in more detail as the technologies evolve. There should no-augmentation zones and location rights established that include regulation against virtual squatters (like those who owned .com URLs before the Internet became mainstream).

Fraud Protection With the quality and volume of digital cloning increasing, there is the potential for more license infringement and misuse of data. Safeguarding intellectual property and personal data across these new formats is a challenge that needs to be met at many levels.

Personal Data Advertising Rights Behavior prediction will be much easier with metaverse technologies that integrate eye tracking, gestures, voice commands, body movement, biometric data (including information about pupil dilation), and eyebrow movement. Each can be used to infer and detect the likelihood of interest and purchase. Where is the line drawn? We need to try to avoid the mistakes of social media and always-on smart speakers.

Let's not forget the customer experience of all of this as well. Also, in the Augmented Reality and Brands chapter that Sam wrote, it mentioned the need to establish trust and avoid creepiness.

Trust   With brands having massive amounts of data, the consumer benefit needs to be brought to the forefront of discussions. If mishandled, a brand comes across as invading a potential customer's personal space. Enabling consumer control of the experience should alleviate some of the concerns.

Creepiness   Advertisers already are familiar with how bad advertising can come with an "ick" factor, when it becomes too invasive.

Pay attention to the different needs of your targets based on their personal, professional, and social spaces. There should be a personal data boundary, a professional data boundary, and a social data boundary that can be dialed up and down. More than anything, consciously deliberate how data can be used to improve and not overstep, as likely the legal restrictions for use aren't going to be put in place in the near future.

One addition to this list is overexposure. Visionary Keiichi Matsuda's 2016 concept film *Hyper-Reality* scared many in the industry about how overwhelming and terrible too many AR ads can be. Matsuda deftly highlighted the digital pollution, loss of safety, and general loss of meaning in a digitally gamified space. As the media formats before have shown, there will need to be ways to moderate exposure to ads and branded experiences so that the technologies enhance and not overwhelm us.

There are so many brands and creative ad experiences to spur insights into the possibilities. Katie Hudson, who leads the metaverse and emerging tech product creation at Publicis Groupe, told us "The metaverse is a unique, intimate, immersive, and experiential space. It is unlike any tool that we've ever been able to deploy in advertising to deeply engage people, meaning that we'll need to reimagine campaigns, channels, content, social networks, influencers, brand, products, and the consumer journey. We now have the potential to do far more with marketing than ever before, integrating into people's virtual and real lives and delivering a huge step change in performance if we create meaningful data-driven relationships with consumers."[14]

There are so many creative approaches that brands have already taken when it comes to metaverse technologies. Each example below we chose as they inspired us to think about what is possible.

7-Eleven

The 7-Eleven chain of convenience stores features a AR section in its app since 2018. It's periodically updated with new experiences, such as face filters, volumetrically captured guest participants, and codes that offer 7Rewards points. The stores have partnered on multiple movie releases and with brands such as Dr. Pepper and Cheetos, and sports franchises such as the Dallas Cowboys and the World Cup. In this way, the company created a new, engaging branded channel in an entirely new dimension.[15]

Bored Ape Yacht Club (BAYC)

Although not a brand that might immediately come to mind if you work outside of the tech industry, the BAYC is worthy of every digital marketer's focus and attention. Their NFT collection kicked off the NFT craze and was made of 10,000 images, representing variations of cartoon ape faces, originally priced at $200 each. Tech enthusiasts and early adopters were soon flexing their ownership across social media,[16] as having an ape became a symbol of being a member of that exclusive community.

By April 2022, over $15 billion of those initial designs had been traded and the least expensive BAYC item was worth $300,000–350,000. The company responsible for BAYC, Yuga Labs, received $450 million in seed money to build on the community-driven market they created.[17] They used it to buy other NFT collections, like Meebits and CryptoPunks,[18] and launch a cryptocurrency and a new metaverse-related digital world, where these communities can meet and mingle.[19]

Whether or not you believe in the over-hyped NFT market and Yuga Lab's business choices, Bored Ape Yacht Club's meteoric rise and bumps along the way not only made headlines, they made history.

Burger King

In 2019 in Brazil, Burger King decided to burn competitors' ads. Well, not in physical reality, but with the help of AR. "The Burn That Ad" creative was an app campaign based on a very simple proposition: it recognized competitors' advertising posters and large print ads, and whenever the user pointed their smartphone's camera to such an ad, an AR burning effect appeared and revealed a free Whopper coupon.[20] Although it seems like a very straightforward technique, it's in fact a bit sophisticated gamification approach. The incentives exist for users to interact with the app continuously, which increases the odds of passersby to wonder what's going on. Also, it puts users through the doors of Burger King restaurants to redeem their vouchers.

Dibbs (Previously Known as Snatch)

Dibbs is a great example of the transformative power of a branded experience combined with augmented reality gamification. Their app is focused on gamifying treasure hunts for businesses. It makes users more likely to visit new places and interact between them in their search for rewards. Think Pokemon GO but where you're competing with other players for real-world prizes, like event tickets, brand merchandising, or iPods. The way for users to retrieve these rewards is to find them on the map, go where they are and capture them, but afterward, they will need to run with the loot and keep it safe from other players for a period of time, as all others can snatch captured prizes just by being in your physical vicinity.

Gucci

In the past, luxury fashion brands used to focus only on real-world items, but that's not true anymore. Fashion brands were among the first to experiment with the metaverse and continue to dive deeply. For instance, one of Gucci's most successful metaverse campaigns happened in Roblox in 2021. The Gucci Garden Archetypes included a digital twin of Gucci's palazzo in Florence and attracted preteens to the brand. Avatars within that world could try on and purchase digital Gucci items and move through multiple rooms with different experiences. Gucci also has experimented with limited NFT branded collections and operates a space in The Sandbox. This is just one of the examples how luxury brands can use metaverse technologies to create innovative campaigns and build new audiences. There are many other brands testing digital products in metaverse platforms, like Balenciaga, Burberry, Dolce & Gabbana, and Louis Vuitton, to only name a few. There even has been a metaverse fashion week in 2022; detailed coverage and events from some of the biggest fashion magazines like Vogue, W, and WWD; and multiple fashion-focused research reports including Metaverse Fashion Trends report from Roblox and Parsons (distributed in November 2022).[21]

Wendy's

In early 2020, Wendy's used the popularity of the Twitch streaming platform to amplify a game story within Fortnite. They created Food Fight, a new game mode, within the story that focused on the rivalry between Durr Burger and Pizza Pit, the two Fortnite restaurants. It was spawned by the storage of burgers in the freezer, which is counter to Wendy's value proposition ("fresh, never frozen"). So, they joined in support of Team Pizza in destroying the burger freezers. The Twitch activation was watched live by over 250,000 people and over 1.5 million people within Fortnite.[22] It successfully showed how fast-food brand activations can operate within virtual worlds.

Retail

The next industry to fully explore the possibilities of a metaversed economy has been retail. COVID-19 bred the "most disruptive event to the retail sector in decades,"[23] which forced retailers to cater to potential customers in a different way. The industry is now entering a new era of hybrid commerce. New methods of shopping have emerged, mixing physical and digital touchpoints. Cathy Hackl, a Web3 and renowned metaverse expert (and Sam's coauthor on *Marketing New Realities* [Meraki Press, 2017]) proposed a few hybrid models that move beyond traditional commerce (physical-to-physical) and e-commerce (digital-to-digital). Physical-to-digital happens when your physical purchase triggers a digital effect—for instance, physical tickets that allow entry to both a physical venue as well as a VR party. Digital-to-physical refers to when purchasing a digital good "unlocks" something in the physical world, such as purchasing an NFT of a physical art piece in an online marketplace. Hackl also highlights the rise of a direct-to-avatar model, similar to direct-to-consumer, but where the avatar's needs and context define the purchasing purpose and moment.[24]

Another way to look at the retail industry in the metaverse is to analyze where the actual sale is taking place: digital or physical or hybrid point-of-sale.

Digital Point-of-Sale

A digital point-of-sale can be opened anywhere, at any time in the metaverse. There are no longer physical limitations. There are a wide variety of applications including visualizations (e.g., try-ons, in-home product showcase) and virtual showrooms.

Augmented Reality fashion has evolved from try-on glasses, to try-on sneakers, to, most recently, clothing. Markerless body tracking and Lidar cameras have enabled companies like Snap and the start-up DressX to inspire us all to imagine what's is possible with AR try-ons. Snap's CEO stated, "We are laying the groundwork for an improved online shopping experience. We believe that helping people find the right size and improving the try-on experience could both increase conversion rates as well as reduce the rate of returns."[25] Their report shared that almost all of Gen Z surveyed were interested in using AR for shopping.[26] Most clothes currently match to the physical reality, but expect that to change especially as AR glasses become more ubiquitous.

AR home goods and interior design retail innovation was led initially by Ikea's AR function in their app in 2017. Wayfair, Overstock, Etsy, and Amazon have integrated AR into their sales process. Virtual 3D models have become a cost of doing business in the metaverse. Companies such as Plott showed what is possible in a phygital world. Their product brings "real world dimensions into an app where you can. . .see and make changes. . .digitally before making them in the real world."[27] The sales process doesn't even have to involve an actual physical good, as seen by the billions of sales of video game skins and digital items. Almost 75% of Gen Z Roblox users have spent $20-$100 on one virtual item.[28] Many brands, such as Vans, Ralph Lauren, and Forever 21, offer digital customized outfits. Nike's purchase of the RTFKT, a leading producer of virtual digital-only fashion including sneakers,[29] and the sales of Jordan sneakers in Fortnite[30] demonstrated the importance of 3D digital commerce even for a traditional physical fashion brand.

VR stores also offer a level of customization that is not hindered by physical means. For example, the start-up Obsess took fashion retail and shopping experience into 3D worlds, setting up designer brands in 3D digital platforms. There also aren't as many physical limitations, cost-wise, to house inventory and product types, creating an overwhelming number of potential variations that will need store curation. Although digital retail lacks the full effect of enjoying all of your senses, currently there are opportunities to experiment in VR with spatial sound and, eventually, high quality haptics and advanced digital smell technology could create yet another level of remote shopping.

"With the advent of artificial intelligence, XR, and blockchain, retailers and brands have a unique and powerful opportunity to provide unparalleled experiences in virtual worlds that bring back the joy of shopping.", shares Alan Smithson, co-founder at TheMall, a large virtual retail and entertainment destination, "E-commerce is ruthlessly efficient but it has taken the fun away from discovery and brand engagement."[31]

Let's not forget also that metaverse technologies can also help post-sales of product devices. Maintenance instructions can be overlaid on top of products, and, if these aren't enough, users can make video calls with support staff who can annotate instructions in real time, that appear in front of the user, where they're needed. NFT sales also can become advanced tools for customer interaction, long-term loyalty, and upselling. CEO Matt Smolin of Hang, an NFT membership company, said. "[Brands] can also take a royalty or percentage from each resell transaction as users continue to fast-track their loyalty status, which inevitably will just make them more aligned with that brand."[32]

Physical Point-of-Sale

Although there has been a shift in the way shopping takes place, there is still a lot of room and opportunities for brick-and-mortar sites. Online or digital screen views of products sometimes are just not enough to bring consumers down the purchase funnel. You need to touch and feel a product. Get a sense of what it looks like in person (even if the 3D graphics are of the highest quality).

But physical storefronts don't have to be all physical. There are lots of ways for metaverse technologies to be integrated. There are opportunities for wayfinding tools and games around larger spaces and malls to increase foot traffic. Brick-and-mortar sites can offer exclusive AR interactions to amplify their in-store experience. In 2018, Zara's clothing app ZARA enabled visitors to see the highlights of their next collection in an augmented reality catwalk experience in-store,[33] the same way the ASOS[34] app does. For an eco-conscious brand, videos of the product manufacturing process can be spread around the store, and, for fast-fashion, influencer quotes can be overlaid in AR on top of the physical goods.

Nike is a leading company in applying emerging technologies into their sales process. They have created Snap lenses at the World Cup (2019), offered sure measurements in AR (2019), enabled sneakers to be found in the clouds (2020). Besides their digital footprint in Nikeland in Roblox (2021) and their cryptokicks with RTFKT, some of their famous, scavenger-hunt-like sneaker drops require potential customers to go to a store that had a geo-located access not available elsewhere. In March 2022, they took it to an entirely new level with an actual drone in New York and Los Angeles[35] and a 3D billboard in Tokyo.[36] Although neither are directly at the point-of-sale, they speak to what could be possible integrating technology at physical retail locations.

On the flip side, Web3 startups like Superplastic are jumping into physical reality and creating their own physical stores to sell physical and digital art and educate users on this digital and physical continuum that is the metaverse. "It's all about the intersection of reality and virtual reality and the blurring and then eventually dismantling of that line," Superplastic founder and CEO Paul Budnitz said. "The way we're setting it up is when you walk out the back door, you can continue in the virtual world, and it keeps going."[37]

You also can expand your store inventory and showcase products that are not on the shop floor. A hologram virtual being can be offered as an embodied chatbot with personalized shopping experience based on mining your data. They may be able to provide more convenient help in-store by checking inventory, ordering products, and even talking to customers in their native language, if needed.

Hybrid Experiences

As we've discussed, digital and physical retail experiences aren't mutually exclusive in the metaverse. There will be many companies offering merged versions of their goods packaged with NFT ownership, and the physical items will trigger unique digital experiences or digital giving access to physical items. Splitting the two of them up as separate approaches eventually seem like a "pre-metaverse" way of approaching retail.

We've begun to see hints as to what's possible. Tiffany's sold out Cryptopunk's NFTiffs necklaces.[38] Noah Davis, the head of Brand at Cryptopunk says, "Owning a token does not just mean this JPEG belongs to you. It means you have certain rights with regards to what you can do with your CryptoPunk, what kind of IP you can build around it. There are extremely few restrictions."[39]

Depending on software choices and the level of opt-in/out of your customers, retailers can track interest and even allow for all shopping processes to be controlled on automatic by tracking eye, movement, and several other sensors. This enables stores like Amazon Go or Sensei.tech to be cashier-less and for customers to just grab goods and go, avoiding long lines. Soon these stores will also include AR and/or VR experiences of their own, which is a step toward a vision of metaversed stores.

Customization

It's not just point-of-sale approaches that are changing. It's the products and services themselves. This moves beyond the product customization trends of the past few years. Deloitte developed an opportunity matrix that identified the business potential for different products based on their need for customization and standardization. In that report,[40] automotive, furniture, and apparel are listed as the top opportunities, with makeup and shoes following. On the flip side, home goods, technology, and groceries offered less of an opportunity. Adding this effect to the customization potential of a consumer's data will most probably drive retail to build unique products and unique points-of-sale for the user, created specifically to be meaningful for each consumer.

With the metaverse, the potential for customization moves beyond a matrix of choices and selections. This becomes something that feels truly customized individually. Already, AR versions of makeup and hair color try-on have entered the mainstream. Most of this took place after the purchase of Modiface by L'Oreal in 2018, the first tech company ever to be bought by the corporate giant. Now AR has become a sales platform like web and mobile for the beauty industry with almost every major beauty brand incorporating the tech into their business, e.g., as an April 2022 InStyle article announced, "The Future of Shopping for Beauty Has Nothing to Do With an IRL Experience." Anyone could create and build products or services with low code or no code tools. If it works in the

3D digital world, then it could be 3D printed to order.[41] This kind of process happens now at more of an enterprise design level (e.g., automotive), but as processes improve in speed and technology lowers in costs, the potential for an unprecedented level of customization is likely across many industries.

Gaming

As you easily might guess, there is enough information about gaming and the metaverse to create an entire book. But as we are trying to cover all industries, we have allocated just a small part of the book to accommodate.

Gaming plays a fundamental role in the metaverse. It's no wonder, as it dominates the tech industry. Over 2.7 billion players and a $300 billion value are in gaming, according to an Accenture 2021 report.[42] VR/AR has only begun to make a dent, beyond their gaming engine technology being almost a mainstay of any part of the metaverse. *Pokemon Go's* AR mode kicked off general awareness of graphic overlays. In 2020, VR made some progress, it was announced that the Top 100 VR games made over $1 million each, the Top 20 VR games generated over $4 million, with more than $10 million for the top games across platforms.[43] VR titles like "Half Life: Alyx"[44] or "Beat Saber"[45] already boast millions of players. These aren't big numbers vs. most of the gaming industry, but they are respectful nonetheless.

There are now Web3 metaverse worlds like Axie Infinity or AlienWorlds. They made play-to-earn games popular, where users earn cryptocurrency or tokens by fulfilling goals, quests or adopting specific behaviors inside the gaming platform. Most of the time, these rewards can be exchanged for actual money which of course, builds up user loyalty and gaming time.

Let's not forget the social impact of gaming. It has been attracting generations of users to digital worlds for quite some time, while educating them on how to act socially, use digital coins, and digital items inside them. These gamers are also becoming creators, as platforms like Roblox or KoGaMa provide them with easy-to-use tools to generate their gaming worlds.

A broader distribution of the metaverse will bring the opportunity for game interactions and dynamics becoming even more mainstream:

AR Sports   Teams like ONTOP Studios have already pushed for this new category for their games. "New game genres are being created by mixing video games and sports," shares Nuno Folhadela, CEO of ONTOP Studios. "An alien invasion or a wizard championship can now take place at your shopping mall, gathering thousands of people—or at the comfort of your living room with your family. And no controllers are needed, being each the Player the controller! Get ready to literally jump, squat and run while playing and in the process, maybe you will create a healthier lifestyle while having fun."[46]

Expanded Gamification and Exergames   Turning business applications into games isn't new, but the 3D applications make them more engaging and effective. Specific, health-oriented scenarios have a tremendous impact. Besides physical fitness applications like the Supernatural app, start-ups like Virtuleap develop games to train users' brains and reduce risks of mental disease, like Alzheimer's or Parkinson's.

Greater Diversity of Gamers   Although the stereotype of a teen boy gamer is almost defunct in the 21st century, the demographic distribution of "gamers" is still expanding. KPMG found that kids spend almost double the amount of time as adults in VR, but adults still spend three to five hours a week in a VR headset.[47] If everyone starts wearing metaverse-capable devices that incorporate gaming features in a 3D virtual or overlaid real world, expect the potential for even more gaming niche audiences to arise.

Hybrid Elements   Physical and virtual aspects of games can be used interchangeably, fitting seamlessly into the storylines. Rewards, for example, could range from physical gifts to digital items to tokens, which could be used to build loyalty and/or have real value. Tilt Five is merging tabletop board gaming and AR with their patented glasses. Through them, players can see animated pieces, interactive scenes and even digital parts of the game happening on top of a game board. "You can stick grandma and grandpa into a Tilt5 experience where the grandkids are sitting across the table drawing. Now you have this experience that bridges generations,"[48] shares Jeri Ellsworth, Founder and CEO of Tilt5. As the metaverse building blocks grow and converge, we will see more of these hybrid solutions coming into place, taking full advantage of sensors, robots, and AI to generate new games.

Location-Based Multiplayer Experiences Although many shuttered during COVID-19, there are still many VR companies with business models based on physical spaces (for example, Hologate and SpringboardVR).[49] As AR improves, you will be able to share with your friends in a specified space the same graphic experience. This seems simple, but in order to see these graphics from different perspectives, in real time and with the effects of other users interacting, you'll need the advancements coming with AR clouds and 5G in particular. These will develop in the coming years to make this real-time shared experience more common. Their launch might not be met with fanfare, though, as the group experiences seem intuitive as it's much closer to real life.

No-Code or Low-Code Many tools are coming to simplify game creation. This will allow those without programming skills to create, share, and monetize them, increasing the number of 3D games in the market.

Entertainment

Many people outside of the tech industry believe that the only application of VR and AR technologies are for the entertainment and gaming businesses, with entertainment providing the intellectual property (IP). While it is still true that IP provides a huge value to the tech industry, as seen by the volume of Marvel and Star Wars games, there are many other ways that the metaverse has been used by the entertainment industry.

Production

Movies and TV have embraced metaverse technologies, but not necessarily in ways that could have been predicted. At the highest end of budgets, directors have used game engines and immersive technologies to shoot their movies inside virtual worlds. Jon Favreau's *Lion King* remake was directed this way, by recording all action through a virtual reality headset. On an article from IGN, he shared that "It has the feeling of a live-action shoot, because that's the way I learned how to direct. It wasn't sitting, looking over somebody's shoulder or computer. It was being in a real location, and there's something about being in a real 3D environment that makes it, I don't know, just the parts of my brain are firing that fire on a real movie,".[50] Another example is Favreau's TV series *The Mandalorian*, which uses an LED virtual production stage called "The Volume." Today, a wealth of tech solutions, including Unreal Engine and Helios, allow the directors of episodes to change the background in real time as an episode is being filmed. Of course, using virtual worlds to shoot movie scenes fundamentally changes how producing a Hollywood movie happens, since it significantly diminishes the need to travel to different locations to shoot scenes.

The TV industry, when not using metaverse technologies in their advertising campaigns, has stuck to more of an AR overlay approach. Trying to reach the generations who use photos and videos of themselves integrating graphics via Snap, Instagram, and other social media platforms, MTV Networks applied AR graphics on its performance stages at awards shows to give viewers an amplified experience. The Weather Channel uses AR graphics through its cameras to demonstrate the visual impact of certain weather events without putting its reporters at risks (e.g., the depth of flood waters).

Music and Live Events

Live shows have also been shapeshifting to happen in 3D digital worlds in the last few years, since August 2006, when Suzanne Vega rocked Second Life to the rhythm of "Luka."

The most popular pop artists have performed in front of hundreds of thousands, sometimes millions of fans. Given our collective inability to attend events during the worst times of the pandemic, it seemed more possible than ever that we could be exchanging the experience of a traditional live show for a digital one. And several artists did it, like Soccer Mommy or David Guetta on Roblox, Foo Fighters or Young Thug on Horizon Worlds and many others. In 2020, John Legend starred in a digital concert where his movements were captured and synced with an avatar in real time, right before being broadcast by the start-up Wave. Travis Scott headlined several digital shows on the platform *Fortnite*, with more than 45 million people tuning in during all of his Astronomical Tour.[51]

In the metaverse, a new hybrid space rose, filled with many yet-to-be-discovered creative opportunities. The following are some of the different transformations that could impact the music and live event industries:

Metaverse Storytelling Modes   We have seen interactive VR and AR storytellers. But with the metaverse, it becomes an entire virtual and augmented world filled with opportunities, for both coders and noncoders alike. Potentially new kinds of companies will be created to take advantage of the creative possibilities.

Multi-Reality Shows   Shows can be produced to be seen in different realities simultaneously. The same show might be happening at a stadium in the physical world. "Attending a show" could mean entering a physical world arena, its digital twin in virtual reality, or connecting through the AR glasses of someone at the venue.

On-Demand   3D interactive digital experiences can be captured and experienced nonlinearly, as on-demand video does now, which could be featured in your living room or in a VR world.

See What I See   Real-time call-through VR and AR glasses will give us the ability to tap into the live or recorded point of view of someone else, which is bound to generate several new entertainment formats.

Ticketing   NFTs can reduce the risks of fraud and black-market opportunities for tickets and create a continued relationship and exclusive access with each event attendee.

At this time, several events are leveraging the metaverse building blocks to connect their physical and digital presences. In 2020, one of the most impactful examples of consumer events was Burning Man, with over 100 over-the-top experiences placed across a number of digital 2D and 3D worlds, much like the real Burning Man. The Coachella Fest app gave users access to earn Coachella coins and to a portal into the Coachellaverse, an AR section of the event created in partnership with Niantic.

In the same way, business-to-business events such as conferences are already being organized in platforms like Virbela, Engage VR, or 8agora. Mobile applications also are now an important part of any event. Many events can add AR or VR elements, whether live or recorded, animated or live action (or a mix of the two), at a specific location or location independent.

Casinos and Gambling

The casino and online betting industry in 2021 saw over $60 billion of industry revenue, with results for 2028 expected to move beyond $100 billion.[52] The metaverse, with its potential for almost limitless real estate and access to players, is part of the industry's next growth strategy. A few VR casinos already operate on the market. SlotsMillion, Viva Las Vegas, and Lucky VR allow you to enter different rooms and ambiances to play poker in real time against other players' avatars. You can also decide to jump into crypto casinos like WOLF.BET or Moonbet and start betting Ethereum and 11 other cryptocurrencies on dice, slots, and roulette. These are sought by everyone looking for more privacy.

The metaverse brings some advantages to the industry. One is a more immersive experience, something that casino owners are quite familiar with in the physical world with some of the over-the-top décor lining the casinos of the Sunset Strip (e.g., the Luxor, Caesar's Palace). Casinos can be created using unrealistic environments that encourage engagement and betting. There are the potential opportunities brought about with the improvement in avatars and digital human representation for hosts, managers, and players. There also are simplifications to the payment systems (for example, click-to-bet) and the addition of more digital currencies. Expected transformations going forward in this area include:

Increased Immersiveness   There are many metaverse casino opportunities that move beyond game tables and in-game chats. Haptics, AR, and other sensors will add new layers to players' sensorial experience. Spatial sound and live dealers can help create an experience that purposefully does not resemble real life, creating a new platform for gambling.

New Games   Digital worlds offer a multidimensional canvas for new phygital games to be promoted, as well as new games in virtual reality.

New Regulations   There are many opportunities for casinos within the metaverse, and along with them come the issues of potential exploitation. For example, with the rise of specific AIs that can help players calculate odds more quickly–or even take the turn of players—new rules will need to be created and enforced. Ways to identify underage players and manage addiction will also need to be determined.

Pop-Up Casinos   When XR glasses hit the mainstream, casual gambling might become even easier and an experience in itself.

Adult Entertainment

Although a controversial subject, it's necessary to discuss the pioneering impact of the adult industry on the market. Even if you disagree with the ethics and morals around it, the adult industry is part of the mainstreaming of cutting-edge technology. First with the videocassette recorder (VCR), then with Blu-ray disks, or more recently with VR, it has always been one of the first markets investing in new hardware and new formats, once they are offered to consumers.

Even before Google Glass was publicly released, producer MiKandi recorded an entire adult movie through the smart-glasses point of view.[53] Not even MiKandi's ban from Google stopped them from publishing and promoting a new video format, as there weren't any further restrictions in 2013. Back in the land of NFTs, rapper Azealia Banks was the first to sell the NFT of an audio sex tape for $17,240 just to see that it was re-listed for sale for the unbelievable sum of $260 million.[54]

We see many potential applications powering forward the adult market:

Customized Experiences   Machine learning adult applications may be able to guess and simulate unique situations based on a user's data and preferences.

Hyper-Realistic Avatars   As digital humans resemble real humans more closely, there may be an entire market for virtual erotic entertainers, humanoid or otherwise.

Integrated Experiences   The full potential for haptics is nowhere close to the potential quality and implementation at scale.

Location-Based Entertainment   Strip clubs and other venues for adult entertainment will be able to add a digital element and augment their shows.

New Experiences   Any location is possible in the metaverse, so any place can be created and explored, from the bottom of the sea to the surface of Venus.

As any technologies do, when they are brought into the market, the potential for misuse increases along with it. We can expect that the industry will face regulatory probes, legal and location restrictions (for example, no 3D representation of children), and that unique personalization will increase the addictive properties of adult entertainment. The same will hold true for individualized, hyper-realistic avatars, which could be used for advanced celebrity deep fakes and revenge porn.

Sports and Fitness

Although the idea of exercising and sweating in a VR/AR headset makes some wonder, there are several examples of products improving existing sports and fitness industries and creating new marketplaces.

At Home

Many kinds of experiences have been created for fans at home, from purely promotional to courtside viewing. Today, if you search YouTube, Hulu or Sky Immersive for 360° sports videos, you're bound to bump into several streams of NBA or UEFA games that can be seen directly inside VR headsets. Already in 2018, The New York Times captured 3D images of Olympic athletes while they were performing sports such as figure skating and speed skating to enhance the coverage with AR statistics and player information overlaid on the field. In 2020, the Fox Network created virtual cheering fans to fill the empty stadiums in every sports broadcast, tackling the effects of the pandemic. With the rise of 5G and the opportunity to place volumetric capture-like cameras around stadiums and sports venues, the choice to attend a game either in person or virtually will be harder. Even fantasy football games are already seeing an upgrade in 2022 with Web3, with platforms like Ethereum-based Sorare enabling users to buy, sell and manage a virtual team with digital player cards.

At the Game

Although 5G is not widely distributed across the world (yet), stadiums with access enable telcos and sports teams to test-drive several solutions with audiences. It's possible to enhance the experience from the parking lot, around and within the stadium, during the event and after as well. For instance, Snap created an AR lens that helps Major League Baseball fans find their way around the ballpark,[55] which makes the case for useful and simple immersive applications for all kinds of sports and events. Snap also created fan-friendly lenses like a digital foam number-one finger and virtual sports team merchandise. In 2020, AT&T 5G launched an integrated campaign at the Dallas Cowboys stadium. Larger-than-life, 3D players appeared over the stadium peering in and could only be seen through AT&T's app.[56] Just think of the opportunities (and challenges) when all data from every ticket holder, both remote and local, can be gathered to deliver a custom sports show to each customer.

For Fitness

For those looking to get in shape, there are many VR apps that are happy to help in a very gamified way. *Supernatural,* a title published by Within, promotes an on-demand, full-body, subscription-based inspiring workout program. You are coached by volumetrically-captured trainers who offer words of encouragement during the workout. Dancers program moves that exercise different muscle groups that have you hit virtual balls that explode and move your body through and around large triangles. As of 2022, the Supernatural supportive social community consists of some 50,000 members and several other competitors like VR Workout, Holofit or FitXR are also keeping people fit.

But there are also options that don't require headgear. MIRROR introduced a home fitness product that uses a headset-free approach with a mirror-based AR interface. It was acquired in 2020 by Lululemon for $500 million.[57]

As the fitness market becomes metaversed, we'll see AR data on your health customizing the workout experience based on information from your wearables. Also, expect real-time, individualized fitness coaching by either a AI trainer program, or even a professional athlete holoported[58] to your workout from a remote location.

Automotive, Aviation, and Aerospace

Although putting rocket ships, planes, railways, boats, ships, motor-cycles, and automobiles into one category seems overly broad, the use of metaverse technologies is similar across them all, in various degrees of complexity. Applications span across departments that include collaborative design of parts, 3D prototyping and viewing through XR headsets, simulation and testing in VR environments, training skills with the help of XR and AI technologies (from pilot-ing to cabin crew skills), collaborative research and development, marketing & promotion across showrooms and shopfloor MRO (Maintenance, Repair and Operations) applications, that can accel-erate processes and reduce errors and waste in manufacturing.

It's also worth noting that some of the earliest examples of metaverse technology applications were within these industries. The first heads-up display (HUD) was created by the US Air Force. A HUD was showcased by General Motors in 1965 for their Chev-rolet Corvette concept car, many years before it was integrated into a consumer vehicle.

Since then, automotive, aviation, and aerospace are some of the most advanced industries when it comes to integration of VR, AR, and related technologies for business-to-business (B2B) and business-to-consumer (B2C) applications. The following are cross-market applications that you can find across all these industries:

AR HUD Integration   AR displays have been placed in front windows of cars and planes and in motorcycle helmets, in a very seamless way. By getting rid of physical maps or Smartphone's GPS, drivers and pilots can focus on getting themselves to their destination safely without having to look down at folders and/or maps on their phones. Accuracy is "mission-critical" and the fail-ure rate needs to be zero.[59]

Digital Simulations   In addition to identifying risks and reduc-ing time and cost for testing and development, simulations are extremely valuable for enabling people to practice skills when hands-on, on-location is impossible or unsafe. They enable trainees to learn how to use vehicles in simulated environments.[60] NASA has many immersive centers and labs for training astronauts, including Johnson Space Center (JSC) and Armstrong Flight Research Center. The University of Michigan's Mcity Test Facility is 32 acres of simulated streets designed to test self-driving vehicles and their interactions with the city and with other vehicles. In general, Mcity creates the confidence to apply learned skills to the real world.[61]

Digital Twins Digital twin technologies reduce errors in production and increases efficiencies, either by simulating environments or by helping to connect digital and physical elements. There are digital twins of entire fleets (e.g., KLM's fleet is used across several departments for training, maintenance and other scenarios [62]). Companies like KIT-AR (where Luis, one of the authors is CMO) are reducing the costs of errors in production lines that can go as high as 40 percent of the total operations.[63] In maintenance departments, 3D digital versions make references searchable and reduce the time to locate repair information. Automotive sales teams have incorporated digital twin technologies into their advertising and marketing, opening up experiences at home and at retail.

There are more innovations to come, and the automotive, aerospace, and aviation industries are currently some of the most advanced markets:

Adaptive Holograms Graphics will move into more dynamic 3D designs that adapt seamlessly across any lighting and weather situations.

Distributed Headsets Get ready to see airport, railway, and automotive workers wearing AR glasses at work and working as a team.

New Sales Platforms There are going to be many more opportunities and locations to engage consumer audiences (for example, on the windows on self-driving cars).

"Moving further to a mobility provider and seriously exploring the field of services besides the vehicle will help to detect the added value of the Metaverse—the basic ingredients are already there: digital twins and tons of data delivering context."[64], shares Jan Pflueger, responsible for XR Method Development at AUDI AG.

Military

Military and government organizations have been at the forefront of using and applying emerging technologies, much due to large financial investments. Almost 50 percent of the U.S. government budget allocations for R&D go to the military.[65]

This massive influx of funds has led to many of the consumer products we know today, some accidentally. Super Glue was discovered during the development of a plastic rifle sight in 1942; GPS was developed by the U.S. Department of Defense in the 1960s and then allowed for commercial use in 1980s and '90s; the U.S. government invested billions in creating the ARPANET (Advanced Research Projects Agency Network), which eventually became the Internet; and VR was created in 1979 to help train fighter pilots.[66]

It's no wonder that multibillion-dollar budgets have been assigned to the development of metaverse technologies. The integrated applications have been used for the following:

Collaboration Tools Metaverse technologies such as VR, AR, and haptics can enable teams from across regions to communicate seamlessly.

In-Combat Support Although there are debates about the fairness of certain technologies, many head-mounted devices (HMDs) and drones are used during combat in hopes of gaining an advantage.

Recruitment and Marketing VR and AR are used to showcase what life is like as a member of the military, allowing potential soldiers to have a better notion of the experience awaiting them.

Training Systems These systems offer experiences to help make personnel battle-ready. Combat simulations, however, have their risks, including overuse and the potential of dehumanizing the enemy.

Treatment Programs Simulations can help military members suffering from post-traumatic stress disorder (PTSD) and similar diagnoses. Treatment programs also include stress-reducing biofeedback.

Metaverse-related tools help to save lives outside of combat. The U.S. Government Accountability Office found that from 2010 to 2019, nearly 4,000 accidents happened during training, resulting in 123 deaths. During a CBS News interview, Michael McDowell, father of First Lieutenant Conor McDowell, a platoon leader in the Marines who died during training, stated, "I can accept people dying in combat. But if you're training in your own country and you're dying needlessly in preventable accidents, this is a massive problem which has to be fixed."[67]

Creating a virtual scenario environment can reduce risks and costs in battlefield training. Simulation scenarios have been developed for parachuting, medic training, driving vehicles, and battlefield combat with 1:1 haptic simulated replica weapons. Soldiers can be upskilled in environments that can be changed and updated, without the potential of accidental death. These applications have been used worldwide. The Korea Military Academy is a great example, as they employed several VR and AR companies to build these kinds of simulations.[68] The New Zealand Air Force uses the eight360 VR simulator for training as well.

The investment values in military projects seem mind-boggling when compared to other industries. The U.S. Pentagon budgeted $600 million to test 5G at five military bases.[69] It's estimated that $14 billion is spent per year by the U.S. government just on VR and AR training and equipment.[70] The Department of Defense (DoD) planned to award $10 billion for a cloud computing project for the Joint Enterprise Defense Infrastructure (whose acronym seems on brand: JEDI). The contract ultimately was canceled in July of 2021, but it still speaks to the massive amount of funds in the emerging technologies field.[71]

Warfare-ready AR headsets also mean huge investments, starting with Microsoft's $21.9 billion U.S. contract to create 120,000

HoloLens mixed-reality (MR) headsets[72] (following a 2018 contract of $480 million just for prototyping).[73] A similar AR project is underway in Turkey.[74] Although with some hiccups and delays, these projects are in development and will soon come to fruition.

These applications are not without their controversies, though, and there are different stakeholders expressing concerns.

For example, the developer teams involved in setting up military-grade AR solutions sometimes disagree with this usage of the technology and, once they are aware of that possibility, fight back. For instance, there was resistance among Microsoft employees when they found out through the media what they were working for: "We did not sign up to develop weapons, and we demand a say in how our work is used," they wrote in a letter written to Microsoft CEO Satya Nadella.[75]

Healthcare

Whether you call it the medical metaverse or the Medical Internet of Things (MIoT),[76] the applications within the healthcare and pharmaceutical fields are as wide as the industry itself. In most instances, the goal is to reduce the risks involved in procedures and support both doctors and nurses so that they can provide healthcare in the best way possible. Dawei Yang, Jian Zhou, and a panel of doctors and IT worldwide experts studied results from the application of metaverse technologies in healthcare and found out that, "Through interactions between virtual and real cloud experts and terminal doctors, we will be able to carry out medical education, science popularization, consultation, graded diagnosis and treatment, clinical research, and even comprehensive healthcare in the metaverse."[77]

In their definition of the metaverse, Accenture separates the Internet of Place (focused on simulations and on-job applications) and the Internet of Ownership (distributed data that helps to connect and identify owners and assets) and concludes that "the entire healthcare C-suite should think about tomorrow differently. . .and must now push through a new wave of disruption. . .creating greater access, better experiences and improved outcomes. The applications are far reaching."[78]

Administrative and Logistical

The promise of the medical metaverse is brought by the analysis and insights extracted from extensive personal data. In the near future, remote healthcare will involve sending integrated information to our doctors, our hospitals, and care facilities. We'll be using advanced AI/ML tools as well as digital twins of patients, and leveraging blockchain for more transparency across the whole process. These kinds of tools will enable better remote doctor–patient interactions, potentially leading to metaverse-based hospitals.[79] Ideally each patient will own their own information, protected and stored with access granted only when necessary.

Research, Training, and Education

Digital twins of patients, doctors' offices, and hospitals enable more accurate virtual experiences to train, track, and improve healthcare. All members of the care team can practice and improve with digital versions of real-life simulations. Even patients can better understand their medical future and prepare for it. Metaverse technologies also can enable a new layer of discoveries (e.g., to create and effectively produce drug therapies).

Detection and Identification

Teaching AI the difference between a healthy and an unhealthy body is one of the most exciting applications of computer vision. Machine learning has moved beyond the human capabilities for certain diagnoses and holds huge promise for future applications. For example, Goggle uses VR to explore EEGs more efficiently and diagnose glaucoma more accurately. As body tracking becomes more ubiquitous, the tools can be used not only for physical and occupational surgery, but also for diagnosis based on movement data.

One device that received a lot of press for the simplicity of its solution: Accuvein's handheld system scans the body to locate veins, claiming that it makes the "first stick" 3.5 times more likely.[80]

Pre-Surgery

Although true digital twins of people are still years away, some more generic versions can be used by doctors for practice before the real surgery begins. Some companies are applying simulations in new and interesting ways, such as the VIVATOP project (Versatile Immersive Virtual and Augmented Tangible OP), which creates lifelike models of organs to enable haptic surgery training.

Not only are healthcare providers going to find value with metaverse tech, but patients can also use environment simulations to prepare themselves for surgery. Others help reduce pre-surgery stress using biofeedback and imagery, although the applications can work for any stressful situation, such as chronic pain management. Jason Ju In Chan and the team of KK Women's and Children's Hospital, Singapore, recruited and studied 108 patients about to undergo minor surgery. After seeing VR views of sceneries, background meditation music, combined with breathing exercises, the study concluded that the intervention helped reduce pre-surgery anxiety levels on all patients and that 82 percent even liked the VR experience.[81]

Mid-Surgery

There are solutions available that display relevant medical information in surgery, visible through AR glasses. The Champalimaud Foundation's Breast Cancer team uses AR as a noninvasive technique to guide the surgeon to the location of tumors.[82] Aris MD enables medical exam data to be overlaid onto the patient's body so that surgeons make fewer mistakes.[83] "Did you know that your heart, my heart, your lungs, my lungs, they're all in different places[?]. . .[When doctors] look at medical imaging, be that CT, MRI, any of that sort of imaging, what they do is they look at it in slices. . .[then they] try to composite those images in 3D in their mind. . .We take the images and put them in 3D so that they can view them organically. . .then they can see them live during the procedure. So, [doctors] can see exactly where something like a tumor is without actually having to cut into you," shared Chandra Devam, co-founder of Aris MD.[84] As robotic arms and haptics increase in fidelity, there are more opportunities for remote surgery. Bill Gates–backed Vicarious Surgical uses VR and robots already, but only for minimally invasive procedures. It's the first robot for surgery to be designated as an FDA breakthrough.[85] Because a millimeter can make a huge difference in potential outcomes, the technology needs to be beyond perfect to save lives.

Post-Surgery

"V.R. has this uncanny ability to kind of nudge the human brain in ways that other audiovisual media cannot," said Dr. Brennan Spiegel, Director of Health Services research at Cedars-Sinai Health System. "The bottom line is it motivates us to do things that we might not be able to do."[86] With the help of all available data to track and personalize experiences, IoT and AI, some solutions like InMotionVR or Neuro Rehab VR are already helping patients address anxiety and pain more efficiently in their rehabilitation processes. For example, AppliedVR claims to be the "first on-demand, clinically validated, all-in-one therapeutic VR platform for acute and chronic pain"[87] with over 30,000 patients, 200 hospitals, and 25 randomized clinical trials. Others, like XRehab, delve into remote teletherapy and physiotherapy exergaming or gamified exercise that tries to add a more fun element to the whole rehabilitation process.

Mental Health & Wellness

There are a wide variety of metaverse applications that can support mental health as well. Immersive technologies can create optimal environments for therapies to operate, while AI can track and act upon the reactions of users.

Albert Rizzo, the director for medical virtual reality at the University of Southern California, has studied the benefits of simulated environments on children with focus issues such as attention deficit or hyperactivity. "[W]e built virtual classrooms where we can put kids. . .[where they] have to pay attention to what goes on the blackboard or what the teacher says. . .So, we can begin to measure cognitive performance under a range of challenges [such as "kids sitting next to them fidgeting, throwing paper airplanes, maybe a school bus driving by the window"]. . .where distraction is a lot different than if you're testing a child in a quiet office environment in the therapist's office or the clinician's office."[88]

Exposure therapy like Imotions uses Virtual Reality, Brain-Computer interfaces and even haptics to help trauma victims (e.g. from motor vehicle accidents), by exposing them to specific situations, thoughts, or memories which provoke anxiety or fear and decrease the intensity of their stress responses.

But those aren't the only opportunities. Although seemingly counterintuitive, a recent study found that 30 percent of patients felt comfortable working with an avatar representing the therapist.[89] As its realism improves, that number has a chance to increase even more.

Sarah Hill, CEO and Chief Storyteller of Healium, shared with us that she believes:

> The metaverse is becoming a place of collective healing. Digital therapeutics will no longer be served on a singular 2D app but a multi-user experience where you collectively consume and control immersive content with data that comes from your wearables. Instead of your heart rate being a number . . . it's a spatial asset you can share and manipulate with the avatar sitting right next to you.[90]

Hill's award-winning company uses neurofeedback paired with a graphics-based meditative story to induce the brain into a state of calm and harmony.

On the flip side, remote access removes physical touch between doctor and patient, and with it the benefits of bedside manner. It could even reduce the need for local and family doctors as we know it. There might be increased costs associated with enabling equipment, levels of service, and different kinds of response to emergencies, which could lead to an even wider gap of care between wealthy and poor communities.

Let's not forget that tech tends to create products built on a white or Asian male perspective as they dominate the industry. There is a high likeihood of a risk that certain conditions and patients will not have the same advancements in technology and/or level of applicability.

Hospitality and Tourism

The travel industry seems like a perfect partner for the metaverse industry. Both focus on going to new locations and they're based on exploring new areas, learning, and trying new things.

"If a picture tells a thousand words, then virtual reality tells a whole book,"[91] said Dario Orsini, the general manager of the Sheraton Bali Kuta Resort. Hospitality is not unaware of these trends, and that resort is only one of many that have bought into the potential of XR, as it allows future guests to preview their experience through VR glasses.

Experience is, as in any metaversed business, key for tourism. Both family and business hotels and inns can use their digital dimensions to entertain and educate guests and increase the amount of time they spend using the hotel's services. At New York's Yotel Hotels, this experience starts with a luggage-carrying robot—Yobot, that can handle about 300 luggage items a day.[92]

But from Cape Town's tourism center[93] to Hong Kong's sky100[94] to London's Tower Bridge (www.towerbridge.org.uk/tower-bridge-glass-floor) to Denmark's Viking History theme park[95] to the Ration Shed Museum in Queensland, Australia,[96] hundreds of institutions are leveraging the ability of immersive technologies to add context, rebuild historical tools and objects, or animate historical characters in a way that adds fun and games (most literally) to cultural sites.

Heritage places also are reaping benefits from the metaverse building blocks–starting with the places affected by catastrophes. After the fire in the National Museum in Rio de Janeiro, the Brazilian association XRBR promoted an initiative to collect photos from the museum pieces and, through them, re-create most of the pieces digitally in 3D using photogrammetry. An even bigger digital twin project happened with Notre Dame Cathedral in Paris, after the 2019 fires, which supports a virtual tour and an augmented reality exhibit in 2022.[97]

Travel itself has also been impacted by the metaverse building blocks already. Take the example of TravelX, a Blockchain-based startup focused on allowing users to buy, sell, trade and transfer tickets from wallet-to-wallet, when they cannot travel; or FCM, a corporate travel company whose AI chatbot Sam assists travelers with increasingly personalized information and action.[98]

There are a number of different types of experiences that leverage storytelling and the building blocks of the metaverse to redefine the tourism business:

AR Tours   Gamifying paths for tourists to explore and discovering, step-by-step, new augmented reality experiences can lead tourists off the beaten path and have them engage with lesser-known spaces, objects, and people of interest, like artisans. AR tour guides can be available 24/7, just waiting for you in any corner of the city or in any room of a museum.

Closer to Purchase   There is the opportunity to upgrade experiences such as AR shoppable posts, where you click to order a new experience or a better room.

Digital Concierges   Holographic-like projections are becoming more mainstream and are creating points of interest. There could be volumetrically captured holographic concierges (hyper-realistic digital humans, or maybe the local mascot instead) greeting guests and answering simple questions.

Play-to-Earn   Rewards might be passed on in the form of tokens, which could help cultural places maintain loyalty and build a community of fans across different generations.

Simplifying Experiences AR wayfinding applications can show hotel guests where their room is, customize a ticket holder's journey within a large museum, or direct visitors to a rent-a-car or tour bus station.

Architecture and Real Estate

If any industry can understand reimagining reality and spaces, it's AEC (architectural, engineering, and construction). It's their job to sell a vision of a structure, so that the real estate industry can sell it. This traditionally has been done through 2D imagery, blueprints and drawings, and the occasional 3D model rendering.

Designers and architects have used 3D programming tools to visualize their structures. They can brainstorm the actual size of what is possible and literally walk around their blueprint in VR or AR to identify any potential flaws in a building before it's physically built. Digital twins of buildings will increasingly be relevant during the construction phase, saving costs on changing designs mid-project. Also, physically remote teams can collaborate and review a design from different parts of the world simultaneously. Afterward, the twin can offer a reference for any future maintenance activities. All the previous construction data can be brought into the field of view through AR glasses to streamline the entire process. Overlaying the digital over the physical can identify and solve potential issues (e.g.,, a lever pushed in the wrong direction).

Alex Coulombe is a thought leader in AEC. He is a trained architect for physical theaters and event venues in metaverse worlds, along with the OnBoard XR One Act Festival. He shares that:

> Every designer should be actively designing in VR from conception through completion, starting with VR napkin sketches in Tilt Brush or Gravity Sketch, progressing to massing models, then providing design options with levels of photorealism appropriate to the stage of the project. You should be regularly walking through your projects in VR. You should be grabbing ceilings or railing with code-compliant parameters and moving them around to experience firsthand how it changes the perception of a space.[99]

Real Estate sales teams can use the models for presale or remote sales as the digital buildings and rooms can look and feel real. Many companies have adopted 360 video tours, which are more advanced than photos or 2D videos, which is inching in the right direction. The ability to set up house tours open 24/7 in VR is already an option for Kuula, WeboBook, or Cyango users. As AR models become even more realistic, they can be mapped accurately to allow potential buyers to see and visit the building before any money is spent on construction. As technology evolves and data is infused in these experiences, more customization possibilities can be added to that visit, improving the chance of a sale. Interior design options and even bigger house-renovation options that enable easier and better decision-making also can be previewed by homeowners.

On the flip side, existing physical spaces can be captured to be re-created digitally with tools like LiDAR and then used as reference for decorating and remodeling, as a sales and marketing tool, or even for re-creating the building in a digital world.

As with the metaverse, the entire AEC and real estate industry has begun to change and will continue to evolve. Coulombe says "Virtual architecture, more and more, can service the functional, aesthetic, and psychological purposes of a particular typology while also utilizing the affordances of the digital realm. Walls and ceilings need no longer be structurally stable or tasked with keeping out the elements, but they still serve purpose as space-making tools. Compression, release, light, shadow, color, materiality—all the tools that make us feel a particular way in the real world—can still deliberately encourage user behavior in the virtual through the same phenomenological design principles."

Other examples of potential upcoming changes to the AEC and real estate industry are as follows:

Augmented Services   Buildings themselves could provide walk-in augmented services like AR banks or stores. The location where they'll appear could offer additional (augmented) real estate for the building owner to sell.

Digital Assistants   As with any other market, an AI can help support the team throughout the design, construction, and sales process (for example, helping decision-making, monitoring safety regulations). Bots can evolve into a 24/7 sales support assistant, available both on VR tours or in physical locations with AR versions, almost like holographic AI doormen.

New Designs   As digital twins become more mainstream, buildings can be reimagined by different architects. The same way users will be able to attend art exhibitions, the gallery's building itself can be redesigned by a metaverse architect. Architects can mine data from the usage of the buildings they designed. "What an opportunity to design a space, monitor user behavior in it, and then adjust the design with the regularity of a video game developer patching to fix bugs and improve performance," shares Coulombe.[100]

New Rooms   Physical houses may need a VR exploration space or holo-room with enough space for gestures and users to walk around.

Virtual Architects and Buildings   Metaverse architects and designers could become new careers. As decentralized autonomous organizations (DAOs) sell more virtual real estate plots, there may be a need for virtual architecture firms to set up shop and organizations to establish upcoming metaverse best practices and regulations. Buildings in virtual worlds offer the potential for new and different characteristics, as they allow physically impossible designs to become digitally feasible.

Manufacturing

One of the most useful metaverse applications is the digital twin, technically a real-time 3D digital clone of a physical person, place, or thing. For manufacturing, digital twins (along with an increasing stream of real-time data) are key to recent innovations and foreseeable applications. There are many kinds of digital twins that can be created for manufacturing: asset, component, system or unit, and process. An asset refers to an entire equipment's twin, like a motor;

a component or subcomponent is a twin of a part of a machine; a system or unit is the collection of components and equipment for a bigger function; and a process is a series of functions or activities. They also can be seamlessly integrated with the IIoT (Industrial Internet of Things) and a vast array of sensors.

Smart digital twins within the manufacturing industry have many clear-cut applications. These advancements can support the following:

Assemble Develop digital twin overlays to align on top of machines to speed up product development (e.g., put the right screws in the right place on a rocket ship).

Design Collaborate on product design with preview and feedback, even with worldwide teams simultaneously or not (e.g., when creating a concept car with distributed teams across time zones).

Maintain Streamline processes with AR documentation and instructions, which will reduce on-site issues (e.g., enable more employees to perform maintenance for robotic manufacturing tools).

Optimize Learn and store optimal behavior over time allowing better processes like managing inventory more efficiently and quickly identify the bottleneck of a process.

Oversee Support guidance and repair from a centralized digital control room with integrated tracking and monitoring quality control systems which can reduce human error in defining process issues.

Train Centralize and customize immersive training and upskilling applications from remote locations, even before the equipment is on-site.

Update Make real-time changes to process reducing the need for updated printed or video material and distribution (e.g., creating an AI trainer whose script can be updated and translated for global use).

The metaverse can bring some specific improvements, including:

Empowering a Remote Workforce   Shared digital spaces can be created for remote teams. Employees can do physical work via remote robots connected to production processes. Smart glasses cameras can enable remote inspectors to perform their work, either by pairing with colleagues on the ground or by connecting directly to the workers' glasses themselves.

"Hiring" New "Coworkers"   AI-based digital assistants can support processes and help workers. Cobots can share workspaces to directly work symbiotically in manufacturing processes.

Improving Safety   Metaverse technologies offer more opportunities for training and monitoring.

Increasing Efficiency   Presenting AR overlaid instructions on the point of need and in context removes the need to refer to physical manuals. Gathering all data from production processes, worker biofeedback, and other sensors on the shop floor allows organizations to better identify opportunities for improvement. Also, digital twin prototypes can be developed and used to establish efficient processes before physical models are created.

Lowering Costs   A digitally centralized support center requires fewer physical locations and on-site teams. Moving from the digital to physical, on-demand printing of equipment replicas can also reduce shipment and equipment cost.

Optimizing Production Space   Staging a remodeling of a production space or the expansion of a factory in VR generates more accurate preview and planning opportunities.

Reducing Errors   Real-time accurate twin information can reduce mistakes by even untrained employees.

Physical and digital spaces are already intertwining in factories, and most of the elements needed to push forward a hybrid dimension are already here. Manufacturers like Hyundai[101] are setting up full-fledged digital twins of factories, which can run simulations like new production line layouts, provide helicopter views of the full production chain in real time, or even offer training and upskilling opportunities for workers outside of the production environment but at the same time immersed in it.

"It's a massive amount of data being produced in real time from all the little computers and embedded systems running inside such a factory. Once you can reflect that in the virtual world, we have the ability to teleport." says Rev Lebaredian, one of the key leaders in the industrial Metaverse at NVIDIA. He continues: "Anyone, anywhere, can go inspect an issue inside the factory without actually physically having to go there. If you have a simulator that can predict the near future, things that are about to happen, then you can essentially time travel. You can go into the past by looking at stuff that was recorded, all that data recorded in the past, or go into the future. If you can compute that simulation really fast, then you can potentially explore multiple possible futures, change things around, and test it."[102]

Training and Education

One of the industries where the metaverse has already begun to make a large impact is training and education. The metaverse education market is estimated to be $4.9 billion in 2021, growing to $94.9 billion in the next 10 years.[103] It's no wonder, as studies have shown how impactful it can be. A four-month PwC study demonstrated that what they called "v-learning" made learners 275 percent more confident; they were four times more focused than e-learners and learned four times faster than in typical classroom teaching.[104]

Embodied cognition is one of the key reasons for considering metaverse training and education options. This phenomenon occurs as physical experiences and tactical interactions engage your sensorimotor system. It supports and accelerates the learning process. This is why grade-school teachers get children to move their bodies and play with learning toys to understand concepts. It's why there are simulations for nursing schools. Physical movement has its own kind of muscle memory, and educators can involve more senses in their teaching.

There are many other benefits that apply to both the training and education markets, and some individually:

Better Engagement As most VR headsets track eye, head, hand, and body movement, solutions can use that information to encourage focus.

Dynamic Customization All data available for each student, along with AI tools, can customize training by level of experience and abilities for each student, onboarding new employees, and upskilling existing ones.

On-Demand Teachers or trainers can share a larger variety of educational resources, as they can record or have virtual beings provide on-demand talks and knowledge to their students.

Remote Updates and Access Simulations can be updated easily and allow for training or teaching without on-site staff.

Scalability One experience can be developed for use across headsets and potentially in multiple scenarios (e.g., a digital twin of an oil rig can be a backdrop for training scenarios from remote onboarding to emergency response training).

Testing and Improving Using the data collected from experiences can help improve behavior and/or knowledge.

Visual Memories An immersive simulated 3D action does not need to respect the laws of physics. So there are more opportunities for creative ways of teaching and training.

Training

Metaversed training applications are relevant across all verticals. Some, such as medical and manufacturing industries, have embraced many of the building blocks of the metaverse. Others have yet to identify where it could apply, although the interest is there. There are training simulations for interviewing, public speaking, and even for hiring and firing employees. There are natural-disaster-escape training and construction safety simulations.[105]

One of the key benefits of metaverse professional training is that it doesn't require it to be on location. This is convenient for companies with offices across the world, especially in remote areas. But it's best utilized when the training is for hazardous situations. There's no need to include dangerous materials to be effective, and it can enable faster response times during real-life scenarios.

Still, the market is relatively new as there is the need for employees with multiple kinds of expertise to create them. For example, medical training scenarios require those knowledgeable in "rendering, simulation, haptics, psychology, and physiology."[106] There are few general platforms as they are "typically created according to specific tasks characterized by a fixed procedure and a practical purpose for a specific training target. Thus, their implementations are generally miscellaneous and different from each other."[107]

Companies and organizations such as Caterpillar, Chipotle, Accenture, Honeywell, Verizon, BMW, Toyota, JetBlue, Fidelity, the NHL, the MLB, and the NBA have used metaverse technologies for training employees in different skillsets. It's anticipated that 23.5 million jobs will use VR or AR for training purposes by 2030.[108] In light of its potential, that number actually feels a bit low, especially as costs of hardware decrease and no-code and low-code software becomes more available. The list of potential benefits will increase as training becomes more sophisticated, reducing the need for physical items (e.g., cadavers for learning anatomy) and potentially some trainers themselves (e.g., AI-enabled virtual humans).

"The Metaverse and Web3 in general present valuable opportunities for countries to embrace these trends and put them to use towards economic growth. This is especially true for areas of jobs and skills development as countries can look at the future of jobs and can opt to invest in education and digital skillsets needed to be part of the workforce of the future. People living in developing countries could opt to be part of these opportunities in the same way as any others," said Jimmy Vainstein from his experience leading the Metaverse effort at the World Bank.

Education

McKinsey & Company's research of colleges and universities demonstrated by teachers that adopted virtual classrooms during the COVID pandemic and changed their approach to education.[109] Technology-based learning and assessment tools advanced by necessity, and at the same time opened up both students and teachers to the many possibilities (and issues) of remote learning. The metaverse applications for education are a natural extension of the benefits of training, from pre-school to PhD. AR and online world applications can be used in grade school, as 13 is the youngest age recommended by several brands of VR glasses for usage without adult supervision. Then from middle school on, there can be more immersive experiences integrated into education for any subject.

We are seeing only the tip of the metaverse education iceberg. There are many opportunities for classroom learning, some to be used within physical classrooms and others through virtual worlds. Minecraft: Education Edition is a clear example of precisely that.

Metaverse solutions aren't just for the engineering and technology students. For math classes at every level, there is the possibility of displaying and manipulating three-dimensional data. Science students can create and make experiments that otherwise would be physically unsafe. History teachers can have their students travel virtually to historical locations, with digitally re-created historical experiences. Language teachers can create virtual humans that interact with students in locations, teach through experience, and use as much repetition as needed. Art, design, and drama students can use metaverse in their creative work, such as making sets, drawing costumes, and creating generally open worlds.

There are even more opportunities that the metaverse brings:

Digital Humans as Tutors Teachers could program digital assistants to answer common questions, and recorded lectures could be embodied into them, making test prep multi-dimensional and graphic. Teachers and/or students could also assume different kinds of avatars based on the focus of the lesson to better engagement within the classroom.

Personalized Learning The metaverse enables educators to customize and personalize their approach to each student and to encourage active participation and tracking of students' learning progress. This student monitoring via dynamic data management can lead to adaptive learning tools. Students could eventually be able to choose between auditory, visual, kinesthetic, reading, writing, and/or combinations of them to improve their understanding and retention.

Resources Visualization There are fewer times that you have to say "Imagine if," as you can use tools to create visuals that express what needs to be taught. This can be for people, places, or things: people such as historical figures; places like remote destinations from past, present, or future; or things such as inaccessible, large-scale sculptures. Students also can use the tools to develop and showcase their own creations.

Reward Systems Tokens can be the future of gold star incentives. They can be offered to students and help them achieve their goals in a positive way. They may also be applied to also improve the social and economic fabric of the school.

Virtual Classroom Creating a sense of 3D presence with other students and a teacher can improve the dynamics of a remote classroom beyond a 2D video on a flat screen. Ironically, populating the class with multidimensional simulations can bring more realism to the classroom (e.g., teaching archaeology within a virtual dig site). This multiperson environment can even help with dynamics among students for project team work.

Increasingly schools that have identified the value of the technologies have brought in leaders in the field to build new programs to accommodate potential demand for metaverse skills. Such leaders include the award-winning "Godmother of Virtual Reality," Nonny de la Peña, is program director of Arizona State University's Narrative and Emerging Media program (http://search .asu.edu/profile/3969940). *Forbes* writer and XR pundit Charlie Fink teaches at Chapman University. VR pioneer Jessica Brillhart is director of the Mixed Reality Lab at USC Institute for Creative

Technologies. Already a fixture at Stanford University, Jeremy Bailenson, a research pioneer in virtual reality, has started to teach his class *Virtual People* entirely in VR.[110] Metaverse-related classes are also beginning to be taught worldwide at universities like Nanyang Technological University (NTU), Korea Advanced Institute of Science and Technology, and University College London.

As the technology applications are so vast, some schools have created centers to accommodate metaverse-related majors. The University of Maryland launched an Immersive Media Design major, the first undergraduate program in the country that synthesizes art with computer science to develop immersive media.

Over the past few years, virtual universities have been founded. Initially online-based schools like Oxford University, SEGi University in Malaysia, and Escola Portuguesa in Cape Verde created 3D digital campuses based on the school building's digital 3D replicas. Now there are a number of "metaversities," digital online versions of physical campuses, which launched in fall 2022 by schools including Morehouse College and West Virginia University. Each holds classes in virtual settings that are primarily within the sciences, including astronomy and human anatomy, although there are history classes as well.[111]

However, all this advancement will not be distributed equally among schools. This will likely lead to a metaverse educational gap. Buying all necessary hardware for the continuous update of programs, as well as the contents necessary for students, might prove a financial challenge, especially in the beginning. Add to that the issue of planned obsolescence, where tech companies plan their products to become obsolete within a set period of time, forcing a repair or, most of the times, a replacement of the hardware. And don't forget that all of these experiences need to be accessible to all audiences, including students with disabilities, whose needs VR/AR hasn't had a perfect record addressing. Even so, there are many communities of teachers, like Educators in VR, already betting that the education vertical will be a huge marketplace, as the potential benefits are just too high (www.Educatorsinvr.com).

New Opportunities

Many changes are coming to the marketplace and across industries. The metaverse building blocks, the amount of data being collected, and the increasing number of digital beings will create new trends for businesses across the board:

Continued Experimentation   Like digital photos and videos before, the creation of digital twins will allow scenario testing and simulation, reducing the need for physical experimentation and testing of physical items and environments.

Demand for AI   Machine learning, the "avatarization" of chatbots, and the extreme amount of data on the horizon will demand an increasing amount of AI in businesses. An acceleration of partnerships and acquisitions in this area is coming across all markets, as several professional processes become partially automated. The applications of generative AI are just being realized

Existing Experiences Amplified   Prior to the Walkman, MP3, or Spotify, walking could be a quiet time of contemplation. Suddenly, you had the opportunity to listen to massive crowdsourced playlists of worldwide artists, in addition to making calls or having video chats with almost anyone. Next, AR will bring with it designs and information projected in our glasses or from the people, objects, and buildings around us.

Expanded Virtual Good Sales   Digital fashion has taken off, and other industries and digital products are likely to follow. Some virtual-first items will become physical-next with the help of 3D printing, additive manufacturing, and specialist digital artisans. Along with it, hybrid products will start to appear.

Human Error Reduction   AR solutions and computer vision can complement and supplement existing work and behaviors (e.g., self-driving cars will reduce car accidents, mapping will allow wayfinding beyond roads).

Improved Remote Access   Remote training and education can expand the availability of tools. Robotic solutions for medical and

high-risk situations allow for experts to be present in remote physical locations. This has the potential to disrupt several areas, as
users will be able to perform activities digitally they were only able
to do physically, using third-party services and glasses.

Increased Optimization   With most actions recorded into a
cloud, there is the opportunity to test, review, and improve within
a virtual or augmented digital environment.

On-Demand Hyper-Personalization   With digital twins, companies can create products or services for individuals not just at
retail, but also almost any industry, including medical and pharmaceutical use. Customized solutions will be assumed.

Beyond the improvements and changes it will make to existing verticals, the metaverse brings the opportunity to create entirely
new kinds of businesses, just as the Internet brought with it online
shopping, social media, video sharing services, and cloud computing. None of those industries would have been able to exist prior
to the digital superhighway. We have seen a hint of what's possible
with the metaverse with the sales of virtual land. We can already see
the potential for many variations of data protection firms, hologram
UX design firms, and after-life data management.

The World Economic Forum anticipates new roles like work-
from-home facilitator, smart-home design manager, algorithm bias
auditor, and human-machine teaming manager.[112] Cathy Hackl suggests other job titles like hologram stylist, virtual couture designer,
and autonomous car licensed specialist.[113] Others predict even
more, based on rising personalization and customization needs:
digital currency adviser, personal web manager, food engineer, AI
trainer, and robot operator.[114] Or we might have space tour companies, autonomous ship masters, privacy enforcers, and robot or AI
coaching services.

"Regardless of the particular industry focus (education, gaming,
entertainment, etc.), communities are still made up of people." Sonya
Haskins, Head of Programming at the Augmented World Expo, also
comments on the challenges ahead for any industry. "If you want

a thriving community and a business model in the metaverse, it's important to find a balance of privacy with accountability."

Whatever the future may hold, it is coming and it will impact your business and the market quite dramatically, no matter your industry. The thing about innovation is that you need to be comfortable with being uncomfortable. Those who are the most prolific are willing to admit that they still have much to learn and will change and adapt. Think of this book, this chapter specifically, as just the start of your journey within your industry.

Notes

1. Raja Rajamannar, *Quantum Marketing: Mastering the New Marketing Mindset for Tomorrow's Consumers*. (HarperCollins, 2021).

2. National Endowment for the Arts, "National Endowment for the Arts announces new report on artists' use of technology as a creative medium." June 30, 2021. www.arts.gov/news/press-releases/2021/national-endowment-arts-announces-new-report-artists-use-technology-creative-medium

3. Mickey Rapkin, "'Beeple mania': How Mike Winkelmann makes millions selling pixels." *Esquire*, February 17, 2021. www.esquire.com/entertainment/a35500985/who-is-beeple-mike-winkelmann-nft-interview

4. Rosie Perper, "Beeple believes that we've already stepped into the metaverse," *HYPEBEAST*, December 27, 2021, hypebeast.com/2021/12/beeple-interview-metaverse-nfts-web3-digital-generative-art

5. 4th Wall app. Nancy Baker Cahill Studio, 2022. www.4thwallapp.org/about

6. PRNewswire, "Artist Nancy Baker Cahill selects the Algorand blockchain to mint NFT for 'Mushroom Cloud NYC / RISE,' presented as. . .," *User Walls*, June 2, 2022. www.userwalls.news/n/artist-nancy-baker-cahill-selects-algorand-blockchain-mint-nft-mushroom-cloud-nyc-3318784

7. WA Content, "Krista Kim' Mars house is 'first NFT digital house' to be sold over $500,000." *Canada Architecture News*, March 25, 2021.

worldarchitecture.org/article-links/evzfc/krista-kim-s-mars-house-is-first-nft-digital-house-to-be-sold-over-500-000.html

8. Krista Kim, "We are creating a new decentralized civilization." (Unpublished essay originally posted February 14, 2014, updated 2021). www.kristakimstudio.com/techism-manifesto

9. Anna Codrea-Rado, "Virtual vandalism: Jeff Koons's 'Balloon Dog' is graffiti-bombed." *The New York Times*, October 10, 2017. www.nytimes.com/2017/10/10/arts/design/augmented-reality-jeff-koons.html

10. Miranda Katz, "Augmented reality is transforming museums," *Wired*, April 23, 2018. www.wired.com/story/augmented-reality-art-museums

11. Charlie Fink, *Charlie Fink's metaverse—An AR enabled guide to AR & VR*. Self-published ebook, Charlie Fink, 2018.

12. Louis Rosenberg, "Deception vs. authenticity: Why the metaverse will change marketing forever." *VentureBeat*, August 21, 2022. http://venturebeat.com/ai/deception-vs-authenticity-why-the-metaverse-will-change-marketing-forever

13. Dean Takahashi, "Interactive Advertising Bureau updates guidelines for measuring 3D ads for the metaverse." *VentureBeat*, June 15, 2022. http://venturebeat.com/games/interactive-advertising-bureau-updates-guidelines-for-measuring-in-game-3d-ads-for-the-metaverse

14. Personal communication, July 2022.

15. Caspar Thykier, "Case Study: Zappar brings 7-Eleven 2.7M AR engagements." *AR Insider*, August 5, 2020. http://arinsider.co/2020/08/05/case-study-zappar-brings-7-eleven-2-7m-ar-engagements

16. Taylor Locke and Marco Quiroz-Gutierrez, "ApeCoin is just the beginning: Bored Ape Yacht Club has big plans to enter the metaverse." *Fortune*, March 24, 2022. http://fortune.com/2022/03/24/apecoin-bored-ape-yacht-club-metaverse

17. Jacquelyn Milenek, "Top NFT collections are bringing in millions of dollars weekly but which will survive?" TechCrunch, April 20, 2022. http://techcrunch.com/2022/04/20/top-nft-collections-are-bringing-in-millions-of-dollars-weekly-but-which-will-survive

18. Taylor Locke and Marco Quiroz-Gutierrez, 2022.

19. Taylor Locke, "The Bored Ape Yacht Club metaverse sale was such a mess that it tanked the price of Bored Ape NFTs by 25%." *Fortune*, May 6, 2022. http://fortune.com/2022/05/06/bored-ape-yacht-club-nfts-fall-after-metaverse-land-sale/?queryly=related_article

20. Asena Arica, "Burger King uses augmented reality to "Burn That Ad" digitally." Digital Agency Network, March 20, 2019. http://digitalagencynetwork.com/burger-king-uses-augmented-reality-to-burn-that-ad-digitally

21. https://blogs.newschool.edu/news/2022/11/parsons-and-roblox-partner-to-educate-on-digital-fashion-and-trends

22. VMLY&R, "Wendy's: Keeping Fortnite fresh by VMLY&R." The Drum, January 2020. www.thedrum.com/creative-works/project/vmlyr-wendys-keeping-fortnite-fresh

23. Andrew Lipsman, "US ecommerce by category 2020: How the pandemic is reshaping the product category landscape." Insider Intelligence, July 22, 2020. www.emarketer.com/content/us-ecommerce-by-category-2020

24. Cathy Hackl, "Metaverse commerce: Understanding the new virtual to physical and physical to virtual commerce models." *Forbes*, July 5, 2022. www.forbes.com/sites/cathyhackl/2022/07/05/metaverse-commerce-understanding-the-new-virtual-to-physical-and-physical-to-virtual-commerce-models

25. www.voguebusiness.com/technology/why-ar-clothing-try-on-is-nearly-here

26. https://forbusiness.snapchat.com/blog/how-gen-z-is-reshaping-communication-and-redefining-the-shopping-experience-with-ar

27. https://letsplott.com

28. https://blog.roblox.com/wp-content/uploads/2022/10/FINAL_2022-Metaverse-Fashion-Trends-report_Roblox-x-Parsons.pdf

29. "Nike acquires RTFKT," (press release) *About.Nike.com*, December 13, 2021. http://about.nike.com/en/newsroom/releases/nike-acquires-rtfkt

30. https://esportsinsider.com/2019/05/epic-games-launches-fortnite-and-nike-air-jordans-crossover

31. Personal communication, 2022.

32. www.cnbc.com/2022/07/23/nfts-are-coming-for-loyalty-perks-programs-at-brands-like-budweiser.html

33. Presley West, "Zara AR brings fashionable looks to life in stores." VRScout, April 19, 2018. http://vrscout.com/news/zara-ar-fashion-looks-stores

34. Olivia Houghton, Kathryn Bishop, and Holly Friend, "ASOS launches a virtual catwalk in AR." *LSN Global*, June 26, 2019. www.lsnglobal.com/news/article/24310/asos-launches-a-virtual-catwalk-in-ar

35. www.adweek.com/commerce/nike-drops-free-sneakers-by-drone-air-max

36. www.thedrum.com/news/2022/03/23/ads-the-week-nike-sneakers-go-3d-and-bumble-prints-honest-dms

37. https://digiday.com/marketing/why-web3-brands-are-moving-offline-to-explore-physical-spaces

38. Zoe Sottile, "Tiffany's sells out custom Cryptopunk 'NFTiff' pendants for $50,000 each." CNN, August 7, 2022. www.cnn.com/style/article/tiffanys-cryptopunk-nft-pendants-trnd/index.html

39. www.cnn.com/style/article/tiffanys-cryptopunk-nft-pendants-trnd/index.html

40. Alan V. Cook, Lokesh Ohri, Laura Kusumoto, Chuck Reynolds, and Eric Schwertzel, "Augmented Shopping: The Quiet Revolution." Deloitte Insights (n.d.). www2.deloitte.com/content/dam/insights/us/articles/6367_Augmented-shopping/DI_Augmented-shopping.pdf

41. www.forbes.com/sites/carolynschwaar/2022/01/27/3d-printing-drives-growth-in-on-demand-manufacturing/?sh=525eee821997

42. Accenture Newsroom, "Global gaming industry value now exceeds $300 billion, new Accenture report finds." Accenture, April 29, 2021. http://newsroom.accenture.com/news/global-gaming-industry-value-now-exceeds-300-billion-new-accenture-report-finds.htm

43. Ben Lang, "More than 100 VR games have exceeded $1 million in revenue." Road to VR, February 25, 2020. www.roadtovr.com/100-vr-games-exceeded-1-million-revenue

44. Harry Baker, "Half-Life: Alyx surpasses 2 million owners on Steam, Steam Spy suggests." UploadVR, September 4, 2020. `http://uploadvr.com/half-life-alyx-2-million`

45. Ben Lang, "'Beat Saber' has sold 4m copies & 40m songs, an estimated $180m revenue (and accelerating)." Road to VR, February 2, 2021. `www.roadtovr.com/beat-saber-4-million-units-milestone-revenue`

46. Personal communication, 2022.

47. KPMG, "Go boldly, not blindly, into the metaverse." Consumer Pulse Survey Report, Spring 2022. `http://advisory.kpmg.us/content/dam/advisory/en/pdfs/2022/consumer-pulse-metaverse.pdf`

48. `https://venturebeat.com/games/jeri-ellsworth-and-tilt-five-are-bringing-the-metaverse-to-your-table`

49. Kevin Williams, "LBE rebound takes hold, driven by virtual reality." Vending Times, September 27, 2021. `www.vendingtimes.com/blogs/lbe-rebound-takes-hold-driven-by-virtual-reality`

50. `www.ign.com/articles/2019/05/30/how-jon-favreau-directed-the-lion-king-inside-a-video-game`

51. `www.espn.com/esports/story/_/id/29532117/billboard-travis-scott-astronomical-drew-more-45-million-viewers`

52. S. Lock, "Global online gambling and betting industry market size 2021-2028." Statista, July 26, 2022. `www.statista.com/statistics/270728/market-volume-of-online-gaming-worldwide`

53. Salvador Rodriguez, "As expected, porn industry quick to adopt Google Glass." *Los Angeles Times*, July 23, 2013. `www.latimes.com/business/la-xpm-2013-jul-23-la-fi-tn-google-glass-porn-20130723-story.html`

54. Moises Mendez II, "Azealia Banks and Ryder Ripps' NFT sex tape is being resold for over $260 million by the anonymous RultonFyder." Insider, March 12, 2021. `www.insider.com/azealia-banks-ryder-ripps-nft-sex-tape-resold-275-million-2021-3`

55. Ann-Marie Alcántara, "Snapchat's augmented-reality lenses find their way to the ballpark." *The Wall Street Journal*, October 22, 2020. `www.wsj.com/articles/snapchats-augmented-reality-lenses-find-their-way-to-the-ballpark-11603397554`

56. Alex Edwards, "AT&T is ramping up the interactive fan experience at the Dallas Cowboys' 5G-enabled stadium." Dallas Innovates, November 18, 2020. `http://dallasinnovates.com/att-is-ramping-up-the-interactive-fan-experience-at-the-dallas-cowboys-5g-enabled-stadium`

57. Business Wire, "lululemon athletica inc. to acquire home fitness innovator MIRROR." Business Wire, June 29, 2020. www.businesswire.com/news/home/20200629005789/en/lululemon-athletica-inc.-to-Acquire-Home-Fitness-Innovator-MIRROR

58. Projected visually as a hologram.

59. Ákos Maróy, "How augmented reality can make aviation safer and better." Upload VR, May 13, 2017. http://uploadvr.com/ar-aviation-safer-better

60. Biao Xie et al., "A review on virtual reality skill training applications." *Frontiers in Virtual Reality,* April 30, 2021. www.frontiersin.org/articles/10.3389/frvir.2021.645153/full

61. Anneke Nabben, "Augmented reality taking off in MRO training." NLR, May 31, 2017. www.nlr.org/article/augmented-reality-taking-off-mro-training

62. Mark Caswell, "KLM now offers virtual reality tours of its entire fleet." Business Traveller, December 6, 2019. www.businesstraveller.com/business-travel/2019/12/06/klm-now-offers-virtual-reality-tours-of-its-entire-fleet

63. ASQ, "COST Of Quality (COQ)", *ASQ* (n.d.). http://asq.org/quality-resources/cost-of-quality

64. Personal communication, August 2022.

65. NationMaster, "United States—Defence budget on R&D" NationMaster (n.d.), www.nationmaster.com/nmx/timeseries/united-states-defence-budget-on-rd

66. Thomas C. Frohlich, Evan Comen, & Grant Suneson, "15 commercial products invented by the military include GPS, duct tape and Silly Putty." *USA Today*, May 16, 2019. www.usatoday.com/story/money/2019/05/16/15-commercial-products-invented-by-the-military/39465501

67. Leslie Stahl, "Military vehicle training accidents, many fatal, reveal faulty equipment, poor training." *CBS News*, February 6, 2022. www.cbsnews.com/news/military-vehicle-training-accidents-60-minutes-2022-02-06

68. *The Korea Times*, "Korean military embraces latest tech to train soldiers." *The Korea Times*, May 3, 2019. www.koreatimes.co.kr/www/nation/2019/05/205_268228.html

69. Brandi Vincent, "Pentagon awards $600 million to spearhead 5G experiments across five military bases." Nextgov, October 9, 2020. www.nextgov.com/emerging-tech/2020/10/pentagon-awards-600-million-spearhead-5g-experiments-across-five-military-bases/169161

70. David Layzelle, "Virtual, augmented and mixed reality for defence and public sector." (Blog) *Unity Developers*, June 2, 2021. http://unitydevelopers.co.uk/virtual-augmented-and-mixed-reality-for-defence-and-public-sector

71. Lauren Feiner & Amanda Macias, "Pentagon cancels $10 billion JEDI cloud contract that Amazon and Microsoft were fighting over." CNBC, July 6, 2021. www.cnbc.com/2021/07/06/pentagon-cancels-10-billion-jedi-cloud-contract.html

72. Jordan Novet, "Microsoft wins U.S. Army contract for augmented reality headsets, worth up to $21.9 billion over 10 years." CNBC, March 3, 2021. www.cnbc.com/2021/03/31/microsoft-wins-contract-to-make-modified-hololens-for-us-army.html

73. Todd Haselton, "How the Army plans to use Microsoft's high-tech HoloLens goggles on the battlefield." CNBC, April 6, 2019. www.cnbc.com/2019/04/06/microsoft-hololens-2-army-plans-to-customize-as-ivas.html

74. Goksel Yildirim, "Turkish defense firms strike deal to develop AR glasses." *AA*, October 20, 2021. www.aa.com.tr/en/science-technology/turkish-defense-firms-strike-deal-to-develop-ar-glasses/2397630

75. Olivia Solon, "'We did not sign up to develop weapons': Microsoft workers protest $480m HoloLens military deal." *NBC News*, February 22, 2019. www.nbcnews.com/tech/tech-news/we-did-not-sign-develop-weapons-microsoft-workers-protest-480m-n974761

76. Dawei Yang et al., "Expert consensus on the metaverse in medicine." *Clinical eHealth*, Vol. 5, December 2022. www.sciencedirect.com/science/article/pii/S2588914122000016#bb0045

77. Dawei Yang et al., 2022.

78. Brian Kalis, Jenica McHugh, Kaveh T. Safavi, & Andrew Truscott, "Meet me in the metaverse." Accenture (n.d.). www.accenture.com/_acnmedia/PDF-178/Accenture-Digital-Health-Technology-Vision-2022.pdf

79. Bernard Marr, "The amazing possibilities of healthcare in the metaverse." *Forbes*, February 23, 2022. www.forbes.com/sites/bernardmarr/2022/02/23/the-amazing-possibilities-of-healthcare-in-the-metaverse

80. Accuvein.com

81. Jason Ju In Chan, Cheng Teng Yeam, Hwei Min Kee, & Chin Wen Tan, "The use of pre-operative virtual reality to reduce anxiety in women undergoing gynecological surgeries: A prospective cohort study." *BMC Anesthesiology*, December 2022. www.researchgate.net/publication/345037834_The_use_of_pre-operative_virtual_reality_to_reduce_anxiety_in_women_undergoing_gynecological_surgeries_A_prospective_cohort_study

82. Pedro F Gouveia et al., "Breast cancer surgery with augmented reality." *The Breast*. Vol. 56, April 2021. http://pubmed.ncbi.nlm.nih.gov/33548617

83. http://arismd.com

84. www.forbes.com/sites/charliefink/2019/07/29/aris-md-makes-x-ray-vision-science-fact/?sh=16f2f666577e

85. Amy Feldman & Aayushi Pratap, "Fantastic Voyage-inspired miniature surgical robot aims to revolutionize abdominal surgery." *Forbes*, July 28, 2021. www.forbes.com/sites/amyfeldman/2021/07/28/vicarious-surgical-bill-gates-backed-fantastic-voyage-inspired-miniature-surgical-robot-aims-to-revolutionize-abdominal-surgery/?sh=50a7b71616b6

86. www.nytimes.com/2021/04/21/health/virtual-reality-therapy.html

87. Logan Harper, "AppliedVR series a funding | virtual reality & digital health." *Digital Health Times*, March 23, 2021. https://digitalhealthtimes.com/2021/virtual-reality-and-digital-health-appliedvr-series-a-funding

88. www.apa.org/news/podcasts/speaking-of-psychology/virtual-reality

89. LaKeisha Fleming, "Virtual reality therapy is here—for some people, it's a better option." verywellmind, January 21, 2022. www.verywellmind.com/virtual-reality-therapy-may-be-a-viable-option-5215913#citation-1

90. Hill, S., personal communication, April, 22, 2022.

91. Marketing Interactive, "Sheraton Bali Kuta Resort makes AR and VR push." *Marketing Interactive*, September 28, 2017. www.marketing-interactive.com/sheraton-bali-kuta-resort-makes-ar-and-vr-push/?fbclid=IwAR3gIIdLq5VIKiTWvH59VDFhTyY1ddZN_IcJKtrvFj_AeIlWGzc_WTvgq2I

92. https://aiqom.ai/en/blogs/Robot-Concierges-In-The-Hospitality-Industry

93. Kate Ferreira, "Experience Cape Town in virtual reality." *Financial Mail*, March 14, 2019. www.businesslive.co.za/fm/fm-fox/digital/2019-03-14-experience-cape-town-in-virtual-reality

94. Marketing Interactive, "Hong Kong Tourism Board offers VR time travel." *Marketing Interactive*, November 22, 2018. www.marketing-interactive.com/hong-kong-tourism-board-offers-vr-time-travel

95. Tom Anstey, "Viking theme park takes Norse mythology into virtual reality." *Attractions Management*, September 18, 2015. www.attractionsmanagement.com/index.cfm?pagetype=news&codeID=318145

96. Jess Lodge, "Anzac Day 2018: Indigenous diggers' stories shared through augmented reality app." *ABC News*, April 24, 2018. www.abc.net.au/news/2018-04-25/app-shares-forgotten-stories-indigenous-anzacs/9690766

97. https://redshift.autodesk.com/articles/notre-dame-virtual-tour

98. www.youtube.com/watch?v=bpOB4vE5P5g

99. Personal communication, June 20, 2022.

100. Alex Coulombe, Personal communication, June 20, 2022.

101. Hyundai Motor Company, "Hyundai Motor and unity partner to build meta-factory accelerating intelligent manufacturing innovation." (Press release) Hyundai, July 1, 2022. www.hyundai.news/eu/articles/press-releases/hyundai-and-unity-partner-to-build-meta-factory-accelerating-intelligent-manufacturing-innovation.html

102. https://venturebeat.com/games/gtc-omniverse-panel-the-industrial-metaverse-is-coming-fast-as-digital-twins-take-shape

103. Market Data Center, "Metaverse in education market-technology & vendor assessment (vendor summary profiles, strategies, capabilities & product mapping & regional economic analysis) by MDC Research." *Global NewsWire*, May 4, 2022. www.globenewswire.com/news-release/2022/05/04/2436003/0/en/Metaverse-in-Education-Market-Technology-Vendor-Assessment-Vendor-Summary-Profiles-Strategies-Capabilities-Product-Mapping-Regional-Economic-Analysis-by-MDC-Research.html

104. PwC, "The effectiveness of virtual reality soft skills training in the enterprise." 5discovery (n.d.). www.5discovery.com/wp-content/uploads/2020/09/pwc-understanding-the-effectiveness-of-soft-skills-training-in-the-enterprise-a-study.pdf

105. Biao Xie et al., 2021.

106. Biao Xie et al., 2021.

107. Biao Xie et al., 2021.

108. PwC, "PwC's study into the effectiveness of VR for soft skills training." PwC (n.d.). www.pwc.co.uk/issues/intelligent-digital/virtual-reality-vr-augmented-reality-ar/study-into-vr-training-effectiveness.html

109. Claudio Brasca, Charag Krishnan, Varun Marya, Katie Owen, Joshua Sirois, & Shyla Ziade, "How technology is shaping learning in higher education." McKinsey & Company, June 15, 2022. www.mckinsey.com/industries/education/our-insights/how-technology-is-shaping-learning-in-higher-education

110. Adri Kornfein, "Stanford launches first class taught completely in virtual reality." *The Stanford Daily*, December 1, 2021. http://stanforddaily.com/2021/12/01/stanford-launches-first-class-taught-completely-in-virtual-reality

111. Kyle Melnick, "10 'metaversities' are opening across the US this fall." VXR-SCOUT, April 7, 2022. www.victoryxr.com/ten-metaversities-launching-in-u-s-this-fall-in-first-victoryxr-cohort

112. Robert Brown, "Top 10 jobs of the future—for 2030 and beyond." *World Economic Forum*, May 18, 2021. www.weforum.org/agenda/2021/05/jobs-of-the-future-year-2030

113. Cathy Hackl, "How technology will create these 7 jobs in the future." *Forbes*, June 24, 2020. www.forbes.com/sites/cathyhackl/2020/06/24/how-technology-will-create-these-7-jobs-in-the-future

114. The Money Editors, "Which jobs are at risk of automation?" *The Money*, January 5, 2022. http://themoney.co/which-jobs-are-at-risk-of-automation

Part 4

Challenges

Chapter 9

Understanding Reality

The magic is only in what books say, how they stitched the patches of the universe together into one garment for us.
—Ray Bradbury, Fahrenheit 451

One of the ways that we often envision the future of technological realities is through science fiction and pop culture. This is true of the metaverse, although in most cases it wasn't called the "metaverse" in the movies, TV shows, or books. *Ready Player One, Neuromancer, Snow Crash, Tron, The Matrix, Free Guy* and others allow us to explore new and different worlds enhanced by technology. "The richness of 'storyworlds'— the 'universes' within which [fictional] stories take place—provides us with detailed rules of the context in which a larger reality unfolds that extends beyond a single story, and has the potential to provide us with deeper learning about the underlying systems that regulate those worlds,"[1] say Alex McDowell, creator of the 2002 film *Minority Report* and Peter von Stackelberg, self-described as a "worldbuilder" and "transmedia story architect." These worlds are built either with a utopian purpose, driven by their creators' wish for a perfect society, or out of a desire to tackle an impending apocalypse. From the 1950s through 1980s, an entire genre of science fiction called cyberpunk, which focused entirely on a dystopic future, was at peak popularity. In many cases, the fiction provides enough technical accuracy and detail to satisfy the critical eye of their tech-savvy audience.

This is especially true in the 1992 novel *Snow Crash*, where author Neal Stephenson not only coined the term "metaverse," but he also popularized the word "avatar" as the concept of digital representation of a user. In his metaverse, run by a huge datacenter of computers in the desert, all these avatars hang out inside the simulation to take a break from their daily hardships. (Note that the theme of using immersive technology as an escape from reality seems to be a constant throughout the fictional future.) In Stephenson's novel, readers witness the amazing potential opportunities of the metaverse, but also the concrete challenges it poses, with consequences inside and outside of the simulation. The author clearly means to warn us, rather than inspire the creation of these virtual worlds. There are few (or no) fictional future utopian realities within entertainment properties as most are insights and warnings about where things can go wrong. There are visions of evil corporate overlords who want to monetize the platform (*Ready Player One*). VR being used in an actual war (*Ender's Game*). There's an alternate reality that you can't leave (*Tron*) and one that is created to control humans through technology plugged directly into their brains (*The Matrix*). You become one with the virtual world (*The Lawnmower Man*) or your consciousness can be uploaded digitally (*Neuromancer, Black Mirror*).

Sexism runs rampant, with women in supporting roles (although some are bounty hunters or kick-ass messengers), and cowboy hackers and video game developer antiheroes as the leads. Tech companies are always led by men, usually white men. AI or a robot can be good if it's a female voice (*Her, Blade Runner, Blade Runner 2049, Jexi*), but evil personalities are almost always men (*2001: A Space Odyssey*; *I, Robot*; *Westworld; the Terminator movies*). Granted, there are a few exceptions (e.g., *Ex Machina, The Mitchells vs. the Machines, The Iron Giant, A.I.*).

Seeking New Frontiers

In spite of the many dystopian visions of the future, there's still a clear push to discover and generate new, different worlds for us to create new ways of living. This kind of life-changing innovation isn't new. There was life before the Internet and life after, life before smartphones and life after. There is life before the metaverse and there will be one after.

This desire to establish new roadmaps and territories happens not just in the digital universe. If we delve into some of the world's billionaires' space race plans, we find that fictional warnings were no deterrent to any of them. Elon Musk's SpaceX (www.spacex .com), Jeff Bezos's Blue Origin (www.blueorigin.com), and Richard Branson's Virgin Galactic (www.virgingalactic.com) are betting on developing outer space colonies. The same kind of vision is found in the movies *Interstellar, The Martian, Gravity, Ad Astra,* and one could argue, *Star Wars* and the TV series *Space: 1999, The Expanse,* or even *Star Trek* and the *Alien* franchise, each of them with their own echoes of what outer world life may be. Emma Newman's *Planetfall* book series and the movie *Passengers* depict how even in an outer space colony, our human traits can be our demise.

Back here on Earth, several governments are testing new, real world social organizations in special innovation zones that are run by private corporate entities that are able to create their own laws. Take Próspera (http://prospera.hn), for instance, a Honduran special economic zone on the island of Roatán. Born in 2012 as a ZEDE (Zone for Employment and Economic Development), this "semi-autonomous zone" was conceived to bring in more (libertarian) entrepreneurs who enjoy lower taxation and an open-innovation ecosystem with housing built by Zaha Hadid Architects. Próspera aimed to operate a quasi-autonomous private government and a regulatory and legal architecture anchored in the Honduran constitution, while remaining nimble enough to allow the social implementation of new technological platforms. But in 2022 things changed from the initial vision. The newly elected government voted to cancel the agreement. Vanessa Cárdenas, a leader of a nearby village, said about the effort, "Go pay your tax like everybody else; go and get your permits like everybody else; and [abide by] Honduran law and regulation like everybody else."[2] In contrast, Toyota's Woven City was envisioned as a living lab at the base of Mount Fuji. Located near the picturesque, iconic mountain, this Japanese-branded city looks to allow daily tests of applications, reaping benefits from the tech convergence, allowing people, places, and vehicles to communicate real-time data between each other. The creators openly tout that the effort is "human-centered," a "living laboratory," and "ever-evolving," with the goal to "continuously create advancements that will help better society by accelerating the cycle of technology and development of services." This connectivity will allow Toyota to test out how advanced AI technology works in the real world, with (eventually) 2,000 residents using the driverless cars and personal mobility vehicles. There are also plans to integrate robots, AI health monitoring devices, and hydrogen and solar energy sources, in addition to a partnership with Nissin Foods for "healthy food options."[3] These visions are quite utopic, but they have an uncanny resemblance to that of *The Truman Show, Minority Report,* or even the universes of *The Good Place* and *Forever.*

These space colonies and corporate-governed special zones open new social and economic development opportunities, along with an unknown assortment of risks, as it's not really the technological transformation that is being discovered but societal change. Today, technology seems to be the biggest driver in human behavioral change.

As we advance into the metaverse, technology will enable us to create unlimited digital worlds and re-create ours. Mark Zuckerberg knows that there are many issues to be identified and to be solved ahead. "Interoperability, open standards, privacy, and safety need to be built into the metaverse from day one," he announced while rebranding Facebook to Meta, but without actually detailing how these problems can be solved.[4]

The same executives who are building their own digital worlds and tech advancements highlight several issues, mostly within their competitors' approaches. Elon Musk has dreams of colonizing Mars and using computer chips to interface and literally connect our brains with computers.[5] He has highlighted the health issues that might arise from the daily usage of XR headsets. "You know when I grew up it was like 'don't sit too close to the TV it's gonna ruin your eyesight' and now TV is like literally right here [puts his hand very close to his face].[6]

John Hanke, founder and CEO of Niantic, warns against promoting escapism through virtual reality, as most cyberpunk authors did: "As a society, we can hope that the world doesn't devolve into the kind of place that drives sci-fi heroes to escape into a virtual one—or we can work to make sure that doesn't happen." To tackle that, he champions augmented reality worlds, where the digital elements coexist side by side with the physical ecosystem. This implies "synchronizing the state of hundreds of millions of users around the world (along with the virtual objects they interact with), and tying those users and objects precisely to the physical world," which in itself can bring an array of new privacy and safety issues into our daily lives.[7]

"We should start thinking about it [the metaverse] now," shared Margrethe Vestager, executive vice president of the European Commission. "We're trying to figure out how to ask the right questions."[8] This proves especially important given the several shifts in social behaviors and political regimes social media created and the sheer concept of post-truth.

Post-Truths in the Metaverse

In the past decade, our social behavior has been manipulated. Social media's exponential growth in our lives started to decrease the time we spent with other media and other people. We found that reacting to or discussing the news with friends on social media is much more engaging than watching a newscast on TV or reading an article in a magazine. Being able to browse the news that friends shared, in a way, became a substitute for in-person conversations. We could keep up with their priorities and mindset and remain, at some level, close with them. Hence, it was only natural to see social media becoming gatekeepers to everything news-related and to see the opinions rising from these discussions assuming a dominant role, sometimes occluding facts themselves.

On social platforms, factual content often isn't ranked as high or shared as much as personal beliefs. Emotional arguments almost always trump rational ones. It has created the so-called post-truth society. This effect is boosted by some AI algorithms responsible for selecting the messages we are shown on social media timelines. As users engage more with specific messages that peer-validate their own previous ideas, users feel good and become more confident to engage. The reduction of space for discussion, tolerance, and democratic behavior creates a bigger polarization in opinions, and suddenly, freedom of speech starts to affect freedom of thought. Fake news flourishes, deepfake videos with faces of celebrities and politicians start to be shared online, conspiracy theories like Q'Anon gather user communities around them and are featured in political speeches alongside historical facts.

At the same time, many people are now used to sharing more info about themselves with social media companies. By asking users to either fill out registration forms or click "Accept" in notice boxes that allows their online tracking, these platforms are able to increasingly customize services and ads to each user. Advertising network access also becomes easier for individuals without the need of advertising agencies. These two, combined with what has already been happening within peer groups, enables easy distribution of radical messages, unvalidated and unmediated. This continuous self-validation cycle of radical beliefs has led to the radicalization of the believers. If you only see information that confirms your own opinions and if you only interact socially with people who agree with you, those who do not align with your beliefs begin to become your enemy.

The metaverse could (and most likely will) subject users to this type of behavior, but now everyone will not just read points of view, we'll be able to live them. We will literally be able to create our own custom worlds. The metaverse promise brings with it the concept of more personalization than we have ever had before, leveraging exponentially gathered data that can be used for good or bad. We may evolve from consumers and viewers of fake information to actual witnesses of these, as fake elements might appear inside our field of vision and make us perceive artificially inserted details and preserve memories of them. It may soon be possible that each of us can perceive a specific event in space and time that we could consider "a fact" in a different way from everyone else, reducing the chance of us actually coming to common ground. In the *Cambridge Dictionary*, the word "real" is defined as "existing in fact and not imaginary." But when living in a hybrid reality of digital and physical objects, spaces, and people, that we seamlessly use and own, will it all be real? The memories of our time immersed in those worlds won't tell us otherwise. David J. Chalmers co-directs NYU's Center for Mind, Brain, and Consciousness and argues, "There's nothing fictional about any of this. Virtual objects and virtual events aren't ordinary physical objects, but they're real all the same."[9]

This is complicated by the memory of events. It's no longer about just reading or seeing an ad or video. Experiences bring in more sensory information that can impact perception. There's also context and our own individual abilities to recall short- and long-term memories.[10] And we'll still need to define if every experience can be recorded or if most events will be based on individual recall. There will have to be new rules and laws based on yet-to-be-experienced metaverse interactions.

As Ben Erwin, creator of the Poly Awards and WebXR Summit, says, "The important thing is how we build it. We have many challenges to get right and not repeat the mistakes of previous iterations of the web."[11] These are the stakes in creating the metaverse. However, this time around, we have the benefit of the experience of building the Internet and the time to see how it worked and how it did not. Instead of building the metaverse without foresight, we can look at our previous mistakes and be willing to uncover the short-comings and undesired impacts as we go. There are already several different organizations like the Metaverse Standards Forum and other Web3 initiatives working toward creating global standards. But will these players be able to live up to it? "We'll have to see what will come out of it," shares Alina Kadlubsky, Managing Director at the Open AR Cloud Europe, an organization striving to promote standards to connect the physical and virtual worlds. "Will each be willing to compromise towards universal standards?"

We can pick up our lessons learned of the risks involved and plan ahead for a better, positive metaverse. But to do that, we need to first identify the key challenges ahead.

Assumptions

Outside of the emerging tech ecosystem, most people, when they try a new technology and if not told otherwise, assume they'll have full access to everything. That it will be "plug and play." So, as we're building the metaverse, it's only natural to expect it to have the same level of ease of use and interoperability as the present Internet. Navigating quickly from one web page to another is simple now, so we will expect a similar experience to happen while we navigate between physical and digital assets, spaces, and people seamlessly. This is unlikely to happen anytime soon.

Although the ease of a totally interconnected metaverse seems like an obvious goal, those developing it are still not sure how that navigation will happen. This kind of easily interconnected metaverse seems ideal, but it may not be feasible, at least in the short term. To begin with, we can assume that there won't be one company own-ing the metaverse. However, if you look specifically at the current lineup of tech giants claiming their individual digital stakes, you will see their strategy is not an interconnected one, no matter what their individual hype-machines might have you believe.

This is to be expected, as it has happened before. In the 1970s, there was a debate about the openness and interoperability of tele-communications. North American telecommunications companies like Bell Telephone tried to develop closed ecosystems that ended up competing among themselves. At some point, a customer was only allowed to make phone calls in a specific network through devices manufactured by the same operator that owned the network. That business strategy is called a *walled garden*, defined as a closed plat-form operated by a single party that has full control over the whole system and limits access to it with the end purpose of creating a monopoly. The technology term itself was coined in 1999 by John Malone, whose company Tele-Communications, Inc. was acquired by AT&T. He repurposed the literal term used to describe the hedges or gates placed around an outdoor garden.[12] Walled gardens are not just private areas of a public platform. They are controlled by one business owner who operates and manages a full platform, includ-ing all transactions and data generated within it. This owner can ban users, halt sales, and maintain a detailed profile of each and every registered user in their garden. Users exchange data exclu-sively inside the platform, in a nontransparent way to outsiders. They aren't governed by a community; governance is not decentral-ized. If they have issues, support is mostly automated.

As you read this description, you might begin to acknowledge that companies like Meta run a walled garden as does Alphabet (owners of Google's network of services). Even the tech industry's most valued brand, Apple, is the sole responsible gardener for its iOS ecosystem, which includes an app store, payments, video and audio streaming, as well as all advertising spaces across iPads, iPhones, and upcoming devices, such as smart glasses.

Does this mean that Big Tech players are bound to take over the metaverse, import their business practices into it, and divide it into branded domain areas? Not necessarily, but it's also unlikely that they'll drop profitable business models. With the gigantic amount of biometric data expected to be available in the metaverse (that we'll go through in the next chapter), it's even more likely Big Tech will double down on these practices. Amazon's 2022 purchase of One Medical is only one small ($4 billion) step in the evolution.[13]

But, make no mistake, walled gardens can be useful to onboard new users onto the building blocks of the metaverse. After all, inside them we don't need to make many decisions and the corporation behind it takes care of all issues and liabilities—which comes in handy especially when we're talking about emerging technologies. A walled garden enables the user or developer to connect with a single organizing entity, and it usually implies an easier user experience from onboarding a new virtual world to avatar creation and transactions. Still, it's again the CEO of Meta who states, "No one company will run the metaverse—it will be an 'embodied Internet' operated by many different players in a decentralized way."[14]

Ultimately the metaverse needs to become decentralized, open, and interoperable to deliver on its promise. It will need to be managed in a similar way to the World Wide Web. We need to easily navigate through it, without the hassle of logging into a new application every time we enter a new website.

The Open Metaverse Interoperability Group (OMI Group) is an organization focused on bridging virtual worlds by co-creating protocols to make interoperability possible across the metaverse. Its members include businesses and individuals discussing and exploring concepts surrounding the design and development of virtual worlds.

"True interoperability is not about space racing each other to the moon," says Jesse Alton, co-chair of the OMI Group (http:// omigroup.org). "That's the old school way of doing business. True interoperability is focused on the end-user and their ability to traverse the metaverse into and out of your platform. That requires either everyone 'just' do what one company is doing. Or, it requires companies to come together, cast aside their differences and create the protocols that make it possible in the first place."[15]

Making users navigate the metaverse seamlessly starts with connectivity. That means, effectively, telecommunications availability and standardization. Next, a second step toward interoperability and openness applies to maintaining identity, property, level of privacy, and means of payment across the metaverse virtual worlds—finally, having standard interfaces available in every platform to navigate it.

But Big Tech, social networks, and gaming companies are not that keen on losing control, so most likely, interoperability will come in different levels. As Alton shares, "The natural first step is for the interoperability definition to become the next model update. All these platforms, they are not going to see the light at the end of the tunnel and say, 'You know what? Let's just make this so that anyone can use this.' They're going to incrementally make their way there and users are gonna be excited and [the Big Tech companies are] gonna [make] a bunch of money every step of the way!"[16] Some authors like Kevin Geiger are much more bullish on the idea of a multiverse. He describes the concept as "a dogpile of incompatible, overlapping metaverses staking out divergent commercial, cultural and political claims, within and between nations."[17] Because of the immense complexity of the metaverse, there likely will be steppingstones until a full, interconnected, interoperable metaverse is possible. Most probably there will be a version where open content will mix with several walled gardens, much like the landscape the web has now, not fully decentralized and not fully open.

Still, there is the open question of how we will hop between open and closed ecosystems that will be built to enable the metaverse. On the World Wide Web, its interoperable solution is also its key feature and strength: the link. It's easy to forget that every part of the web had to be discovered. In the 1980s, Ben Shneiderman of University of Maryland created an "embedded menu" or "illuminated links," which eventually became known as the hyperlink. Tim Berners-Lee even referred to it in his 1989 creation of the web.[18] This miracle of hypertext allows us to move around all online pages, unless of course individual walled gardens demand login.[19]

"We have to drive towards that while building the underlying network and ensuring we bridge the gap," shares Alina Kadlubsky. "What we can see emerge are closed systems that lack an underlying core language. Learn from the web area and constantly improve, striving to create a better future for all of society. The mindset of being fast and breaking things doesn't apply to the big challenges we are facing."

As of this writing, there isn't a standard generally accepted to jump between open and closed platforms in all the diversity of social networks, VR/AR platforms, blockchain worlds, and massive multiplayer online social games.

One standard though is already enabling virtual reality and augmented reality via the web. It's called WebXR.[20] This isn't the first of its kind. As we mentioned earlier in the book, VRML allowed websites to integrate 3D animated graphics and create links between 3D worlds, but only more recently have navigation programs (that is, browsers) started integrating these standards and creators have begun developing more complex and integrated online services in immersive environments. "The significance of WebXR is that it allows developers to create immersive experiences that are accessible across devices, that they can build and maintain themselves, just like a website with no app stores as gatekeepers,"[21] shares Ben Erwin.

Open source projects like Mozilla Hubs (`http://hubs.mozilla.com`) allow you to access and create your very own, fully customizable VR chatrooms on the web, using a headset or a common desktop browser, and to move in and out of these rooms through a link. As the VR/AR industry understands the value of WebXR tools, the products and services are increasing in number and diversity, as seen yearly at the Polys Awards (`http://webxr.events`), the first awards fully dedicated to WebXR.

A Protocol and an Engine

Navigating between the physical and digital worlds via the web might be the first step in building an open, interoperable metaverse. Will there be portals for users to teleport in and out of each world? Maybe a voice-operated digital assistant, to which we can tell where we want to go next? There will be interface experimentation and likely mistakes along the way, but one thing's for sure: It's not just about making it 3D and fully available online. All your metaverse experiences need to be explored in a specific space, your physical space. Your home, your office, the manufacturing floor, the road where you are driving, the street where you are walking. As the metaverse is a merging of physical and digital. Your current surroundings are a part of it. With AR, you will see your space. With VR, you won't see the real world, but computer vision will need to accommodate and adjust to it regardless.

In 1999, Tim Berners-Lee described an extension set of the WWW standards called the Semantic Web,[22] whose main purpose was to provide better search results and overall to allow AI to take care of bureaucratic, administrative, and repetitive processes in our everyday lives. In it, he advised that every website should include metadata (underlying details and directions, unseen to common users of the web) that computers could read to predict, interpret, compare, and recommend solutions.[23]

However, to do that, he relied on site owners to create consistent, usable metadata syntax and vocabulary that offered meaning to the machines so they could read it.[24] This proved extremely complicated to scale, as there was no immediate gain to site owners for the added amount of work they'd have every time they added a new text, image, or video. So, the Semantic Web never actually grew and although there are a few semantic-web-annotated websites today, there are not nearly as many as were expected in 1999.

Making the upcoming metaverse interoperable implies associating context with content, as some digital experiences will be overlaid on top of the physical world (in AR) and as digital twins may show specific information for the physical equipment or object they represent. There also is the added complication of context between people as well. It still makes sense to include information about digital spaces, assets, and owners of an experience, effectively metadata. According to Gabriel René and Dan Mapes, "Web 3.0 will be a semantic web because we will embed 3D spatial intelligence into everything."[25] Whether because some of the information will be needed to create the metaverse experiences and functionalities, or because users will also be able to contribute to this metadata, the bottleneck for the 1999 Semantic Web becomes necessary for the success of the metaverse.

There will be several additional interoperability issues to be solved. Just gathering and referencing the spatial information of our physical places, assets, and people, for instance. It is assumed at this point that it will be gathered and made available by AR clouds, which would enable real-time persistent augmented reality experience. Meta LiveMaps, Magic Leap's Magicverse online, Microsoft's Spatial Anchors, Apple's AR Cloud Anchors, Niantic's Lightship, and Earth Cloud Anchors from Google are all ongoing, generously funded initiatives to position digital objects persistently in the physical world. They are effectively putting down the first building blocks of the AR-based metaverse experience. Given the sheer size of the opportunity, there likely will be several other entrants to the market, each potentially with their own proprietary formats (thus, more walled gardens). So, the interoperability issues of putting these platforms all into contact and enabling users to seamlessly benefit from them all may continue to increase in complexity before they are simplified and solved.

How data and content will need to flow across several platforms also will need to be solved so that each digital world doesn't require separate profiles, separate friend lists, and separate messaging services. Bringing our identities and property along to every part of our experience is really important to ease the burdens we're now feeling within the current version of the Internet. Even payment services and which cryptocurrencies are accepted might be differentiated across these platforms, creating even further complications. Signing up a few times is manageable, but imagine having to sign up for each website you surf. It needs to be easy to use and as seamless as possible.

The Open AR Cloud (www.openarcloud.org) was founded to help address some of these foreseeable issues. It is a nongovernmental organization whose "mission is to drive the development of open and interoperable spatial computing technology, data and standards to connect the physical and digital worlds for the benefit of all."[26] It is creating an open standard for geospatial discovery that already allows several European cities to enjoy multiplayer augmented reality experiences. The organization also developed an Open Spatial Computing Platform infrastructure that enables localization and discovery in spatial services for persistent positioning and interoperability.[27]

Governance and Access

Interconnecting all the corners of the metaverse isn't just about people, places, and assets. There is the hope that we can sync these three with the blockchain. This would enable more transparency and give each of us the power to rule our own identity and data through wallets that are accepted worldwide. Throughout this idealized metaverse, fiat and cryptocurrencies would be accepted, and NFTs would be standard contracts. The metaverse could even be governed by users themselves through a gigantic DAO, where each could vote and directly contribute to every major decision.

"The tension between decentralized and centralized is growing, and it's hard to imagine how they will co-exist. On the other hand, it's even harder to imagine a future where one or a few monopolies own it," shares Alina Kadlubsky. She continues, It's interesting to see that in the past, decentralized alternatives emerged after centralized systems were in place. Now we have those being established in parallel."

The blue-sky thinking around a total decentralized metaverse is exciting, but complete decentralization is highly unlikely. Governments and standards organizations will impact the potential for interoperability within the metaverse, as they can and will create standards and enforce them as well.

Beyond the technologies and standards for moving from world to world, the metaverse also needs a version of a spatialized search engine. Remember the web without a search engine, back in the 90s? We had directories that were fed by human hand and results were either repeated, nonrelevant, or too few. The ability to extract relevant results and to bring users directly to what they needed brought the World Wide Web, not only to our mainstream but to our daily usage as well. Then Google became a verb, e.g., "I'll just Google that." Search engines totally transformed our relationship with the web. With the metaverse, the ability to filter experiences and search for the services and applications one wants will be instrumental in making it a commodity. How that search engine will look and how it will work is still being thought out, with voice recognition being a leading contender as an interface.

The evolution of the web search engine was awkward and clumsy at first, so we can expect a similar trajectory for metaverse search. Literally multiple dimensions of complexity are being added. It's no longer just Internet and mobile devices, but it also needs to include your headset, operating system, browsing experience, your current and past environments, the context of your request, and potentially even more information.

The metaverse won't miraculously appear worldwide either. Different regions, states, and countries will join the in-construction metaverse at different times and at different rates. Access might even be limited by several other forces outside of the technical scope, similar to the distribution of the Internet. As we will be operating in 3D spaces likely with gestures, cultural norms might become more of an issue than they are on the web. Although we can overcome the language barriers through the power of artificial intelligence's automatic speech recognition (ASR) and natural language processing (NLP), cultural aesthetics and behavioral references might communicate in different ways to different audiences. For instance, female avatar dress and behavior might be a concern to some Islamic societies. Some nations might be altogether banned from accessing specific content, or just decide to become isolated from all other ones, like North Korea does currently. Governments are bound to create specific laws that might hinder how businesses operate across the metaverse. Even individual users might hinder complete and transparent interoperability. Either by themselves or by organizing themselves in communities, users will be able to create invite-only content or apply community filters that could provide safe and private spaces or an entirely new version of spatialized isolation that results in post-truths. So, although the future of the metaverse is starting to take shape, with many players and billions invested, how it will interconnect is still yet to be determined not just within the emerging tech ecosystem, but also the world.

Notes

1. Isabel Fernández Peñuelas, "Science fiction narratives and future studies." *BBVA OpenMind*, April 6, 2022. www.bbvaopenmind.com/en/technology/future/science-fiction-narratives-future-studies

2. Laurie Clarke, "A crypto-libertarian paradise just lost an existential battle with Honduras." *Rest of World*, May 11, 2022. http://restofworld.org/2022/crypto-libertarian-prospera-lost-legal-battle-honduras

3. Iain Robertson, "Inside Japan's smart city of the future." *Innovators*, June 14, 2022. www.innovatorsmag.com/inside-japans-smart-city-of-the-future

4. Meta, "Founder's letter, 2021." *Meta*, October 28, 2021. http://about.fb.com/news/2021/10/founders-letter

5. Through the mission of neuralink.com

6. Tech Desk, "Elon Musk mocks 'Metaverse' idea, says nobody wants a screen strapped to their face." *The Indian Express,* December 23, 2021. http://indianexpress.com/article/technology/tech-news-technology/elon-musk-mocks-metaverse-idea-says-nobody-wants-a-screen-strapped-to-their-face-7686834

7. John Hanke, "The metaverse is a dystopian nightmare. Let's build a better reality." *Niantic*, August 10, 2021. http://nianticlabs.com/news/real-world-metaverse/?hl=en#:~:text=As%20a%20society%2C%20we%20can,Niantic%2C%20we%20choose%20the%20latter

8. Pymnts, "Metaverse may pose new competition challenges, says EU antitrust chief." *PYMNTS*, January 20, 2022. www.pymnts.com/news/regulation/2022/metaverse-may-pose-new-competition-challenges-says-eu-antitrust-chief

9. David J. Chalmers, *Reality+: Virtual Worlds and the Problems of Philosophy*. W. W. Norton & Company, 2022.

10. Carley Marie, "Here is why two people see the same thing but have different memories." *The Versed*, January 28, 2019. www.theversed.com/94513/two-people-see-thing-different-memories/#.57QhagX4go

11. Personal communication, August, 2022.

12. www.techopedia.com/definition/2541/walled-garden-technology

13. Shauneen Miranda, "Amazon buying One Medical is only its most recent dive into the health care industry." *NPR*, June 26, 2022. www.npr.org/2022/07/26/1113427867/amazon-one-medical-health-care

14. "Interview: Mark Zuckerberg on Facebook's metaverse," interviewed by Casey Newton, podcast, July 22, 2021. *The Verge*. http://podcasts.apple.com/br/podcast/interview-mark-zuckerberg-on-facebooks-metaverse/id430333725?i=1000529701945

15. Interview of Jesse with Luis, May 2022

16. Jesse's interview with Luis, May 2022.

17. Kevin Geiger, "Metaverse = multiverse." (Blog), *AWN*, May 11, 2022. www.awn.com/blog/metaverse-multiverse

18. Gary Klein, "The invention of hyperlinks." *Psychology Today*, January 4, 2018. www.psychologytoday.com/us/blog/seeing-what-others-dont/201801/the-invention-hyperlinks

19. Ben Shneiderman and Catherine Plaisant (Eds.), "Hypertext research: The development of HyperTIES." July 2018. www.cs.umd.edu/hcil/hyperties

20. The Immersive Web Working Group/Community Group, "Links to our specifications, samples, and tools." http://immersive-web.github.io

21. Personal communication, August, 2022.

22. W3C, "W3C semantic web frequently asked questions." W3C Semantic Web. www.w3.org/RDF/FAQ

23. Frank van Harmelen, "The semantic web: what, why, how, and when." *IEEE Computer Society Digital Library*, March 4, 2004. www.computer.org/csdl/magazine/ds/2004/03/o3004/13rRUwInvEB

24. Frank van Harmelen, 2004.

25. Gabriel René and Dan Mapes, *The Spatial Web* (self-pub, 2019), author's edition.

26. Open AR Cloud, Building a better reality together! www.openarcloud.org

27. Lily Snyder, "How the Open AR Cloud enables the metaverse." (Blog) *AWEXR*, January 17, 2022. www.awexr.com/blog/434-how-the-open-ar-cloud-enables-the-metaverse

Chapter 10
Privacy and Safety in the Metaverse

Most human beings have an almost infinite capacity for taking things for granted.

—Aldous Huxley, Brave New World

B etween creating an interoperable way to completely access its full extent and linking open areas with several different walled gardens, one of the main promises of the metaverse is to provide you with a customized version of it—being able to wander around and interact with digital and physical elements in an increasingly bespoke way. The metaverse takes personalization to a whole new level. What powers that individual experience? Data.

Much of the discussion around data in the news today is focused on what is gathered via the Internet. There is data from social media, search engines, online retailers. The data that's collected goes well beyond the information you provide on registration forms. It's data about what you search for and your journey through the Internet— each and every time you log in. This kind of data improves your experience (for example, not having to look at the same news stories, not having to reenter your credit card information). The size of data you alone provide is massive, even if you don't see it. There is a constant debate about how much data should be tracked, as we don't want Big Tech to know "too much" about us. But on the flip side, we want our Internet experience to be easy and personal. It's ultimately about the value of a customized experience versus how much data is being tracked.

Data is actually one of the most important parts of the digital world. In 2014, *Wired* predicted that "Data in the 21st Century is like Oil in the 18th Century . . . for those who see data's fundamental value and learn to extract and use it there will be huge rewards."[1] In 2017, *The Economist* declared, "The world's most valuable resource is no longer oil, but data."[2] It's data that powers Big Tech business, and, generally speaking, it's data that has changed how society works and how value is created and distributed.

As we move from a 2D Internet experience to a 3D spatialized one, the amount of data becomes exponentially greater. VR, as it stands now, is said to offer 2 million data points of any user within a 20-minute experience. Although this might sound high, consider that it's no longer data about just what you are typing or clicking on or even your GPS location. Data will be gathered on your movement, gestures, voice, your point of view, and everything in it, including your home, your workplace, your family's, friends', and coworkers' faces, and so on.[3]

The main benefit of capturing your location (home, work, etc.) is for this metaverse spatial tracking for the creation of a unique experience customized to each of us. The customization level achievable will be directly related to the amount of contextual data and machine learning algorithms at work, many yet to be developed.

Data will fuel each interaction in the metaverse. Let's say you are looking through your AR glasses at a building and would like to receive information about the building based on your current interests and your past behavior. If you are a real estate agent or in the market for a new place, your experience will be completely different from that of an historian or someone who used to live in that particular building. Data capture and processing will enable this personalized point of view of the world.

Data is about to become even more central and valuable in business settings. Each person working on the construction of a building may need to view different information. Some will need the architectural drawings, others the pipe locations, others the wiring. Some may need all or a combination of just a few. The same would be true for a medical procedure. The nurses, the anesthesiologist, the doctor, all would need different information applied within the physical context around them (in AR) or in shared simulated environments (VR).

There will also be data beyond work and home. Facial recognition could be activated for everyone you know, or even those you don't recognize. This goes beyond the facial tracking software that is available on a mobile phone photo search. But, how much information will you want or need for each person? How much information do you want to give to other people? You may want or need to share personal health information with a family member, but you wouldn't want exchange the same information with your boss.

And yes, there is advertising. The recent global debate has been around how Big Tech has used surveillance techniques to mine personal data for advertising and marketing. It's gathered to enable brands to get much more efficiency from their ad budgets, while improving the customer experience. Ad-serving networks use this information to plan advertising campaigns that target you, that have you see or get you to learn more about a product or service and buy it. By knowing your preferences, data-powered advertising programs can place ads for a new pair of shoes that you might actually like based on your previous purchasing behavior. By knowing your location, a nearby shoe store can be suggested for where you can go to buy it. This will become more personalized, more customized, and based on more of our personal data in the metaverse.

This kind of experience can get pretty creepy, pretty quickly, so much that the term "surveillance capitalism" has been used to describe it. "[Data capture] typically occurs outside of our awareness, let alone our consent. . . [For example,] every time we encounter a digital interface, we make our experience available to *datafication*, thus *rendering unto surveillance capitalism* its continuous tithe of raw-materials supplies,"[4] says Shoshana Zuboff, Harvard professor, author of *The Age of Surveillance Capitalism*. User behaviors became the raw materials for a new industrial model but the goal for advertisers is to make it seamless, so your reaction is of delight, not of disgust.

If you are generally comfortable with allowing your data to be tracked, you may forget that you—well, more specifically, the data you generate—are the product companies sell. Meta's and Google's core products, including Instagram, Gmail, and Google Maps, don't charge you for their use. You have given them your personal data in exchange. But, you are left in the dark about the amount of information collected, who gets to look at it, what they infer from your behavior, and what it's worth to sell it. Your consent for this usage is often given with a click or an easy digital toggle, without a full understanding of what you're getting into. Instead, you sign off to a very complex or oversimplified terms of service, designed to be inconspicuous to the average user.

You may say you might not care about some of the data you're sending, but as technologies accelerate and converge, a new digital persistent plane of existence comes into play and wearables, IoT, cameras, and other headsets start tracking you, the data you are offering will become more and more personal. It goes from an on-screen, 2D experience where you know you are logging on, to something that you forget as it enters your personal and private spaces.

Data Issues

Collection of your data isn't always something you have consented to a company to gather. Today, through a common smartphone, someone you don't know can take a photo or record a video of you and post it on social media without your permission. Even if you aren't directly tagged, you can always be recognized and the social network company itself will know that you were in that specific time and place, whether or not you want them to. You can thank facial recognition algorithms for this.

This interaction gets more complicated with headsets or smart glasses. You might not know when you are being identified. For example, Ray-Ban Stories, a set of glasses on sale since 2021, was built to ease up social media sharing via your mobile phone. They have a camera built in to enable capturing and then sharing photos and videos of what you're seeing. There's a tiny LED white light on the side of the Ray-Ban smart glasses that warns us the glasses are recording, but the Irish and Italian governments,[5] for instance, found it too small and insufficient to safeguard anyone's privacy.

On the other side of the spectrum, in 2018, China added more cameras to their 170 million CCTV camera system: more specifically, the ones included in the smart glasses of Zhengzhou's police officers.[6] These enable them to perform facial recognition on the fly and more easily identify wanted criminals and cases of fake IDs.

If this still doesn't concern you much, don't forget the recent history of data breaches and misuse of data by tech companies. According to the Identity Theft Resource Center's Annual Data Breach Report,[7] 2021 saw the greatest jump in data incidents year to year: 1,862 breaches, up 68 percent from the previous year. The biggest data leak in 2021 happened at Comcast and alone represented a loss of a whopping 1.5 billion private records.

Even if data breaches are prevented and we find a solution for the protection of personal and interpersonal data ownership, data usage still has a potential negative impact. Although the ability to target based on engagement might be helpful to create personalized experiences, too much reliance on data and targeting results become a problem. Social media has shown that what seems like simple customization can go very, very wrong, including the following:

Deep Fakes If videos and media resources are edited to feature a person or an element that is not actually there, it's referred to as a deep fake. Recently, deep fakes have been created and shared socially, such as placing Steve Buscemi's face on Jennifer Lawrence's Golden Globe interview in 2019 and the viral Tom Cruise video. Although it brought a lot of attention to the capabilities of the tech, we have yet to understand fully how the technology could be used to manipulate public sentiment. Deep fakes could be used to create videos or photos that could impact the social, professional, and political livelihoods of any of us. Platforms sometimes set policies to stop deep fakes, but not all organizations commit means to enforce them with third parties.

Fake News   There was much discussion around fake vs. real news in the 2016 United States presidential election. The fear within tech is not about the validity of well-known organizations, but instead about the companies that are created to further a particular agenda, without integrity. If all the news information you see is only peer-validated, there is room for inaccurate, deceptive "news" that leaves out details, shares misinterpreted information, or deliberately creates arguments to propel private agendas.

Filter Bubbles   As people are served more and more of what they like to see, they are not exposed to different opinions or points of view. This disables the opportunity to understand each other's reasoning, making consensus much harder to achieve and opinions much less open for discussion.

Post-Truth   After many accept inaccurate information as true, several start accepting it as the truth, without having any historical criteria or background check.

Social Polarization   If social media algorithms consistently share extreme information, it can strengthen the resolve and the beliefs that the "other side" is wrong, effectively destroying any solution-building process and the ability to accept any other option than their own.

Data collection is the cornerstone of most business models in Web 2.0, as well as the many social issues they bring. The ongoing convergence of exponential technologies will likely increase privacy and social issues also exponentially. We must prepare for it and create mechanisms to predict, and protect us as the metaverse comes together.

Your Internet of Things

One of the most likely sets of private data enabled by the metaverse will be our own digital twin. This isn't just the data collected by a 3D scan of your body or the creation of an ultra-realistic digital avatar. Instead it is a collection of real-time data and historical info about your body from a medical and behavioral perspective.

The following are some of the data you likely already give to organizations, that you may not even realize:

Behavioral Data captured from your actions inside an online platform.

Biometric Data captured from your gestures, the face recognition safety locks on your smartphone, selfie photos, videos, augmented reality filters, and your wearables (e.g., fitness trackers, smart watches).

Gray areas Data captured or inferred without your consent, although technically legal.

  • **Inferred Data** Data extracted by interpreting the context of other data (i.e., if you search on your mobile phone for sneakers and your geographical data shows you're near a shoe store, the data implies you likely are looking to buy new sneakers.

  • **Registration Forms** Any of the information you included when subscribing or joining online platforms.

Third party Data gathered about you on other websites and platforms, besides the ones you're originally registered on.

Today, data is also being captured by several different devices besides smartphones, most of them screenless: doorbells, hallway cameras, smart locks, smart watches, Bluetooth devices, toasters, refrigerators, pace counters, or even cars that have several kinds of sensors and monitors that add more detail about our lives.

This exponential growth in individualized, personal data requires a term of reference: "Your Internet of Things." For seamless, real-time, personalized interactions anywhere between physical and digital in the metaverse, even more data capture and analysis are needed to enable those. Our spatialized interactions and experiences will generate data of their own. HMDs will track our gaze and see where and for how long we look at something and even what makes our pupils dilate. Also, the gestures and body movements we make—that is, where we point and what we pick up, regardless of it being physical or digital—can be tracked. Finally, it will be possible to monitor our tone of voice, our pauses, in addition to what we say. All might reveal information regarding our state of mind and opinion toward a specific person, topic, product, or brand.

Our every action, if done with smart glasses, could be recorded or lifelogged and be part of a memory disk that we could log into and rewind at will. We will have the ability to check, when needed, all information regarding one specific conversation, for better or worse. It could help identify a friend or loved one's preferences or the details of an argument. There also will be the data gathered from our interactions with our family, friends, community, and workplace, which can be logged and referenced.

All this data generated from lifelogging activities will need to be stored for a given period of time. A new service will probably be created, and possibly in the future, personal walled gardens could hold the memories of users' lives. The avatar versions of these digital twins might stick around after death and allow, for instance, more dead celebrities to be featured in Hollywood movies, like Stan Lee, who is being placed in future Marvel films after his passing. Or maybe these digital twins might be available as some kind of digital oracle to families (e.g., a beloved grandmother could live forever in digital human form). This opens up the opportunity to create an entire market around capturing and mining memories.

Some might opt out of constant data tracking, or even just change their behavior. In a 2015 research study, volunteers who wore lifelogging cameras were observed over several days. Several privacy concerns were unveiled, most specifically for the camera wearer. As they became mindful that they were being recorded, they started paying more attention to who they talked to, who they watched, and what screens were captured on their personal computers. Anxiety kicked in, as they were always alert about their behavior, and that had an impact, not only on their need to safeguard their privacy, but also on their mental health.[8]

And who will manage "Your Internet of Things"? Initially businesses who will charge for your data protection. Eventually a version of a personal AI assistant.

It's a dazzling amount of data that each of us will create. There's also the information generated by connecting every object and equipment with each of us and with each other so that AI services will be able to automatically manage services for best efficiency and performance. For example, cars would generate relevant data for traffic management. Buildings would supply relevant data for the hygiene and safety of everyone in them. Nearly every place and object could have a sensor and scanner. This massive amount of data capture isn't all bad. Automated services open up a huge number of possibilities for location-wide services and logistics (e.g., building- or city-wide) to talk, communicate, and provide a better, more impactful service. Local governments could allow citizens to vote immediately on multiple matters, in either a centralized or a decentralized manner.

As so much information is being gathered, maintaining user privacy has stood out as a major social issue in the last couple of years, especially by creating some legal ground for key personal data types, like medical records or children's information. As we walk into the metaverse, privacy and safety risks are bound to increase.

Security

Policies like the European General Data Protection Regulation (GDPR), National Institute of Standards and Technology (NIST) guidance, Family Educational Rights and Privacy Act (FERPA), and Children's Online Privacy Protection Act (COPPA) were just the first of several initiatives that aimed to promote and regulate the Internet. We can develop and try to apply the policies of Web 2.0 to the metaverse, but probably not all the policies, as the experience, interaction with digital beings and avatars, and the immense diversity of data being gathered will be unlike anything we have seen before.

When it comes to Web3, decentralization of all data might be the answer to reducing risk. Attaining sovereignty is a core tenet of this model. Take, for instance, Bitcoin's creator Satoshi Nakamoto's identity. It is still not known, but anyone can keep up with the transactions via his wallet's address.

However, there are those who believe that the blockchain is not as secure as the hype tells us it is. Some say not all privacy is safeguarded, as your property, cryptos, and NFTs are visible on the chain. The Secret Foundation's co-founder Tor Bair tweeted earlier in 2021, "Web3 requires you to give up privacy entirely. NFTs and blockchains are all public-by-default and terrible for ownership and security."[9] Even users who don't typically make their wallet addresses and identities known can be traced thanks to professional data-gathering experts.

Social and Emotional

Some of the risks of a future metaverse can be identified based on the issues that have arisen with the current and previous version of the Internet as well as gaming and existing VR and AR experiences.

One clear one is addiction. Games are often designed to make you want to play more, encouraging you to reach new levels of gameplay. Each time you get excited about moving past an obstacle, your brain releases dopamine and provides you with a pleasurable feeling. Likes on social media feeds also lead to the same kind of chemical reaction.

In the metaverse all interactions generate a lot more stimuli, as immersive environments will allow for fully immersive experiences and rewards. Remember, users will be able to edit and increasingly interact in customized worlds, which increases the chance of larger dopamine spikes and the desire to stay in the metaverse and continue your interaction with digital humans and avatars. Likely this kind of interaction is going to be much more exciting to our brains than interactions with real humans in the real world.

The desire to create and live within a digital world that is fully customized to your wants and needs makes complete sense. However, if, ultimately, you choose to spend more time in that digital world than the physical one, then problems arise. What if you can digitally replicate friends or celebrities who exist in the physical world but in a version where they're focused on your interests and desires and always positive about your opinions? What would then happen to the perceived relationship between you and these people? This editing potential can change the way we interact or expect to interact with one another—as consumers, as professionals, as business owners, and as parents and citizens.

This is going to start to confuse many of us. There will begin to be multiple "realities" in which we all will live. This concept tinkers with the foundations of our life, the physically based reality that we were educated to believe was always there. We'll be able to digitally enhance our role in it, or at least convince our brains of that effect. How this will impact our mental health is still to be determined.

Harassment

Anonymity and plausible deniability have led to some terrible behavior on the Internet. But in a spatial environment, there is a greater likelihood of more physical kinds of problems. "The issue of harassment in VR is a huge one," shares Frances Haugen,[10] the whistleblower who, in 2021, exposed how much Facebook knew about the safety and privacy issues happening on its platform. Demeaning behaviors and abuse can have a bigger impact on users when felt in immersive worlds, especially when they are minors.

Horizon Worlds, VRChat, and Rec Room have put tools in place that help reduce this risk. Some allow users to set up an invisible bubble of personal space to prevent other users' avatars from closing in; others allow muting or even blocking what you don't want to see. Most of these platforms even have moderators who can report abuses, and sometimes, users can vote to kick someone out of a VR space.

Still, according to Haugen, "There's going to be whole new art forms of how to harass people that are about plausible deniability. The tech company would need to hire substantially more people, and likely recruit volunteers, to adequately deal with this problem."

Harassment could even become trickier as digital beings could be programmed to abuse a particular target/s. As AI technology evolves, more sophisticated digital humans will also create new challenges for harassers' detection and identification.

Digital Cloning

Given the amount of data available about each of us that will be gathered in the metaverse, we need to look beyond some of the parallels of personal data issues on the web. Digital twin data brings with it even more concerning issues.

Meta has filed many patents to help ensure dominance of our virtual social experience. One specific patent from Meta reveals an "avatar personalization engine" that has the power to generate 3D avatars based on a user's photos, including what they refer to as a *skin replicator*. According to *TechRadar*, Meta's goal is to "create digital replicas of users, with the aim to make the metaverse's avatars seem indistinguishable from real people."[11]

Of course, this cloning potential is being explored by many corporate players, not just Meta. Eventually every pore, every micromovement could be replicated. Users will have, through this and other services, the ability to create hyper-realistic avatars and don them across the metaverse. It will make the line between the physical and the virtual almost invisible.

But users will be focused on the benefits these digital twins and Your Internet of Things will bring. If medical teams can test-run procedures, for instance. If you include lifelogged memories and artificial intelligence, you might have a virtual assistant copy who could anticipate and accommodate your needs. If you take that further with historic data of your interactions, you could test out different scenarios before making any decision—almost like a continuous life hack. It's hard to resist the charms of these future opportunities and overlook the likely issues.

Hacking

Having digital twins of every person, place, or thing brings in many additional issues and threats.

As today, payments will definitely be an area where security will see an upgrade. Let's say you are buying something at an AR store; you might need some sort of PIN, have an eye scan, or even open your crypto wallet to effectively perform payment. All of these moments might allow data to be copied by a hacker, if no safety guards are in place on the user side, on the spaces themselves, and on the metaverse technological solutions.

There are more potential opportunities for bad actors to copy different physical-to-virtual parts of you. A research team at Rutgers University published a study on how virtual reality headsets are vulnerable to attacks on voice commands, known as eavesdropping attacks. Yingying "Jennifer" Chen, Associate Director of WINLAB and Graduate Director of Electrical and Computer Engineering at Rutgers University, says, "Our research demonstrates that Face-Mic can derive the headset wearer's sensitive information with four mainstream AR/VR headsets, including the most popular ones: Oculus Quest and HTC Vive Pro."[12]

These attacks might not just be stealing data, but they might also install specific, personalized trackers that could send information to the hacker when you're connected. They could lifelog a user's full metaverse experience and ultimately create their very own virtual copy of them.

Hackers also may interfere with your perception of the metaverse. For example, they might alter your field of view and perception of the world. This could be a short-term change or a longer one, with access to stored details like your credit card number or crypto wallet access.

As graphics become more sophisticated and harder to determine if they are real, all of the issues around deep fakes and fake news can have an even broader impact. Any kind of reality can be created to strengthen bias and hatred toward a specific race, nationality, or religion. Worse even, the filter bubbles that are primarily now about news stories could become 3D re-creations. This would be even harder to counter as, from their perspective, they actually saw it happen.

Society

As the metaverse brings opportunities to support our everyday activities: driverless cars to avoid accidents, real-time information about work colleagues or business partners to build closer relationships, grocery shopping details sent from your kitchen based on your personal preferences and meal history. This will begin to seem like part of our daily reality.

It also presents a huge opportunity for the poisoning of this information. Location filters or product or person identifiers could be altered. They can even remove objects or people from view, erasing them in real time. This is called *diminished reality (DR)*. DR allows the removal, concealment, or elimination of real-life objects from users' vision, with seemingly believable backgrounds or 3D reconstructions that make you unaware of what is missing. This could be good (e.g., avoid advertising you don't want to see), or bad (e.g., removing stop signs in your field of view).

It's hard to imagine what hackers may or may not do. But if Internet history is a predictor of the future metaverse, there may be virtual destruction or defacement of schools, cemeteries, police stations, churches, temples, and hospitals. A hacker could even place adult materials in front of minors.

Children's Safety

There are a growing number of emerging tech platforms and services aimed at children, both for education and entertainment purposes. In Christmas 2021, Shawn Whiting from Rec Room announced that in the 60 hours after Christmas Day, a million new VR players joined his platform.[13] Google "Oculus Christmas gift" or "VR Christmas gift" and you'll stumble across unboxing videos with an Oculus Quest 2 or some other VR device. Common Sense Media reported that 17 percent of children 8–18 in the United States had a VR headset and some 25 percent have tried VR.[14] Creating a service for this audience requires a set of skills that takes into account the specific needs of children, as well as knowledge of policies and laws that keep younger users safe.

As of now, tech companies have begun to split headset access to people over 13 and children under 13. In the Oculus store, you need to be above 13 to use VR apps. Most of the XR headsets establish either 13 or 7 years as the lowest age threshold for a VR user, although there aren't any ways to effectively confirm a user's age at this time.

There likely are many potential issues for children when it comes to the metaverse. Some haven't been studied enough, like the effects on the biological development of a child's eye when exposed persistently to VR and AR interfaces. Still, bringing screens close to their retinas consistently is bound to have a deleterious effect. There are several other considerations already identified when it comes to children in the metaverse:

Real vs. Unreal   Children who are still in their years of magical thinking will risk confusion when seeing digital beings talking through AR headsets.

Abuse   Without age verification, abusers have been posing as children with the hopes of grooming them.

Adult Content   Children might be exposed by accident to mature themes or pornography.

Bullying   Children might be more likely to bully behind the guise of an avatar.

Fraud/Phishing/Malware   Just as with the 2D Internet, innocent-looking elements might be activated without any intention by younger users.

Right vs. Wrong   More realistic experiences could peer-validate bad behavior and, as often has happened with tech, reinforce stereotypes or prejudice.

Trauma   Intense or violent experiences may lead to terrible memories, especially due to the amplification that sometimes happens with dedicated immersive experiences.

Safety Controls

To enable health and medical benefits based on metaverse technologies, organizations will need to capture our data on body movement, eye tracking and pupillary response, hand gestures, voice, facial scans, and even internal biometric information such as heart rate, body temperature, and more. This is as personal as body data can be, and therefore it is important for businesses and professionals to identify the best methods to handle this personal health information (PHI) and personally identifiable information (PII).

Offering personal keys and continuously updating digital safety measures need to be standard business practice. As the metaverse ecosystem is growing and changing, it's also important to continuously keep up to speed on the policies, regulations, and laws, and even predicting those that have yet to be created. Some of the responsibility will be passed to business owners in the near term, and while Meta, for example, has invested or plans to invest billions in the metaverse, as of now, it has only $50 million allocated to privacy.[15]

Whether your company or industry has ventured far into these technologies, there are a few things to consider while transitioning into being ready for the metaverse and enabling your business to start coping:

Assign Ownership Make sure that someone within your organization begins to plan for future privacy issues and follows updates to standards.

Clear Opt-Ins Make sure that users of your services are aware of what you are tracking and what value it brings to them, and allow them to choose accordingly.[16]

Data Protection Plan for security breaches via AR/VR, AI, and offer security tools to employees.[17]

Partner Audit Identify when and where your company is responsible and make sure to understand (and influence) the policies of your partners.[18]

Privacy Policies Draft and share your company's approach to all kinds of data, assuming that there may be misuse.

Notes

1. Joris Toonders, "Data is the new oil of the digital economy." *Wired*, July 2014.www.wired.com/insights/2014/07/data-new-oil-digital-economy

2. *The Economist*, "The world's most valuable resource is no longer oil, but data." *The Economist*, May 6, 2017. www.economist.com/leaders/ 2017/05/06/the-worlds-most-valuable-resource-is-no-longer-oil-but-data

3. Shelly Kramer, "Metaverse privacy concerns: Are we thinking about our data?" *Forbes*, June 1, 2022. www.forbes.com/sites/forbestech council/2022/06/01/metaverse-privacy-concerns-are-we-thinking-about-our-data/?sh=253900f4ffb8

4. Shoshana Zuboff, *The Age of Surveillance Capitalism*, Profile Books, 2019, p. 233.

5. Euronews and Reuters, "Italy data authority seeks clarifications on privacy from Facebook over its new smart glasses." *Euronews*, November 9, 2021. www.reuters.com/technology/italy-data-authority-asks-facebook-clarifications-smart-glasses-2021-09-10

6. Jon Russell, "Chinese police are using smart glasses to identify potential suspects." *TechCrunch+*. http://techcrunch.com/2018/02/08/chinese-police-are-getting-smart-glasses

7. Identity Theft Resource Center, "Identity Theft Resource Center's annual data breach report sets new record for number of compromises." (Blog) Identity Theft Resource Center, January 24, 2022. www.idtheftcenter .org/post/identity-theft-resource-center-2021-annual-data-breach-report-sets-new-record-for-number-of-compromises

8. Roberto Hoyle et al., "Sensitive lifelogs: a privacy analysis of photos from wearable cameras." CHI '15: *Proceedings of the 33rd Annual ACM Conference on Human Factors in Computing Systems*, April 15, 2015. dl .acm.org/doi/10.1145/2702123.2702183

9. Dashveenjit Kaur, "Why Web3 isn't the privacy panacea we think it is." *Tech Wire Asia*, February 9, 2022. http://techwireasia.com/ 2022/02/why-web3-isnt-the-privacy-panacea-we-think-it-is

10. Queenie Wong, "As Facebook plans the metaverse, it struggles to combat harassment in VR." *CNET*, December 9, 2021. www.cnet.com/ features/as-facebook-plans-the-metaverse-it-struggles-to-combat-harassment-in-vr/#ftag=CAD-09-10aai5b

11. Michael Beckwith, "Facebook Meta patents would fill the metaverse with ads." *TechRadar*, January 18, 2022. www.techradar.com/news/ facebook-meta-patents-would-fill-the-metaverse-with-ads

12. Emily Everson Layden, "Rutgers researchers discover security vulnerabilities in virtual reality headsets." *Rutgers Today*, February 10, 2022. www.rutgers.edu/news/rutgers-researchers-discover-security-vulnerabilities-virtual-reality-headsets

13. Harry Baker, "Developers share record VR player & sales numbers across Christmas." *Upload VR*, December 30, 2021. http://uploadvr.com/vr-player-sales-numbers-christmas-2021

14. Nelson Reed, "What are kids doing in the metaverse?" *Common Sense*, March 23, 2022. www.commonsensemedia.org/kids-action/articles/what-are-kids-doing-in-the-metaverse

15. Shelly Kramer, 2022.

16. Shigraf Aijaz, 2022.

17. Shigraf Aijaz, "How we can mitigate the potential threat to data privacy in the metaverse." *VentureBeat*, April 12, 2022. http://venturebeat.com/2022/04/12/how-we-can-mitigate-the-potential-threat-to-data-privacy-in-the-metaverse

18. Norton Rose Fulbright, "The metaverse: The evolution of a universal digital platform." *Norton Rose Fulbright*, July 2021. www.nortonrosefulbright.com/en-us/knowledge/publications/5cd471a1/the-metaverse-the-evolution-of-a-universal-digital-platform

Chapter 11

New Rights and Regulations

It's almost like stealing people's data and giving it to a hyper-intelligent AI as part of an unregulated tech monopoly was a bad thing.

　　　　　—*Mark Bowman in The Mitchells vs. the Machines*

Unforeseen effects of technology can generate unwanted transformations that ultimately tilt our lifestyle. Even if it's uncomfortable, we need to discuss how emerging tech can be monitored and regulated. We don't have to cross our fingers and hope that Big Tech companies figure it out themselves (again).

As an article in *ZDNet* puts it, "You can be anything you want in The Metaverse, you just can't be in control."[1] The 2020 documentary drama *The Social Dilemma* brought to light how the best intentions for new technologies can have terrible consequences. Through these "based on a true story" movies and the interviews given by social media platform creators, it becomes scarily clear how small innovative discoveries and implementations can have negative societal implications.

For example, social media's data-driven, advertising-based business model influenced and still influences consumer behavior.

237

As the saying goes, "If you're not paying for the product, then you are the product." VR's founding father Jaron Lanier describes its power in the movie as "the gradual, slight, imperceptible change in your own behavior and perception that is the product." There is a very fine, almost imperceptible line between meaningful advertising and consumer manipulation. In the words of Harvard Professor Shoshana Zuboff in the movie, 'It's a marketplace that trades exclusively in human futures.'[2]

For a while, tech companies could say that the terms and conditions and privacy policy notices protected all parts from any repercussions. This kind of blind consent may be legal, but *legal* is different from *ethical*. Lifestyle-changing platforms like social media bring in new behaviors and ways for people to relate, so it's only natural that rules evolve and adapt as our behaviors transform these same platforms and aim toward trustful relationships. We have the benefit of hindsight into what went (and still is) wrong with the business models of the last technology revolutions, in order to best prepare the next stage of the Internet. No one believes that the transition will be smooth or without issues, but awareness and action can go a long way to reduce the risks and negative impacts.

Crypto Scams

We have seen safety issues stemming from the crypto marketplace. In the beginning, decentralized currencies were promoted as safer and more protected. In a 2018 article, NASDAQ listed "10 Ways Cryptocurrency Will Make the World a Better Place."[3] This included reducing the risk of fraud, keeping companies and individuals accountable for their actions, as well as increasing safety and reducing instability of currency.[4]

But the yearly value of cryptocurrency stolen by scammers almost doubled in 2021 as $14 billion[5] worth of tokens were transferred illegally. Crypto losses were 60 times worse in 2022 than five years earlier.[6] Decentralization is sold as safer, yet it also means the opportunity for wallets to be opened without having to present valid identification, a national tax ID, such as a Social Security number; or an address and contact information.

Still, at present, and unlike bank accounts, which are heavily regulated, you won't find the same levels of fraud protection on decentralized transactions. When you're scammed with cryptocurrencies, most probably the only way to recover your crypto is for the other user to willingly give it back to you—which is highly unlikely when you're dealing with a scammer.

While mainstream crypto-exchange platforms boast better fraud security measures than smaller ones, there's still no safe way to recover stolen crypto.

Crypto scams can assume several forms. The following examples show how creative scammers have already become:

Dating Scams   According to the U.S. Federal Trade Commission, about 20 percent of the money lost in romance scams from October 2020 through March 2021[7] was sent in the form of cryptocurrency. In most cases, the victims thought they were actually making an investment in a business held by someone they were romantically involved with.

Phishing Scams   The "Nigerian prince"-like phishing scams have entered the metaverse, with some nuances that weren't present before. Messages are sent to bait recipients into clicking links and sharing personal details and passwords, or in the case of a user's wallet, its secret key. Unlike most passwords and usernames to bank or trading accounts, this one private key rules over your blockchain wallet and is the only way for you to regain control of your wallet, if you were to lose access. This is part of blockchain's decentralized design, ensuring that one entity cannot control your information, but it poses an issue if someone else gets ahold of that same key.

Pump & Dump   New cryptocurrencies are constantly being minted and offered in initial coin offerings (ICOs). An organization or individual may announce this once-in-a-lifetime opportunity to invest in a new form of crypto with guarantees X percent returns. Demand is apparently very high as the issuing organization is also the one making most of the buying through different wallets. After the price soars, the owner sells all the coins and fraud happens.

Rug Pull   New services being launched (for example, play-to-earn games or through DAOs) lure potential newbie investors to become early birds in a newly minted coin or newly created token. Sometimes, the creators of these tokens, after the project receives an initial sum of funds, sell all their holdings, loot the organization, and empty the value of the currency.

And this is likely just the start of scamming schemes. If there is a way to make money and lots of it quickly, bad actors will find innovative ways to do so even if it is illegal, especially since there is no centralized authority looking to stop fraud and the transactions are not reversible.[8]

Money laundering with crypto is another real issue today. As the financial system is decentralized and global, it's no wonder that cybercriminals have started exploiting it. Privacy idealism inspired the creation of Monero, a cryptocurrency that saw a sharp growth in its value, as well as in the number of developers dedicated to guaranteeing that true fungibility is attained and its transactions remain untraceable. And, although there are ways to "mark" NFT transactions done with shady funds, their origins can be masked. Then, by selling the NFT, criminals trade it for new crypto and funds can become clean. Although this looks like a nifty little scheme that could be quite popular among criminals, according to *Traders Magazine*, Bitcoin has been used less for money laundering than plain old cash[9] and accounts for less than one percent of these crimes. . .so far.

Why is it important as a business owner to understand these new (illegal) behaviors? Acknowledging and keeping on identifying these new challenges will allow you to address them if you come across them, as well as to make the correct decisions when encountering these scenarios. It is key to develop and maintain trust for both professional and personal purposes, especially as we are shifting into an innovative way of business, where digital and physical come together.

New Medium and Platform Risks

Whenever people start working in and with a new medium, it's natural to refer to it in terms of the previous one. Think radio versus newspapers, TV versus radio, online video versus TV. Often the first creative work developed seems almost the same as the last. Eventually creators begin to understand the medium better and their work adapts accordingly. The same is true for rules and regulations.

VR and AR experiences themselves are still being compared to their on-screen counterparts. Most of the regulation available for all things digital and on a screen is applied equally to immersive worlds. However, users are already seeing a difference. There are parallels, yes, but the present version of the Internet is not the same as the metaverse.

Take, for example, pharmaceutical industry advertising within Europe. Physical advertising, such as cardboard cutouts, or *standees*, of pharmaceutical products within pharmacies is prohibited in several countries across Europe. Digital advertising enables a bending of that regulation. People waiting in line to get their prescriptions can receive ad messages on their phones or be exposed to these products while playing casual games.

Now if you consider augmented reality under the same regulation as digital advertising, there could be a 3D ad floating in the middle of the pharmacy. Currently, you will just see this ad on the screen of your mobile phone, but it will be visible in the coming years through other devices like headsets or smart glasses. Should this 3D ad follow the same regulation of a tiny ad served on your smartphone? What if that ad is persistent, almost like a physical object? What if it's interactive and you can play with the ad somehow? What if several users can play with it?

Should AR pharma advertising be regulated like a physical advertisement, like a digital one, or should a new setting be created? If all parts of the world are digitized and have the potential of advertising, should there be regulations as to what and where, even before it becomes possible? Should we allow metaverse ads to be viewable in schools, graveyards, or churches? Should we allow every kind of messaging anywhere? There are a ton of specific situations that need to be addressed and framed correctly so that the social and individual disruption we're going to feel is minimized. We need to have some guidelines in place before the bulk of the metaverse business opportunities arrive. We can't only rely on existing policies based on past assumptions. That is why organizations like the Interactive Advertising Bureau is already working on advertising standards for the metaverse.[10]

Metaverse Dark Web

The web has a dark corner, the notorious *dark web*, which is often featured in crime dramas with a black background and white, purple, bright green, and red graphics from the early 1990s. The likelihood of a metaverse version is quite high, or there could even be one as of the writing of this book.

The dark web was used initially to protect information without data tracking and monetization. This use wasn't what made it famous, though; it was child pornography, arms trafficking, drug dealing, neo-Nazi and extremist groups, counterfeit documents and goods, malware, hacking for hire and all related, criminal marketplaces. In 2011, Bitcoin currency was used.[11] Governments took action against the dark web and worked to remove user's anonymity. [12]

There is a justifiable fear that the metaverse will offer up a new, anonymized location and marketplace for illegal activities, that can now be more persistent and decentralized. Advocates for free expression and privacy need to be aware and not ignore this risk. When there is a new kind of medium, it's almost guaranteed that there are going to be bad actors exploiting it for profit illegally.

Challenges and Risks

Proactively looking at potential issues is a discipline known as *risk innovation*. Just as innovation is all about applying creativity to address specific needs and leverage opportunities in a new way, risk innovation is a concept that deals with the other side of the coin, acknowledging how creative approaches generate new challenges in our businesses and lives and how we can address them. Luckily, methodologies are available.

Arizona State University has created the Risk Innovation Nexus (http://riskinnovation.org). The framework, which is available on the website, asks you to identify the value that you want to obtain for your enterprise, investors, customers, or community. It then helps organizations navigate several kinds of existing risks, unintended consequences, and social and ethical factors through a set of specific tools. Its analysis also includes orphan risks, the ones easily overlooked, but usually the ones separating successful from unsuccessful businesses. Orphan risks include the consequences of emerging tech's ethical missteps, privacy abuse, public services disruption, and several other topics that most entrepreneurs tend to put outside of their sphere of interest but that frequently end up having a massive impact on their business outcome. The framework asks you to answer the what, why, and how to approaching specific risks—simplifying the approach to difficult potential problems.

Trust Across Worlds

Unfortunately, there isn't a quick fix or simple solution to any of the potential issues that will likely arise with emerging technology. "Our report emphasizes that nobody should treat AI as the solution to the spread of harmful online content," said Samuel Levine, director of the Federal Trade Commission's Bureau of Consumer Protection, upon presenting an FTC report, "Combatting Online Harms Through Innovation," in June 2022.[13] The report continues, "Combatting online harm requires a broad societal effort, not an overly optimistic belief that new technology—which can be both helpful and dangerous—will take these problems off our hands."[14] The same can be true for spatial computing and the next generation of tech.

Most services being rolled out have privacy policies that comply with legislation already passed and in effect across several countries.

In the United States, this legislation includes the Health Insurance Portability and Accountability Act (HIPAA), the Children's Online Privacy Protection Rule (COPPA) and the Fair Credit Reporting Act (FCRA); in the European Union, the General Data Protection Regulation (GDPR); in Brazil, the very similar General Data Protection Law (LGPD); in Canada, the Personal Information Protection and Electronic Documents Act (PIPEDA); and the Personal Information Protection Law in China (PIPL).[15] But these legal frameworks don't offer most of the answers to all privacy and safety issues arising from the metaverse.

Meta's Director of Human Rights, Miranda Sissons, explored this topic on a panel called "Human Rights and the Metaverse: Are We Already Behind the Curve?" saying, "Many of the salient risks are related to our behaviors as humans . . . . And many of those behaviors can be mitigated or prevented through guardrails, standards and design principles, as well as design priorities."[16]

Many believe that the UN Guiding Principles on Business and Human Rights should be considered a guideline for conduct worldwide as the metaverse develops and grows. This is particularly the case when it comes to communication and surveillance technologies that could interfere with free expression. Access Now and the Electronic Frontier Foundation (EFF) recommend using "strict data minimization" and "privacy-by-design" principles as a way to manage future potential problems.[17]

But just the mere fact that organizations use personal data in the metaverse the same way as they do on Web 2.0, to customize visual and sensorial experiences in order to promote their private interests is a level of neuromarketing that can unfairly influence individuals beyond their free will. Safeguarding the right for free thought in the metaverse is today a topic for discussion and, most probably, we'll need to protect more areas of our digital experience. For instance, one morbid example: digital death. Can a platform decide unilaterally to ban you from access to your avatar or outright delete it? Can a state decide to permanently ban a citizen's digital identity? Investors, activists, researchers, and communities, in addition to governments and businesses, are required to adhere to human rights standards and responsible practices with metaverse technologies.[18] One of the non-governmental organizations (NGOs) working to map out the privacy and safety issues that immersive worlds are bringing to businesses is the XR Safety Initiative (XRSI; http://xrsi.org). Besides continuously promoting best practices for privacy and safety in the metaverse, XRSI launched the first Privacy and Safety Framework in XR, a set of free and globally accessible ground rules created by a diverse set of experts. It is a baseline set of standards, guidelines, and best practices that are regulation-agnostic, and it includes requirements drawn from multiple global initiatives (for example, GDPR, the National Institute of Standards and Technology [NIST], the Family Educational Rights and Privacy Act [FERPA], and COPPA) and is bound to be updated periodically and as new regulations come into effect.

The framework is not a law itself, although it can inspire regulation, but is a tool to enable businesses to promote trust in the metaverse. It is divided into four focus areas: assess, inform, manage, and prevent.

Assess

Organizations and users inside them should understand how their devices use sensors to collect and use data. Privacy risks must be assessed to determine the impact on organizational operations, mission, and functions while taking into account other risk factors, such as human, societal, informational, and financial. The following are questions adapted from XRSI to help organizations assess their vulnerabilities:

Types   What are the various types of data required by your platform, service, or app? What is being collected, processed, and shared?

Legal   What is the legal basis for storing personal and sensitive data?

Third Parties   Which third parties will the data be shared with, and how will they be processing the data? How will they store it?

Process (Storage)   How long will the data be retained? What processes ensure that the data is stored securely? Where will it be stored (for example, on a device, on the cloud)?

Process (Safety)   Will the personal and sensitive XR data be encrypted, disidentified, obfuscated, and/or aggregated before storing or processing?

Process (Outside Company)   What processes are in place to communicate to customers, collaborators, and regulators what data is being collected and why?

Process (Breach)   What are the processes for responding to a data breach or any privacy incident in a timely manner?

Pipeline   What is the data collection pipeline?

Inform

As we discussed, tech companies often ask for consent for data usage, but the current practices are opaque to most. As the metaverse brings even more intimate types of data into play, like biometrics, consent becomes fundamental.

- Designing why, when, how, with whom, and where you intend to use data is key to empowering your customers to make informed decisions about how their data is processed. Your organization should strive to present this information in a clear, accessible, accurate, and timely manner. Even the design choices should be given careful thought to make the process easier for your customers. This is especially true for procedures that protect children's data.

- The Electronic Frontier Foundation's Katitza Rodriguez suggested additional training for tech employees: "You have to educate and train engineers, marketing teams, etc., on the importance of human rights and the consequence of their product to society. . . . How to mitigate human rights risks? Avoid including face recognition in the product. These are difficult choices to make."[19] Does mandatory digital human rights training need to be required by companies? We don't think that is the solution.

A broader perspective on potential human impact should be interwoven into the organization's business practices and accepted by all employees as metaverse data becomes an essential part of many, many parts of our lives.[20]

Manage

Your workforce and third-party partners should perform duties and responsibilities consistent with yours so that your customers are safeguarded from unnecessary risks from all sides:

- Organizations should establish and implement the processes to identify, assess, and manage privacy risks related to special data types, like biometrically inferred data (BID), such as:
  - Dactyloscopic data (fingerprint verification)
  - Ear shape recognition
  - Facial recognition
  - Gait analysis
  - Gaze analysis (eye-tracking)
  - Handwritten signature analysis
  - Iris scanning
  - Keystroke analysis
  - Retinal analysis
  - Voice recognition

This kind of data enables companies to create and develop "biometric psychography," which can reveal our inclinations and desires, even if we don't know them or want to know them. We should be understanding and regulating the diverse kinds of data harvesting before they begin being collected, before we realize all the potential for harm.[21]

Prevent

Security and privacy policies (for example, purpose, scope, roles, and responsibilities in the data processing ecosystem and management commitment), processes, and procedures are maintained and need to be updated. These policies should limit access to data and devices to authorized individuals, processes, and devices, as all good security policies dictate.

Consider adopting data security measures, such as encryption or pseudonymization, if necessary. Look into XR minimum security standards (for example, SANS15, NIST16, ISO17, CIS). Disaster recovery plans also should be set in place to address incident response and security breaches. Depending on the nature of your company, you should have detailed content moderation policies that, at a minimum, contain rules regarding violent/extremist content, hate speech, and other unlawful content.

New Rules for New Ways

Only covering your business practices, however, doesn't account for the decentralized systems that are being developed within the metaverse. There are still many questions to answer, such as:

- **Control:** Who controls decentralized personal data? Will each user be accountable, will there be custodians or even intermediary parties for this data?
- **Storage:** Where would the decentralized data be stored, since that can determine location and jurisdiction? Take DAOs, for instance—will they be responsible at any level for any data generated by their own activities?
- **Access:** How can a DAO respond to legal access requests, and which entities are required to respond in the case of such requests?
- **Deletion**: Who can delete or change personal information on and off the blockchain?

Privacy in the metaverse will become a key issue, and it's best to play both offense and defense with this new business reality.

As of this writing, there has not been an internationally coordinated regulation of crypto, although attempts have been made to define it. International organizations and central banks and regulators already are working in this field as countries from China to El Salvador are currently implementing different regulatory options. The Australian consumer advocacy group CHOICE is already acting on securing their future interactions with crypto: "Crypto assets are complex, volatile and high-risk products that can cause harm to Australian consumers," CHOICE stated. "Strong consumer protection laws are urgently needed to protect people from the significant harms."[22] The call for watchdog interventions and awareness campaigns as well as the establishment of age limits for investors were floated as possible measures to diminish risk in the field of cryptocurrency investment.

But there are also many regulatory gray areas on the metaverse:

Separating NFTs from the Purchased Item Itself   An NFT is a digital contract, not the item itself. It's similar to purchasing a house or a car or some artwork: You get a deed to certify you're the owner. The NFT is stored separately from the assets you purchased, it is on the blockchain—but not your item. So your item could be deleted, repossessed, or hacked, making the related NFT worth little or nothing. The law has not yet addressed this scenario for NFTs broadly. In the existing virtual worlds, metaverse property ownership is governed by contractual law, not property law, thus making the platform owner legally allowed to remove or transfer an item by unlinking the digital asset from the original NFT identification code under the terms of service.
Interoperability limitations also further restrict your ownership because most platforms do not allow users to export these items easily across platforms.

NFT IPR (Intellectual Property Rights)   Some buyers of an NFT think they own the property rights to the actual art, code, or product associated with the NFT. But most probably that is not the case. The only person with the right to copy, distribute, alter, or publicly display the art, for instance, is the creator of the art. So, when you buy the NFT, you're buying that item but not the copyright. So, you can profit from the sale of the digital goods you bought but not the licensing of it (for example, for merchandising).

Today, every buyer needs to conduct thorough due diligence, and if necessary, seek legal advice, to ensure they understand each and every aspect of an NFT purchasing process.

Royalties Payments   There are many benefits to artists when it comes to NFTs (although there are quite a lot of issues, such as people selling artwork that they don't own). One of the biggest ones is a change in the way that art is sold. Traditionally, artists financially benefit when their art is sold initially, but not in the resale market. This means that, in theory, if you are an artist who sold your piece for $1,000 today, you get the $1,000. But, a year from now, if your buyer sells your artwork for $10,000, they get all of the profit. So, you remain a starving artist, and the gallery owner or broker makes a handsome profit.

With NFTs, royalties can be paid to the creators each time an NFT changes hands. This means whenever an artwork is resold through an NFT, the contract might have a clause stating that the original artist gets a fee of the full transaction. This offers a great incentive to artists to continue to make work. However, even if such an obligation is placed within the agreement, enforcement is required, as some sellers might just choose to ignore it.

NFT Trading Rules   There aren't legal frameworks that safeguard NFT sales, especially given the international nature of them. Also, NFT sellers' and traders' authentication is being done in several ways across NFT online marketplaces, without observing any international standard, which helps the appearance of bad actors.

Data Protection   As we moved up the hype cycle for NFTs, there have been a lot of uses created for these blockchain-based contracts. Some NFTs may contain personal information, like photos or personal documents, which might violate data protection, laws. For instance, GDPR grants all European citizens the right to be forgotten[23] and to erase or amend their personal data. But in the case of NFTs, where everything is on the chain, that is not possible as there is no governing body, by definition.

Anything on the blockchain has the same potential issue, such as digital twins and behavioral data. This has received very little legal consideration as of yet. So, in the meantime, you need to understand how your organization approaches data privacy and safeguarding (for example, the amount of data and information that can and should be shared and registered on the blockchain).

NFT Taxation　This is one of the most notable areas of law that is lagging behind the development of NFTs, although governments are always very interested in obtaining new financial means to support their policies. While some accountants argue that profits and losses relating to NFTs are liable for capital gains tax and that NFTs themselves can be inherited, there is no official position from any government at this time and, again, the global nature of this trading makes it difficult to create a broad, international legal consensus.

Digital Beings　When our main interface with the metaverse is voice-activated, interactive, and can resemble humanoid figures, the way we'll interact with content will change, not just mechanically, but also as a whole social behavior. Organizations with access to the right data could create digital assistants able to mimic all the characteristics that a user finds interesting in other human beings.

As conversational AI evolves, digital assistants will be used to promote and sell in the metaverse. By analyzing a real-time user's facial expressions and vocal inflections, they're bound to pitch more skillfully and adapt their emotional tone in real time. There must be some way to differentiate digital humans and their AI-based algorithms from the real ones, like a metaverse version of #ad from Instagram. Regulating this relationship will be key to creating a trustful avatar ecosystem.

Ultimately, governments and regulatory institutions must address that our reality will increasingly operate in two converging dimensions, physical and virtual. There must be a multidimensional legal infrastructure for rights and compliance obligations. Regulators and lawmakers must gain a deeper knowledge of these technologies and their risks to support the creation of a safer, fairer, and more inclusive metaverse for all of us.

Notes

1. Tiernan Ray, "The Metaverse is a human rights dilemma." ZDNet, November 28, 2021. www.zdnet.com/article/the-metaverse-is-a-human-rights-dilemma

2. www.thesocialdilemma.com

3. Due.com, "10 ways cryptocurrency will make the world a better place." NASDAQ, January 16, 2018. www.nasdaq.com/articles/10-ways-cryptocurrency-will-make-the-world-a-better-place-2018-01-16

4. Due.com, 2018.

5. Chainalysis Team, "Crypto crime trends for 2022: Illicit transaction activity reaches all-time high in value, all-time low in share of all cryptocurrency activity." Chainalysis, January 6, 2022. blog.chainalysis.com/reports/2022-crypto-crime-report-introduction

6. Emma Fletcher, "Reports show scammers cashing in on crypto craze." Federal Trade Commission, June 3, 2022. www.ftc.gov/news-events/data-visualizations/data-spotlight/2022/06/reports-show-scammers-cashing-crypto-craze

7. Emma Fletcher, "Cryptocurrency buzz drives record investment scam losses." *Data Spotlight*, May 17, 2021. www.ftc.gov/news-events/data-visualizations/data-spotlight/2021/05/cryptocurrency-buzz-drives-record-investment-scam-losses

8. Emma Fletcher, 2021.

9. Martin Cheek, "Is cryptocurrency making money laundering easier?" *Traders Magazine*, June 19, 2021. www.tradersmagazine.com/departments/regulation/is-cryptocurrency-making-money-laundering-easier

10. https://martechvibe.com/news/iab-updates-guidelines-for-measuring-3d-ads-for-the-metaverse

11. U.S. Immigration and Customs Enforcement, "Ross Ulbricht, aka Dread Pirate Roberts, sentenced to life in federal prison for creating, operating 'Silk Road' website." U.S. Immigration and Customs Enforcement, May 29, 2015. www.ice.gov/news/releases/ross-ulbricht-aka-dread-pirate-roberts-sentenced-life-federal-prison-creating#

12. Aditi Kumar and Eric Rosenbach, "The Truth about the Dark Web." September 2019. www.imf.org/en/Publications/fandd/issues/2019/09/the-truth-about-the-dark-web-kumar.

13. Federal Trade Commission, "Combatting online harms through innovation." Federal Trade Commission report, June 2022. www.ftc.gov/reports/combatting-online-harms-through-innovation

14. Jose Rascon, "FTC report warns about over relying on artificial intelligence." MeriTalk, June 21, 2022. www.meritalk.com/articles/ftc-report-warns-about-over-relying-on-artificial-intelligence

15. i-Sight Software, "A practical guide to data privacy laws by country [2021]." i-Sight, March 5, 2021. www.i-sight.com/resources/a-practical-guide-to-data-privacy-laws-by-country

16. Derek Robertson, "Human rights in the metaverse." *Politico*, June 7, 2022. www.politico.com/newsletters/digital-future-daily/2022/06/07/human-rights-in-the-metaverse-00037853

17. www.accessnow.org/human-rights-metaverse-virtual-augmented-reality

18. Katitza Rodriguez et al., 2021.

19. www.politico.com/newsletters/digital-future-daily/2022/06/07/human-rights-in-the-metaverse-00037853

20. Derek Robertson, 2022.

21. Katitza Rodriguez et al., 2021.

22. Josh Taylor, "'Complex and volatile': Cryptocurrencies should be regulated by financial watchdogs, say consumer advocates." *The Guardian*, May 30, 2022. www.theguardian.com/technology/2022/may/31/complex-and-volatile-cryptocurrencies-should-be-regulated-by-financial-watchdogs-say-consumer-advocates

23. Intersoft Consulting, "Right to be forgotten." *GDPR Key Issues*, n.d. http://gdpr-info.eu/issues/right-to-be-forgotten

Chapter 12

The New Humanity

Reality exists in the human mind and nowhere else.
—George Orwell, 1984

One of the most exciting parts about working in emerging technologies is a sense of contributing directly to creating the future. In the coming years, we will be able to explore hybrid spaces and interact in physical and digital ways we are just starting to discover. Some of these societal transformations will be harder to perceive, while others can have a much larger impact on our entire world. Think, for example, how the Internet and mobile computing created an always-on culture. We didn't realize how much of a change it made until it had already happened. We know already that the metaverse will change the way we work, we socialize, and we live. We won't be able to say how much until it happens.

The Impact of Data

Beyond the technology advancements themselves, we already established that the data generated will play the most important role in the upcoming metaverse and how we'll deal with it will define the future of business and society. "You can't manage what you don't measure" are words of wisdom usually attributed to W. Edwards Deming and Peter Drucker, repeated year after year in management schools across the globe.

This belief in data as the absolute solution to one's business—and to societal challenges in general—is referred to as *data-ism*, a term coined by *New York Times* writer and political commentator David Brooks.[1] It implies that by analyzing big amounts of data, we can efficiently solve any problem, any dilemma we might encounter in complex organizations and, yes, in society. As such, it's almost similar to an ideology where data is more important than any other human measure or value and the reasoning behind gathering or analyzing it is self-justified by the benefits it brings. So, issues like personal privacy are pushed aside in the search for the necessary data to solve problems.[2]

Big Data is a simplified term used when there is so much data that it can't be analyzed easily given the parameters needed. In these cases, you need algorithmic support, like AI and ML, to process that raw data and extract the necessary insights for decision makers. Algorithms digest it, analyze it, and identify patterns, no matter how subtle, so they can provide meaningful analysis.

Big Data brought about several business model shifts. It birthed Amazon, for example, changing the bookselling business, and eventually all of retail. Amazon demonstrated how live customer and sales tracking could predict how potential and current customers navigated the website, which product links were clicked the most, and how much promotions, reviews, and page layouts influenced each and every sale. Traditional retailers were left behind, mainly because gathering this information was simply not feasible in a brick-and-mortar location. Big Data before analysis essentially put many retailers out of business.

This didn't happen just in retail. "A typical . . . intensive care unit (ICU) generates an estimated 160,000 data points *a second*," shared Steve Lohr, *New York Times* journalist and author of the book *Data-ism*. "Amid all that data, informed and distracted by it, doctors and nurses make decisions at a rapid clip, about 100 decisions a day per patient, according to research at Emory. Or more than 9.3 million decisions about care during a year in an ICU. So, there is ample room for error."[3]

Basically, more data doesn't mean better decision-making. It does mean more opportunities to track and more opportunities to analyze, but this is not inherently a more effective business. Although sometimes users decide to delegate decisions to automated services, it's important to remember that AI remains a tool, not a decision maker.

The overwhelming amount of Big Data on Amazon or in that ICU unit is small in comparison to the unprecedented amount that will be generated by metaverse services. The initial challenges will be to gather, process, and analyze this data at a heretofore unheard-of speed. It's not surprising that new data sources are already becoming available, as we use biometric commands (for example, gesture or voice) and access immersive experiences anywhere.

Our behavior changed with the Internet through data usage, and we will shift again. It likely will change how we experience and remember the world we live in. It also will bring about even more debates about how we create, store, access, and analyze data individually, socially, and collectively at work, and how we are governed through it.

The move to the metaverse will be focused not just on data gathering, analysis, and predictions based on our search and purchasing behaviors and social media, as with the Internet. It will reap the data from our interactions within the physical world as well, as digital and physical will be interwoven; it will gather information from every object, building, space, and entity, be it physical or digital, that we interact with.

The amount of potential change and unanswered questions about how data affects the metaverse is overwhelming:

Access   How important will data technology be in our work life? Will it be like having a computer and Internet connection, or will it become a basic human right? Will there be gatekeeper services for data in the metaverse, digital beings that can help users enforce their data preferences?

Creativity   If we can program an algorithm to make an artwork, is it any less art? Are there going to be new kinds of hybrid instruments that musicians can play? If AI corrects or adds to our creation process, are artists still true artists?

Data Storage and Use   Beyond the massive amount of location and power needed to handle the metaverse dimension of our lives, more personal issues will crop up. For example, how long and where do we keep all this data? If we have a decentralized way to maintain control over our data, will we have to support costs of storing it or will it be another public service to consider? And how much of it will be tradeable? Will that open a new market by itself?

Foresight   Will we begin to rely on AI and ML to make predictive models so accurate that we can surrender minor and even bigger decisions to it? How much of our data are we willing to provide in order to get better decisions? Will we delegate some of our daily decisions to digital assistants? The same way we can program our smart fridge to order milk when several conditions apply, can we also program an assistant to cast a vote for a political party if a specific set of conditions are met?

Friendships   Is it possible to build meaningful relationships with digital beings? If we only recognize someone virtually by their avatars, can they still become really our friends if we haven't met them in our physical lives? As the metaverse draws closer and this hybrid dimension allows us to socialize at a distance but spatially, will new forms of relationships be born from this? Will there be a new name for these kinds of friends?

Governments   Who will be in charge of digital locations? Who will enforce law and order in the metaverse? With currencies, strong communities, and a decentralized view of society, will we see the rise of digital nations? If users can create digital and hybrid worlds aligned with their social beliefs and their ethics, what kind of motivation will they have to drive change in our old, physical one as citizens?

Immortality   How far are we willing to push science and technology and let data change our lives? What if data is used to ease the grief of a lost loved one, as it enables a digital twin of that very same person, run by an AI that is able to talk with us and reply to questions in the same way that person did?

Learning   If we can travel to any destination virtually or make any physical object appear in AR in the classroom, how does that change teaching techniques and lesson plans? What about when there are more sophisticated AI versions of teachers? If digital humans of celebrated economists, scientists, and business-people can help teachers in the classroom and be valuable educational resources, how will that change the profession and the way teachers follow up on the learning needs of their students?

Memory   If we can record and bring up the exact capture of a situation, do we need to rely on our biological memory anymore? How do our conversations and interactions change if we have data stored about all of our interactions that we can easily access? Will it be good to have "total memory recall" and tap into a backup of each and every conversation? What about privacy—how will it be safeguarded in this scenario?

Work   If we can send digital beings to work on our behalf, is that legally understood as work or is it more like how we treat a computer? What kinds of new jobs will be created for digital humans? By owning and controlling several digital assistants, and owning their data, will we need to fulfill specific conditions?

Reality   If this new digital dimension is able to create shared experiences and shared memories and inspire us all to do more, won't this new dimension feel real? Digital is not physical, but how will we redefine the word "real"?

Socialization   How do our interactions change if we all experience others interacting with digital objects and people we cannot see physically? How does that affect conversations and ultimately relationships?

Travel   Will we need to visit a physical location to have it be a trip? Or could we be going to virtual locations for a vacation? With our data, each tourism experience can be customized to best fit our expectations, from the digital tour guide that explains to us what we see, to the augmented reality experiences on location.

How will we share these experiences? Will we still share photos from our vacations or volumetrically captured, interactive experiences instead?

Reality, Digital, Technology

The huge opportunities and the many debates around data gathering, use, and analysis in the metaverse usually focus mostly on the digital side of it. This following outlines a few of the technologies that will generate data from the physical side of the metaverse.

IoT (Internet of Things)

We have touched on IoT several times in this book. IoT consists of the networks between objects and devices connected to the Internet via embedded technologies, usually in combination with AI/ML and cloud computing. IoT uses multiple kinds of sensors (for example, temperature, pressure, motion, humidity, chemical, and optical) to monitor devices and the environment, and the sensors use algorithms to define when to take action. In this way, they are data generators and processors.

You can find IoT examples in the home, such as kitchen appliances, as well as industrial IoT, focused on business and industrial applications. M2M (machine-to-machine) applications are built on top of IoT in order to optimize the efficiency and reliability of more complex systems that are behind the move toward smart cities.

Already today, lighting poles, roads, and traffic lights generate data that can be cross-referenced with other data sets. Already a large number of cities like Lisbon, Toronto, and Chennai have their own Open Data available, where they share some of this wealth of information in the hope new services can leverage public data and be offered to the population. Increasingly, more equipment will be added to the network, and smart cities will become fully interconnected places that can communicate with us, make us safer, and engage with us to participate in the community.

Wearables

Sensors aren't limited to inanimate objects. We actually wear them too. VR and AR glasses are themselves wearable technologies and they aren't the only ones. Fitbit, the Apple Watch, and heartbeat or blood pressure monitors are other examples. If you have smart headphones, or some smart sneakers like Xiaomi Mijia shoes[4] or a piece of smart clothing like Levi's Commuter x Jacquard jacket,[5] they also are wearables. Companies like Neuralink, Neurable, and NextMind are investing in brain–computer interfaces (BCIs) that process data signals streaming directly from our brain. Technologies in use today include EEG/EMG (electroencephalography/electromyography), ECoG (electrocorticography), and functional magnetic resonance imaging (fMRI).

There are three levels of BCIs: *noninvasive* (for example, EEGs), *partially invasive* (implanted within the skull but not in gray matter), and *invasive* (surgically implanted technologies). There are active devices that issue commands and passive devices that primarily monitor.[6] BCIs are mainly being used in the treatment of Alzheimer's, Parkinson's, major depression, epilepsy, and there are also efforts in development to give paralyzed patients robotic limb movement, "sight" to the blind, and "hearing" to the deaf.

Data about human brain activity can then be gathered and processed along with the other data we mentioned. Their benefits are touted for health and well-being. Of course, this is where we need to draw a line. What kind of data will be acceptable to gather and who will own it? For example, as sensors improve, our wearables warn us to go to the doctor before we even feel it ourselves. But how much health data do you want to share? Is there a right amount? Will we begin to treat symptoms that aren't necessary because the data shows it's an issue? Or because the algorithms created by health providers push for that?

"The next frontier in technology is inside our own bodies," shares Amy Webb in her book, *The Genesis Machine*. "Should there be limits to human enhancements? What cyber-biological risks are looming?"[7] Biologists and other scientists will have the ability to decipher the secrets of the human body. More data flows and more machines enable faster and more meaningful data processing power, that will then become accessible to AI services. These technology platforms will potentially understand biological humans much better than we understand ourselves and, again, we might feel tempted to delegate decisions about our health to them on our behalf.

Naturally, the invasive implantable end of the spectrum of BCIs tends to invoke the most ethical debates. Elon Musk talks about implantable technology as if it's an inevitability for all of us.[8] But of course, it is not. Data collection can and most probably will have a bigger impact on our physical bodies. Just how much is what we need to decide. Before understanding how this data can be used, we need to answer the bigger ethical questions around a seemingly elective surgery for healthy individuals. Do benefits outweigh risks? Do we know the impact? What kind of information will be public or private? How will it be regulated?

Robotics

Robots will also be part of the metaverse. They'll offer much more data for analysis, because they can perform tasks autonomously and continuously send a flow of data from specific processes, or they can act as the physical surrogate of a person within the metaverse (for example, an operator at home connects via virtual reality to operate a robot remotely). CEO and co-founder of InOrbit Florian Pestoni stated in *Forbes* that the Robotverse is already here, while we wait on the metaverse to be created. Examples shared are autonomous mobile robots (AMRs) that manage simple tasks and cobots which are collaborative robots that perform tasks side by side with human operators.[9]

Robots' data will connect to the rest of the metaverse's in many ways and will be generated from the six primary areas of any robot: operator interface, its mobility, its programming, its perception, the manipulators, and the effectors.[10] The interface is referred to as the human–robot interface: It could be a gaming controller or, in an enterprise, a touchscreen through which a human operator controls the robot. Mobility refers to the robot's ability of moving around a designated area. It can have several humanoid movements or animal-like movements, like those of Boston Dynamics, or flying drones or wheeled rovers. Perception refers to the sensors that help a robot control its situational awareness and fulfill its predetermined tasks. Finally, effectors and manipulators are the robot's ends that interact with the environment it's in, like an end-of-arm-tool (EOAT), hand-like, for gripping or grabbing purposes.

As many machines become more sophisticated and perform more tasks, the promise of more comprehensive data to be reaped also increases. A stream of data can be sent without interruption from any of these machines, which usually hold a host of sensors and cameras. Specifically, self-driving cars and exoskeletons are two of the most innovative types of robotics today that could have a large impact on our experiences in the metaverse. Remote operations also can have a huge impact on the medical and manufacturing industries as well as the military.

Self-Driving Cars

At the Consumer Electronics Show (CES) 2022, Hyundai's CEO made the direct connection to the metaverse by referring to what self-driving cars do as "metamobility."[11] As drivers will be turned into passengers, a whole host of new experiences can happen inside a car:meetings to games to new ways to enjoy the trip itself through AR windows. These experiences will leverage the data from multiple sensors embedded in the vehicles (for example, Lidar [Light Detection and Ranging], radar, computer vision, GPS) plus inertial measurement units (IMUs), such as accelerometers and gyroscopes, to detect movement.[12] The cars already use this data to make their own autonomous decisions in what is called *sensor fusion.*

The data from these autonomous robotic trucks and cars will become available in the Big Data melting pot of the metaverse, or, hopefully, just in your own private data pool. Google has already used self-driving cars to support its map development, and it's likely that all autonomous cars will crowdsource this effort in the long run.[13] Where you are going, what you are doing, when you are stopping, and who you are with can all be a part of your digital twin—all gathered and assessed and analyzed with future behaviors inferred to give you a more seamless and optimized experience or an extremely invasive look inside your life.

Exoskeletons

Exoskeletons are another type of robotics, but one that is directly connected to our bodies. These wearable mechanical suits or devices encase an operator's body and assist its movement, while augmenting its physical capabilities. Exoskeleton discussion explores the sense, the decision, and the execution of an action. There's cognitive human–robot interaction (cHRI) concerning how they are controlled and then the physical human–robot interaction (pHRI) focused on how they act[14]—once again, with lots of sensor data that can be integrated and analyzed for white or black hat means.

As of this writing, there are 128 companies working worldwide on building and supplying exoskeletons for both business and consumer audiences.[15] Common uses are to help a person walk or reduce physical hindrances; enhance muscle work and help in physical rehabilitation processes; aid in training professional athletes; or allow safe heavy lifting for human workers by leveraging the power existing in robotic arms.

It's All Connected

Eventually all of these devices and data sources will be interconnected. There won't just be an integration of real and virtual, but also the technology around, on, and in us. We won't just be tracking where we are going and what we are doing, and all of it will be available to be analyzed by a superpowered AI engine, cross-referencing data in the digital and physical planes, as a physical person or as an avatar.

This analysis isn't just overwhelming to think about; it will be overwhelming for technology companies to manage. We know that in the metaverse, the amount of data needed to enable the synchronization between digital and physical alone, enabling a true hybrid world, is unimaginable. "Big" isn't a strong enough term to define it. There's also all the data from transactions happening between users and these services or between users themselves. This dataflow can and will be constantly captured by cameras, sensors, and microphones and fed into processing systems.

If you already think there are so many opportunities for mishap, think again. We are just beginning to grapple with what's coming. It's no wonder that the data-ist view considers data as a being. In the words of historian Yuval Noah Harari, "In its extreme form, proponents perceive the entire universe as a flow of data, see organisms as little more than biochemical algorithms, and believe that humanity's cosmic vocation is to create an all-encompassing data-processing system—and then merge into it."[16]

Where's the Line?

Data has helped us create new digital experiences and will eventually create a new, persistent one called the metaverse. So why is it important we keep innovating and gathering more data for these experiences? One reason is that we want to improve the human condition; to progress as a society; to be faster, better, stronger; and to prevent sickness. We want to reduce the number of mistakes, to improve capacity, to increase our speed for analysis. We also love to find new things, make new insights and discoveries, and use creative tools. But some technologies beg the question of where we draw the line. When are we going beyond a need to a want or desire?

Singularity

Raymond Kurzweil, an acclaimed futurist and Google's Director of Engineering, believes that the pace of technological innovation is picking up and that the next 50 years are bringing not just a set of disruptive technologies but a major one that will fundamentally change the nature of human beings. He called it the *Singularity*:

It's a merger between human intelligence and machine intelligence that is going to create something bigger than itself. It's the cutting edge of evolution on our planet. One can make a strong case that it's actually the cutting edge of the evolution of intelligence in general, because there's no indication that it's occurred anywhere else. To me that is what human civilization is all about. It is part of our destiny and part of the destiny of evolution to continue to progress ever faster, and to grow the power of intelligence exponentially.[17]

Kurzweil even calculated the year when this major transformation is set to happen: "I have also set the date 2045 for singularity— which is when humans will multiply our effective intelligence a billion fold, by merging with the intelligence we have created."[18] He also claims that "By 2029, computers will have human-level intelligence.[19] Singularity in this context refers to that point in time when all advances in technology, particularly in artificial intelligence, will lead to machines smarter than human beings. He adds, "Today, that's not just a future scenario, it's partly here, and it's going to accelerate."[20]

Some have said that the Singularity already happened and that in some ways machine intelligence leveraged all data available and has already passed human intelligence. For instance, the late Stephen Hawking claimed that the Singularity happened in 2014. Others believe it was in 2016, when Google DeepMind AlphaGo defeated Lee Sedol, the Go world champion.[21, 22]

Besides being a heated debate around a table of developers and tech executives, the discussion of the Singularity focuses on how sophisticated will technology become and what should we do when it becomes sentient and smarter than we are. When AI becomes smarter than humans (note that it's no longer an "if it does"), what kind of decisions should be given to AI and what should remain solidly in the capacity of humans? Just because AI could eventually make all our decisions doesn't mean it should.

Post-Humanism

After a discussion around AI optimizing human decisions, the conversation soon turns to a debate around creating superhuman powers.

This decision isn't a fantastical Marvel or DC Comics–like choice between a radioactive spider (Spider-Man), Super-Soldier Serum (Captain America), or implanted claws (Wolverine). There are actual everyday examples of human augmentation currently in place or on the near horizon. Let's separate them into three categories that are presented in order from least to most debated:

Replication   When technology is created to imitate our physical capabilities and help us compensate for losses (e.g., reading glasses, hearing aids).

Supplementation   When we wear technology or even implant tech in our body (e.g., wearables, exoskeletons).

Exceeding   When the goal is to surpass human abilities (e.g., nanobots, artificial blood cells, artificial limbs).

The first two are generally accepted by most people familiar with or who use technology. The third comes to light when people discuss post-humanism. It is debatable whether post- is the right prefix— probably a comparative-level prefix would be more accurate (for example, meaning a "better" human). Someone with a post-human trait is defined by having "a general central capacity greatly exceeding the maximum attainable by any current human being without recourse to new technological means," according to philosopher Nick Bostrom, who spearheaded the concept and identified in 2008 three main areas of our lives where we can be technologically enhanced:[23]

- In our health and life span, by remaining fully healthy and active throughout the years, both mentally and physically
- In our own intellectual capacities, such as faster memory, analysis, and calculus functions in our brains, as well as our deductive thinking
- In our emotions and our capacity to enjoy life, understanding humor and music, and creating new meaningful forms of expression

Post-humanity isn't about life after humanity but about how to push the human race beyond its natural limits. Those who follow post-humanism believe that this is ultimately the goal of humanity.

According to Bostrom, transhumans are the first step to this movement. To become a transhuman, he says, is to see human evolution as "a work-in-progress, a half-baked beginning that we can learn to remold in desirable ways . . . by responsible use of science, technology and other rational means . . with vastly greater capacities than present humans."[24] There is a focus on making technological symbiosis evolutionary. Transhumanists state that not only *can* we be amplified through technology but that we *should* do it so that we can achieve the greater good and strive for the improvement of the human condition as a whole. So, natural evolution should give way to a human-guided evolutionary process.

As expected, artists have begun to experiment in the space. The artist Neil Harbisson overcame his full color blindness with the help of an antenna-like sensor implanted in his head, which translates different wavelengths into vibrations on his skull, which he then perceives as sound. Dubbed as the world's first official cyborg, (since his official passport photo includes his headgear), Harbisson sees technological augmentation as something that expands his connection to everything else: "My understanding of the world has become more profound. The more you extend your senses, the more that you realize exists. If you're in the same house for years, there's a repetition of what you perceive there. If you add a new sense, though, the house becomes new again."[25] He considers his antenna to be a part of his body.[26]

The limits of what the metaverse and technological convergence can be are still being explored, but positions like these aren't as obscure as you might assume or what your gut might tell you. Post-humanist research and institutes are being funded by billionaires like Peter Thiel and technologists like Vitalik Buterin and Ray Kurzweil, and there is a transhumanist political party present in more than 10 countries.[27] So although it's not likely to be a discussion in your boardroom, understanding the topic helps you envision the far horizon, keeps you prepared for future challenges, and can help you make better decisions.

Those who disagree with the beliefs of the post-humanism and transhumanist perspective question their outright focus on making technological enhancements a central part of our evolution, and, morally, a central part of our purpose as human beings—whether doing so clashes with human rights, deontological codes, and ethical standpoints. Do we really want to become a world filled with cyborgs and a metaverse that taps into the biggest data pool ever to feed digital assistants and make our lives easier but less private? That's essentially the debate.

We Don't Know . . . Yet

Because we are faced with so many unanswered questions and unsolved technical challenges, there should be no shame in saying, "I don't know" or "We don't know" when asked about the future. That type of answer tends to make everyone uncomfortable. No investor wants to hear that. Probably your shareholders wouldn't be thrilled either. But not knowing has led to a lot of debate about what comes next. This question could have hundreds of answers depending on your role and your field. Being willing to understand the uncertainty is expected can make one more willing to look for and find answers.

The potential is great for inaccurate information and opportunities for people to say that they can predict the future. The idea of the metaverse, John Carmack says, can be "a honeypot trap for 'architecture astronauts.'" Those are the programmers and designers who "want to only look at things from the very highest levels" while skipping the "nuts and bolts details" of how these things actually work.[28]

But everyone must learn to deal with this challenge. Stress testing the reality of a future vision. You can have blue sky plans and ideas—you can wish and hope for the best, easiest, most sophisticated technology solutions, but what is possible now and what is possible in the near future operates with a given budget. These so-called architecture astronauts make Carmack "just want to tear [his] hair out . . . because that's just so not the things that are actually important when you're building something."[29]

Although only a relative few are building the tech, it isn't just those talented creators who will impact our future. But the metaverse will change all of us, whether or not we can code. And code is not the most important part, we are. For better and for worse, we are in this together.

Notes

1. David Brooks, "The philosophy of data." *New York Times*, February 4, 2013. www.nytimes.com/2013/02/05/opinion/brooks-the-philosophy-of-data.html

2. www.techopedia.com/definition/14808/data-ism

3. Steve Lohr, *Data-ism: The Revolution Transforming Decision Making, Consumer Behavior, and Almost Everything Else.* HarperCollins, 2015.

4. www.androidcentral.com/xiaomi-mi-smart-shoes-review

5. www.levi.com/US/en_US/sale/mens-sale/outerwear/levis-commuter-x-jacquard-by-google-trucker-jacket/p/286600000

6. Amaia Benitez-Andonegui et al., "An augmented-reality fNIRS-based brain-computer interface: A proof-of-concept study." *Frontiers in Neuroscience*, April 28, 2020. www.frontiersin.org/articles/10.3389/fnins.2020.00346/full#

7. Amy Webb and Andrew Hessel, *The Genesis Machine: Our Quest to Rewrite Life in the Age of Synthetic Biology.* PublicAffairs Books, 2022.

8. Jeremy Kahn and Jonathan Vanian, "Inside Neuralink, Elon Musk's mysterious brain chip startup: A culture of blame, impossible deadlines, and a missing CEO." *Fortune*, January 27, 2022. http://fortune.com/longform/neuralink-brain-computer-interface-chip-implant-elon-musk

9. Florian Pestoni, "Forget the metaverse — the roboverse is already here." *Forbes*, February 16, 2022. www.forbes.com/sites/forbestechcouncil/2022/02/16/forget-the-metaverse---the-roboverse-is-already-here/?sh=5b054d674229

10. George Brown College, "Understanding the 5 primary areas of robotics." Robotics Technician Training Center, July 22, 2020. www.onlinerobotics.com/news-blog/understanding-5-primary-areas-robotics

11. CNET, "The future of physical robots in the Metaverse explained by Hyundai exec." YouTube, January 4, 2022. www.youtube.com/watch?v=-AGd_6WS71g

12. Udacity Team, "How self-driving cars work: Sensor systems." Udacity, March 3, 2021. www.udacity.com/blog/2021/03/how-self-driving-cars-work-sensor-systems.html#

13. Mark Bergen, "Google won the last maps war. Self-driving cars give other mapmakers a chance to find their own way." *Los Angeles Times*, February 22, 2018. www.latimes.com/business/technology/la-fi-hy-self-driving-maps-20180221-story.html

14. Konstantinos Sirlantzis, Layla Bashir Larsen, Lakshmi Krisha Kanumuru, and Paul Oprea, "Exoskeleton (robotics)," excerpted from *Handbook of Electronic Assistive Technology*, Donna Cowan and Ladan Najafi, eds., Academic Press, 2019. www.sciencedirect.com/topics/engineering/exoskeleton-robotics

15. https://exoskeletonreport.com/exoskeleton-companies-and-organizations-directory

16. Yuval Noah Harari, "Yuval Noah Harari on big data, Google and the end of free will." *Financial Times*, August 25, 2016. www.ft.com/content/50bb4830-6a4c-11e6-ae5b-a7cc5dd5a28c

17. Ray Kurzweil, "The singularity: A talk with Ray Kurzweil." *Edge*, March 24, 2001. www.edge.org/conversation/ray_kurzweil-the-singularity

18. Christianna Reedy, "Futurism: Building the future together." *Futurism*, October 5, 2017. www.kurzweilai.net/futurism-ray-kurzweil-claims-singularity-will-happen-by-2045

19. Christianna Reedy, 2017.

20. Christianna Reedy, 2017.

21. Unikey Word, "Technological Singularity." *Unikey Word*, January 29, 2015. unikeyword.wordpress.com/2015/01/29/technological-singularity/comment-page-1

22. Dirk Schulze-Makuch, "Reaching the singularity may be humanity's greatest and last accomplishment." *Air & Space Magazine*, March 27, 2020. www.airspacemag.com/daily-planet/reaching-singularity-may-be-humanitys-greatest-and-last-accomplishment-180974528

23. Nick Bostrom, "Why I want to be a posthuman when I grow up." In *Medical Enhancements and Posthumanity*, Bert Gordijn and Ruth Chadwick, eds., Springer, 2008. https://nickbostrom.com/posthuman.pdf

24. Nick Bostrom, "Transhumanist ethics." nickbostrom.com, n.d. https://nickbostrom.com/ethics/transhumanist.pdf

25. Michelle Z. Donahue, "How a color-blind artist became the world's first cyborg." *National Geographic*, April 3, 2017. www.nationalgeographic.com/science/article/worlds-first-cyborg-human-evolution-science

26. Neil Harbisson, "I listen to color." YouTube, July 20, 2012. https://youtu.be/ygRNoieAnzI

27. H+Pedia, "Transhumanist political organisations." *h+pedia*, July 23, 2020. https://hpluspedia.org/wiki/Transhumanist_political_organisations

28. Brendan Sinclair, "Oculus' John Carmack skeptical about efforts to build the metaverse." gamesindustry.biz, October 29, 2021. www.gamesindustry.biz/articles/2021-10-29-oculus-john-carmack-skeptical-about-efforts-to-build-the-metaverse

29. Brendan Sinclair, 2021.

Part 5

Preparation

Chapter 13
Building the Metaverse

Life doesn't happen to be something that just happens to us.
—*Guy (played by Ryan Reynolds), Free Guy*

We shared with you our vision of a fully grown metaverse: a hybrid universe with a physical world filled with gateways to a persistent digital dimension where users can use, own, trade, search, and co-build new kinds of objects, relationships, and spaces. Digital humans will populate these worlds and will be our primary access points to goods and services. Our identity cards, avatars, data, currency, and property will increasingly become persistent elements in our phygital experience. A regulatory, legal, and governmental framework needs to come into place to establish the trustful environment we all need to do business and work safely.

This vision is being enabled by the technology building blocks being developed as you are reading this. The distribution and advancement of these underlying technologies is happening every day. Technical acronyms abound while this happens, much like the early days of the Internet, when the infrastructure and tools were being built, and most people didn't have a clear understanding of how to use a browser. Remember when the word "google" didn't exist as a generic replacement for online searching?

In March 1998, *Harvard Business Review* warned readers of the coming shift in business practices with the rise of that weird platform called "the Internet":

> Established businesses that over decades have carefully built brands and physical distribution relationships risk damaging all they have created when they pursue commerce in cyber-space. What's more, Internet commerce is such a new phenomenon— and so much about it is uncertain and confusing—that it is difficult for executives at most companies, new or old, to decide the best way to use the channel. (. . .) Nonetheless, managers can't afford to avoid thinking about the impact of Internet commerce on their businesses. At the very least, they need to understand the opportunities available to them and recognize how their companies may be vulnerable if rivals seize those opportunities first. To determine what opportunities and threats the Internet poses, managers should focus in a systematic way on what the Internet can allow their particular organization to do.[1]

Today, you can almost replace the words "Internet" and "cyberspace" in this quote with "metaverse."

Now we have the experience of creating and building digital platforms, and this time around, we have the experience and the time to plan ahead. We can create the version of the metaverse we think is best, and we can make it better than the present version of the web. Can you imagine what could have happened if we actively worked our way to prevent the effects of fake news on social media? Or anticipated the habits we acquired with smartphones? We have the opportunity to build a metaverse that can operate as a business tech universe, yet still create a safe, private, and trustful economic environment, without significantly increasing personal, business, and societal risk to every stakeholder involved. This is a goal we all need to set from the start, as there will be a number (dare we say trillions) of opportunities.

Start Your Immersion

After reading the previous chapters, you caught a glimpse of what is possible. But in order to really understand it, you should add another dimension to your perspective. We want you to put this book down and try the technologies for yourself, to own your experience of each one of them. (And then, of course, pick our book back up again—we aren't done yet.). In the words of Joanna Popper, Chief Metaverse Officer at the Creative Artists Agency and former Global Head of Virtual Reality at HP, "Experience games, try immersive experiences, hang out in virtual worlds socially +/or professionally, take a class, start building to learn, follow and engage with communities, buy or mint a NFT. As you're experimenting, think about your plan of action."

You need to immerse yourself in many different experiences so that you can envision the different ways each technology works and impacts your business. Only through this will you be able to foresee the way these technologies will interconnect.

Play Video Games

If you haven't played games in the last six months, please start. Even if you aren't a gamer, even if you think you're past the age limit (believe us, you aren't), it's worth trying just for a bit especially if it's part of an online digital world. You'll see that, even as you set up a profile, you'll begin to understand from a business perspective the importance and value of avatars, gaming currencies, skins, and power items. Notice the dynamics of communities, which will be one of the most powerful driving forces in our future.

If you are ambitious, try a range of consoles and hardware to see how your experience varies. Play games on handheld systems, computers, and gaming consoles. If you have doubts, access Twitch or YouTube to watch professional players livestreaming their game-play, and read all the community's comments. You can also ask most gamers how to play, *if* they aren't playing while you ask them. Go and play games in different screen sizes and resolutions and with a different number of players.

Resist the urge to think "I get it, I get it." It is uncomfortable to learn something new. But this is also the part that makes the difference between using future-forward decision-making and basing your decisions just on your own understanding of the world. Take the time to compare and contrast the experiences and identify the benefits and the drawbacks of each. This exercise will demonstrate how the future citizens of the metaverse are spending their time now.

Try Virtual Reality

You also have to try VR. Yes, put on that headset. We know it's really hard for some people—they worry they'll look silly or bang into a piece of furniture. Having put many nontechnical executives into VR, we know they almost always start out slightly embarrassed and apologetic (something no executive wants to feel or do publicly). Find someone to onboard you in the VR navigation to kickstart the experience, make you familiar with it from the very beginning, and help you find the right experience.

Guaranteed, if you find the right kind of experience (avoid roller coasters, shoot-it-ups, or zombie scare horror experiences), you'll come out nodding and agreeing it was different and better than you ever imagined. "I get it now," you'll say, and then you'll start to imagine what it can mean to your organization in a much clearer way. We've seen that happen countless times before. VR is something that needs to be experienced to be appreciated.

At tradeshows, many business-to-business (B2B) companies will also be available to share their VR with you. If you're looking to hire a company and do your own experiment, try at least three experiences of the immersive technology you are considering. Remember not every company has worked with every industry. You may need to be creative when thinking about the potential applications for your business. This is still emerging technology, so not knowing yet is how you set the standard for your industry.

Get Social in VR

In addition to stand-alone VR experiences or games, you should give social VR worlds a try. Feel how it is to be present with other people in VR. You'll likely be surprised that it really does seem like you are in the same room. Try to meet a friend or colleague in a VR room. Even with a low level of graphical fidelity, you can have verbal and nonverbal communication with another avatar. Given the current level of graphics commercially available, it will be harder to identify your friend or colleague visually (unless you can read their avatar's name label). But once you find each other, you will see how easily you relax in conversation. Notice how you talk after the experience: "I met my colleague at such-and-such," as if you met in the same physical space.

If for some reason you happen to encounter someone who trolls you in social VR, take that as a learning experience. See the importance of moderation and management. Although unlikely, do your best to avoid shutting down VR as a medium and say it's "not for you." Just because it might not be your medium of choice, it could be for your colleagues, employees, and customers now and in the future.

Try Haptics

If you get the opportunity to test VR with high-quality haptics, like gloves or haptic suits, do it. If you don't get that opportunity, search for it. These are bound to get much more available over time, but by trying it now you can get an edge over the competition. Note: If it doesn't feel real, it's not a good haptic solution. The most advanced haptics move beyond simple vibrations, air movements, small shocks, or temperature changes. Granted, you might not need the highest-fidelity haptics for your company, but trying the best gives you the perspective of what is possible.

Remember that haptics doesn't live on its own in the metaverse. It's about syncing the touch technologies during the visual and audience experience. Great haptics will make you feel as if you were given the gift of touch again.

Try Augmented Reality

AR experiences are much more convenient to try. AR apps and filters are available right at your fingertips, on your smartphones or on your computer. You can try AR filters on or around your head. You can make the background of your video calls look different than your actual room. You can populate your living room floor with fantastic creatures or measure your space and use digital furniture to envision your décor. Now take those experiences, especially the ones placed within your room, and start imagining what is possible for your business. You could put digital AR instructions on top of a physical product to be assembled or needing maintenance. You can measure your warehouse and create simulations to improve your storage planning. You could place AI assistants on your showroom floor to help with potential customers.

Experiencing AR only through your phone doesn't showcase all that is possible with the technology. Many AR enterprise applications need hands-free AR. So, try out AR glasses for yourself at a trade show, event, or ask AR companies to demo their product for the executives at your company.

Although AR headsets and smart glasses do exist, their form factor, price tag, and overall performance are not yet suitable for every-day consumers. They are almost exclusively used by businesses. Eventually you're likely to see more AR consumer headsets available with your cellular service, as 5G will power them. Also, while they may seem part of science fiction, AR contact lenses by companies like Mojo Vision already exist and will also start to appear in the market. Opticians themselves likely will become a part of the push.

And, Yes, Crypto

Cryptocurrency is next. Luckily, no significant investment is needed or required to understand it. To give it a try, place only the amount that you are willing to lose. This could be as little as $10 or €10. Too many people get carried away thinking there is only an upside to crypto. But remember that any investment anywhere, whether virtual, digital, or physical, fungible or non-fungible, has an element of risk.

Find a platform where you can create your wallet (for free), explore different cryptocurrency options, and explore NFT marketplaces. At this point, you can browse artwork, fashion and lifestyle products, travel packages, and more. Some traditional companies have started using crypto in their direct payments, although many users just register for crypto-linked credit cards.

If you are still open and willing to try something new, you can also enter and explore the already existing Web3 worlds where virtual land is still being traded. Often joining is free, but you'll need a crypto wallet, some time to find your way around everything being built by brands. Unless you have a ton of discretionary income, best to avoid trying to get yourself a virtual mansion next to a celebrity's.

Artificial Intelligence and Machine Learning

Most of the experiences we have mentioned so far incorporate AI and machine learning (ML) at some level. AI and ML are used to recognize your face, body, and environment through computer vision and to place something on, around, below, above, or behind you. AI is the technology that is used to take the mapping of world and computer vision and calculate the information needed for self-driving cars. But it has also powered search engines, social media, e-commerce, and financial analysis for years already. As we shared, AI is a very, very broad term.

Free tools are available online that can help you understand the diverse powers of AI and ML. You can write commands and play around with the possibilities. You also can watch videos created by data science experts. Review the topics we raised in our previous chapter, and heed the warning of Elon Musk in 2018: "Mark my words—A.I. is far more dangerous than nukes. Far. So why do we have no regulatory oversight? This is insane."[2] So, once again, the choices you make as an executive can impact the world beyond your business.

Learn to follow all related topics in the news—and there are many to follow.

Wearables

Although you might not have heard of the term "wearable," you probably have put one on. A Fitbit or an Apple Watch would be considered a wearable. Any device that monitors your heart rate is a wearable. In order to understand how these technologies apply to the metaverse, imagine the data being collected not just being available to your mobile app tracker. It could be integrated within your Internet of Things (IoT), meaning that your smart kitchen would know how much exercise you got (or didn't get) that day and predict what you might want to eat or drink. Your data would be connected to your medical digital twin that your doctor or surgeon would be able to access and they would be able to track your progress. This would make us all more accountable, but also it could become really invasive really quickly. Do we all really want to know how those chips or dessert impacted our health in real time? Do we want our doctors to know as well?

Ubiquitous AR Cloud

We still don't know how long it will take for a global, worldwide AR cloud to become a reality due to a lack of standards and regulation. In the meantime, you can catch a glimpse of the effects of a global AR Cloud by playing Pokemon Go or any other games by Niantic. Meanwhile, tools are already available to enable some level of integration between metaverse worlds and we will see more integration and interoperability between virtual worlds as the AR cloud is built.

Avatars and Digital Beings

Avatars and virtual beings already exist, mainly in gaming and social media. There are some companies that are using them as well, as the embodiment of their brand persona. There are millions of fans of virtual influencers and VTubers. However, the applications beyond entertainment and advertising have just begun within industries like the medical field.

As the technologies evolve, there are still a lot of issues to be resolved (e.g., identity theft) and standards to be established (e.g., cross-platform use). There also are social expectations to be established (e.g., which avatars are appropriate for a workplace).

The variations of these avatars and digital beings could be as wide as our imaginations, from fantastic creatures to exact replicas of people. The quality can run from entry-level UGC (user-generated content) to continuously updated AIGC (AI-generated content) hyper-realistic graphics. The ability to generate and edit them efficiently will prove immensely important in the metaverse, as it will also bring its share of legal and regulatory issues along with it, as you might expect by now. So how should any business professional leverage these momentaneous waves and identify more value for their own business or work? Well, we suggest a simple methodology for you to use and reuse across any emerging technology:

Define   See if you can identify what you don't know. These could be terms, companies, recent innovations. Sometimes it's just a few terms or acronyms that will help to get you started. Identify the top players in the technology industry. Discover what other companies in your industry are doing (or not) with the technology you have identified. Determine your objective in your research. Although it (likely) might change, it will help to identify your initial direction.

Research   Pick a handful of tech companies to monitor and analyze. They could be within your market and/or those adjacent to yours when it comes to emerging technologies (e.g., communities, creators, new tokens). There's no need to go in depth yet. Just understand that the tech is always shifting and that you need to keep up. Don't just look at the big headlines, but see what the trades and the snarky pundits are saying. Ask yourself and your tech-savvy friends and colleagues. Consider if what the company is doing is ethical (but more on that later).

Identify   Determine the companies that seem the most aligned with the goals for your organization. They might not have worked in your industry before, but that is OK if you are willing to share your insights. Have a few companies do demos for your company. Be reasonably excited by the opportunity but skeptical. Push for more examples with results, although the more innovative, the less likely they will have them to share. Push to understand what can be delivered in the next few months and what is a year, two years or more away. It will likely evolve and be easier to integrate their tech later, but that's when your competitors might have caught up. If the tech companies are cutting edge, anticipate signing some non-disclosure agreements (NDAs).

Understand   Now you have a deeper knowledge of what's in the market and what emerging tech companies are seeing in the new future. Imagine what is possible for your company, if you had a healthy budget. Even if you can't implement your concept immediately, you can determine the steps until eventual integration. Establish what processes in your organization might change and how. Anticipate what's ceasing to exist and what's coming.

Acknowledge   This won't be as easy to do as with an established technology and a mature company. It will take more work, there will be more "problems" than you will face in other projects. There likely will be more emotions involved as well. There will be those within your organization who will advocate for the change, whom you should get more involved in the project. There also will be the naysayers. There are always naysayers for emerging tech, so prepare to convince them more slowly by asking a lot of questions about their department's needs. The best you can do is hope that they will begin to see why the change might make their role a little better or easier eventually. They won't advocate for the integration, but they won't go out of their way to stop you.

Budget   Chances are that the first round of innovations will have a larger cost, at first. Some organizations are OK with that, as they consider it to be an investment in the future. Others might need convincing that the costs will reduce expenses. For example, high-quality haptics are an investment, but it reduces the need for printed prototypes.

Test   Given the place where you are in the metaverse layers, do controlled experiments based on your assumptions. Identify ways to prototype or pilot with clear goals and key performance indicators (KPIs) and assess results as quickly as possible so that you can replicate those results. Document what you are doing as those tests can be used not only for determining the best outcomes, but also for thought leadership marketing content later.

Expand   As you see what is working, start bringing more of your colleagues into the fold. This could be initially by just sharing your results. Then ask for their thoughts and opinions to allow them more ownership of the process. See where efficiencies can be created. For example, a digital twin of a building or engine can be used across multiple departments. A company that builds those twins could present to individual departments or the entire organization. If you have shown good results already, share them to encourage other departments to give something new a try. They might be more likely as you already vetted the team and the technology.

Start Again   Go back to research, validate your findings, and keep building an efficient model to scale your presence in the building blocks of the metaverse while it's being built. So you and your company can be there first.

It's a continuous validation cycle, as Rafael Pavon, the award-winning Immersive Creative Director at Nexus Studios, tells us: "The most important thing we can do right now to improve the metaverse is to observe people inhabiting these early stages and learn from them. How do we behave? What frustrates us? What are we missing? What do we remember? Where do we find value? Spending valuable time inside this digital landscape will help us improve our future steps towards a better metaverse."

Ethics, Trust, and Risks

"I run an unethical business," says no executive ever. Same with "I don't care if my customers trust me." Because trust and ethics are such a big part of standard business practices, it's odd that it becomes something that puts executives on the defensive. "Of course, I'm ethical and trustworthy," says everyone.

But saying you are both and then acting in a way that benefits your business and employees over anyone outside your organization likely results in something less than perfect. No matter your opinion of Big Tech business, one of the biggest issues has been just that—it's big. It's too big. How is it possible for Big Tech businesses to monitor each and every person's behavior all the time, no matter where they are or what they are doing, without ever violating anyone's individual rights? Even still, companies still should strive for better and customers should require Six Sigma levels of ethical behavior.

We are about to enter a time where it's impossible to fathom the amount of data points that will be available to track each person. There are about to be exponential ways of potential ethical issues arising. Just spend a few minutes imagining that you are wearing glasses that are tracking your movements, what you are looking at, who you are talking to, and what you are saying. Imagine the same thing happening with a colleague or a family member and then everyone you are passing on the street and then everyone at work. Getting a sick feeling in the pit of your stomach? Now remember that feeling when you have the opportunity as an executive to decide what your glasses will see and not see and record and not record. Starting to feel a little better? Good.

It's no wonder that one big word that has always been in the active vocabulary of all metaverse pundits (and, truth be told, of all Internet pundits before them) is ethics. The use of the word *ethics* might vary slightly dependent on use, but when it comes to the metaverse, more often than not it boils down to data capture and its usage. Where do we draw the line? What professional standards do we want to establish that protect our individual rights? This is the challenge we face as we enter the metaverse. Personal and interpersonal human standards are different than professional standards. The former is about how we treat people in any situation, and the latter is connected to growing shareholder value and avoiding risks to profitability. Decisions made about data capture and use in the metaverse impact both.

This isn't a time to become a passive participant. Just announcing that you're an ethical player does not make you one. Announcing grand, nonbinding principles and rules, and pointing to them should any challenge arise, doesn't really do anything besides produce a momentary bump in interest. Consumers are becoming savvier, and decentralization is bringing another level of data sovereignty for each individual. It seems inevitable as activists are demanding a clearer and much more consistent approach to data and technology use. It's the cost of doing business in the next digital age.

Prepare

In general, it's best to take a first-do-no-harm approach. You may not be able to solve the world's problems, but you definitely don't want to be the one causing them. A technology executive once said (anonymously) that she didn't want to be the next person testifying in front of Congress apologizing for the issues that her technology had caused. Although an extreme example, it is worthwhile to think about what can go wrong alongside what can go right. Stress-test what you are doing.

- Openly discuss metaverse business models, data capture, converging technologies, safety, and privacy within your organization.
- Outline your key ethical redlines as if your job depends on it, because it will.
- Anticipate that regulations are coming, and lead your company to set and beat the coming standards.
- Assign team members to be accountable for actions, especially those that will be automated and AI-powered.
- Create auditing processes, with the goal of testing for efficiency and safety.
- Track the data you're gathering and make sure you are able to justify its collection from the user side and not just from the business side.
- Return often to seek out any bias and potential ethical issues with algorithms, data sets, or processes. Finding and fixing them is a win; ignoring them causes damage.
- Actively seek out new and diverse perspectives to make sure that you and your team have not lost yours within the data sets.

Resist passing on the liability to users and letting them determine for themselves what data they want to give and what the algorithm should mean. Making the user accountable has been a get-out-of-the-ethical-jail card to date. A little toggle to say "it's OK" for eye tracking isn't enough to approve data capture. A scroll through multiple pages of legal documents to approve doesn't do it either. Big Tech tends to say their technology is not the problem—that users hold the power to use it wrong or affect any unexpected outcome algorithms may produce. At the risk of sounding a bit extreme, we don't want to end up saying, "Data capture didn't cause the downfall of society—society did."

Inherent in these discussions is how we each don't always act in our own or society's best interests. We all enjoy the dopamine hits of scrolling social media and receiving "likes," but the extremes of that behavior is what we need to be wary of with emerging tech. How much time should we allow people to spend in VR? How much time should be spent wearing a haptic suit? How much data should be captured? None of these have right or wrong answers. But there are more right or more wrong answers. We need to define the answer of what is "not too much."

At this point, there are a lot of metaverse regulations that have yet to be put into place. This mean opportunities exist for misuse and abuse without legal ramifications. There are some follow-if-you-want recommendations issued by non-governmental organizations (NGOs) and professional associations. However, many uncomfortable situations can arise before the rules are put in place, such as hacking of what you see through your glasses, how you are represented, and what types of extreme communities and irrational behaviors are permitted. The potential is, at this point, seemingly limitless for bad actors as well as good. No metaverse laws exist that mimic and expand on the real-world ones. It's not pleasant, but deviancy, hatred, prejudice, and immoral behavior doesn't yet have consequences beyond just kicking people off a virtual world platform. Still, you need to be aware of how wild the metaverse will be at first as you begin to make business decisions, and you must do your part to mold the metaverse into a more ethical and professional medium.

First Steps in Each Market

There are specific hurdles for each market to start integrating the metaverse into its value chain. Not only is each professional audience very different, but also the metaverse challenges to overcome in each area depend on the current framework in which professionals are working, the kind of data being professionally gathered and the speed of technological convergence. To bring you meaningful insights, we tapped into our network of industry players and tried to find out.

Art and Performance

Although several digital artists are already digitally savvy, traditional and established artists, gallerists, and art teachers still need to start tinkering with the technologies to explore the possibilities of the metaverse. "Not everybody is going to have the same point of entry and that's OK. The most important part is that people recognize the advantages of this new space rather than the disadvantages," says digital artist Tupac Martir.[3]

This can be achieved by increasing the availability of physical and digital art marketplaces where artists can showcase their new work and enable more education opportunities for artists, art enthusiasts, and collectors. More digital and NFT exhibitions, along with more hybrid art pieces with larger use of AI creation tools, will most probably be some of the starting points for this market.

Advertising, PR, Marketing

There are already inroads made by the communications industries. The next steps involve standardization and regulation. Several attempts at creating standard formats for advertising across the several metaverse building blocks and platforms have been made, from virtual reality billboards to advergames (games created in partnership with brands or included in wider campaigns). But all this effort is still in its very beginning, and the reason is pretty simple—the metaverse is not here yet.

The regulatory and public service officials have yet to provide guidelines and guardrails for business activities. Studying the multiple and, in many cases, still unknown impacts that advertising will have on each market, in civil society, and overall in our lives, will be key to avoiding more pain down the line. Some of the (potentially biased) research will be undertaken by Big Tech themselves, as they are already working on this matter on their own and inside standards organizations like the Interactive Advertising Bureau (IAB).

"Just look at the organic way in which the Internet developed. I think over the next few years the metaverse will remain unstructured and somewhat wild, which isn't necessarily a bad thing as we will learn a lot," shares James Watson, Chief Marketing Officer at The Glimpse Group. "But, in time, agreement on standards will become a priority as it becomes clear that the lack of structure will be holding back a truly interoperable metaverse."[4]

Retail

Beyond the existing changes at the cutting edge of retail, the number of expected disruptions awaiting this market is massive. Not only will new channels and distribution platforms pop up, but new customer journeys and added elements, like visual comparison, digital assistants, and a host of blockchain tokens. Each will start contributing to the customers' decisions. The opportunity to sell physical, digital, and hybrid products will transform the ability to generate distinctive value for any brand. Virtually any retail brand can benefit from becoming metaversed. According to Alan Smithson, co-founder and CEO of MetaVRse, "With the advent of artificial intelligence, XR and blockchain, retailers and brands have a unique and powerful opportunity to provide unparalleled experiences in virtual worlds that bring back the joy of shopping."[5]

On the regulatory side, as taxes begin to be discussed for the metaverse retail market, much more governmental guidance will need to be put in place for fair international trading, bringing crypto payments and hybrid products into the mainstream, create trustful marketplaces, mediation services, and consumer protection in each sector of this market.

Entertainment and Music

AR clouds, gamification, and social tokens will bring hybrid entertainment to new heights across the physical, virtual, and augmented worlds. Telcos see the opportunities here and are now supporting the efforts to more widely distribute entertainment and music experiences—most probably they will be one of the main drivers to bring the metaverse into the mainstream in this specific vertical.

One of the main trends will also be community co-creation of experiences, of spaces, of worlds. As Vince Kadlubek, Founder and Director at Meow Wolf, shared, "The Metaverse will fundamentally shift the nature of storytelling by placing each individual into the central role of an ongoing, co-created narrative. Storytelling has always been a reflection of the human experience, and this coming shift will reflect the human experience's transcendence into a fully new dimension of consciousness."[6]

News

"Today, immersive experiences and the metaverse are not more than a topic for journalism," says Marco Magnano, multimedia journalist and adviser at XR Safety Initiative Europe. "When the immersive technology hits the mainstream for real, this [view] will probably start changing, and the metaverse will turn into a medium."[7]

Other trends include newsrooms expanding beyond what the Internet has provided. Artificial intelligence applications and algorithms are helping journalists with repetitive chores and with identifying fake news. Journalists themselves are understanding more about the VR and AR points of view possible when covering newsworthy facts in digital worlds. These trends imply a need for new techniques and skills training, and that should be a focus for newsmakers preparing for the metaverse.

As more data about human behavior is tracked, expect fake news and deep fakes to improve and generate truly believable stories, where digital replicas of human beings might be making calls or taking actions in place of real human beings. These stories will be presented in such a realistic way that they will be almost undistinguishable from actual news stories. We need to address this huge societal challenge as quickly as possible and not just by creating regulatory frameworks. "There needs to be an Associated Press for immersive storytellers. A group which is providing relevant 3D content as the world needs it," shares Henry Keyser, Director of Innovation at DemocratizeXR and former Director of XR Editorial at Yahoo. There also is a need to create more products, services, and companies that enable us to spot and filter out deep fakes.

Events

With so many new formats for shows, venues, and presence, and even with the rise of hybrid and digital artists, event producers will need to become proficient across physical and virtual venues. Creating new digital and phygital venues that provide support for both artists and their fan base means new core skills must be added to production teams. There are more opportunities within the metaverse that have yet to be discovered. For instance, NFT tickets seem like a fairly easy entry point use case for live shows, but they will always need to be integrated with existing systems, as well as venue-only augmented reality experiences or digital beings.

Award-winning filmmaker and immersive artist Kiira Benzing highlighted the need to support and educate the industry on digital and physical events. "The way that we value the cost of entertainment is constantly changing. Society is always looking for free content, but a society that values art will reflect that value in a way that respects the artists. From the world builders to the virtual stage managers to the performers themselves, there is an entire industry that needs to be economically developed."[8]

Casinos

Gambling in VR and in virtual worlds has begun, but decentralized and crypto gambling is liable to cause industry disruption. There will be the need to define jurisdiction for licenses, regulations, and taxes across physical and digital platforms. Governments will have to ensure that trust mechanisms are in place and, while they're not, take measures. It's important to trace not only the money changing hands, but also to control access to this service (for example, identifying minors or addicts).

Adult Entertainment

Moral judgments aside, the adult business will extend its reach within the metaverse, making pornographic content available in 3D, in an immersive way, and with decentralized access. A standard ratings system like the ones we see in movies and games could be a start. There is a need for simpler, standard ways to identify content, for permission to be given, and for specific physical areas (such as schools or religious buildings) to be off limits for these kinds of experiences.

Sports and Fitness

These technologies lend themselves to the sports and fitness industries. Many companies in this space have already begun to explore what fandom is like in the metaverse and verified that communities have a powerful drive to bring together people interested in doing sports together and exploring new hybrid sports, based on VR or AR. Growing the visibility of these communities and services is a path to accelerate the growth of this market in the metaverse.

These technologies will also continue to support athletic and physical training. This could be via advancements in the competition experience simulation and to progress tracking. Headsets may become available at gyms or facilities being built specifically for metaverse experiences. In a virtual setting, you could join other people for a workout, some joining virtually, with detailed tracking of your progress.

There's also the potential of holoported or AI personal trainers who will make sure that you are getting the fully customized benefit of your workout. Using your data, they could select the best kind of exercises for you that day and make it easier for you to embrace a healthy lifestyle. Of course, with all of this data tracking comes the need for legal regulation, as the tech companies will then have access to specific and important health and physical data for each user.

Travel and Tourism

With the metaverse, there is the opportunity to take travel and tourism to new dimensions, both real and virtual. Beyond avatar-led experiences, augmented reality tourism, for instance, is a huge opportunity.

Museums and cultural institutions have begun exploring what is possible. Robin White Owen is a creative producer at MediaCombo and shared with us her take on this matter: "As a producer of digital interactive experiences in museums for many years, I've observed enormous changes in the way cultural institutions try to attract and engage the public. Due to the immersive nature of virtual reality, the metaverse offers opportunities to profoundly deepen and expand engagement. For example, VR will make it possible for visitors to examine and interact with 3D versions of art and artifacts in ways they can't in real life, and to see historical objects in virtual versions of their original environments. Furthermore, in the metaverse, I'd like to see museums reinvent themselves, going beyond the preservation and interpretation of global cultural histories to becoming centers of creative activity—by using their collections to inspire people to dream big, share ideas and apply their new understanding to improve life in their communities, virtual and physical." Gamifying travel experiences might become more prevalent. Think play-to-earn routes that can take users through the same physical places but with different levels of gameplay—so they can keep returning to the same spaces but benefit each time from different experiences and memories. Tourism might also begin to take place in metaverse worlds that can enable us to visit remote places on Earth or fictional ones.

As it happens with the physical world, the hybrid world will also have its own wonders to visit. Landmark digital experiences and art installations will be points of interest to visit and most probably a new part of humankind's history books.

Garnering the storytelling skills that can effectively create these narratives for each POV is the gamechanger in this area. "As we create a more technologically advanced society where more people spend time in headsets, it is imperative that we create experiences that cause people to value their physical world. The metaverse cannot be dystopian and escapist. It is up to us to create metaverse experiences that are utopian, uniting, and inspiring. Hopefully experiences in our digital world enhance our physical world." These are the words of Elena Piech, XR and Web3 producer at ZeroSpace, with which we agree wholeheartedly.

Architecture, Engineering, and Construction (AEC) and Real Estate

The AEC and real estate sectors have started to incorporate metaverse technologies from creation and ideation through sales and interior decoration through maintenance and repair. However, many still are using 2D models of 3D spaces or 2D screens to showcase 3D spaces. As rendering speeds and hardware distribution increase, we should expect that to change with more architects pulling out AR glasses on-site and construction workers with headsets attached to their hard hats.

The overall trend toward the integration of physical and digital also may require a new metaverse space at work and/or at home. This could impact the layout of offices and increase the need for virtual office spaces. Some large homes may be outfitted with a holodeck room, like those who have home theaters or gaming rooms.

But, in the short term, tangible, immediate value is prioritized. This is confirmed by Emily Olman, CEO at Hopscotch Interactive, who says, "For my technophobic clients metaverse talk only makes them feel even more like they are behind the 8-ball. I think finding approachable ROI-generating products that make sense and are the way to engage the Real Estate industry is the way forward. I see lots of potential for Unreal Engine, virtual humans and [building] pre-visualizations, but not yet in a scalable way."[9]

In the meantime, there are still ways to prepare for the arrival of the metaverse. Professional standards need to be put into place. For example, what kind of avatars are appropriate for your business? There's also the opportunity of digital buildings and real estate, which has the opportunity to grow into new divisions in AEC or tech business in the coming years.

Transportation

"The future of mobility is an open playing field as automotive titans from BMW to Audi and Tesla to Volvo are jockeying for positions taking on tech giants Google to Apple in the race for autonomous vehicles. The biggest names are moving quickly, investing billions of dollars into developing prototypes, software safety testing, and hardware integration. The biggest challenge for one of the most important industries for the U.S. economy is the cultural adoption of autonomous vehicles," shares Angeli Gianchandani, founder and mobility expert at Mobility Girl. "The metaverse will supercharge the development to tackle the complexity of autonomous vehicles."[10]

The experience of a self-driving car will eventually transform itself and create opportunities for these metaverse technologies to become increasingly available. This is a task for both manufacturers and cities, as they become more sensorized and AIs become more effective in managing this information. ˙

Beyond just self-driving, there are an increasing number of shared-transportation and mobility offerings that will require the establishment of responsible uses of these new ways of transportation. Also, AI taking over driving doesn't mean that individuals will lose responsibility for the actions of their vehicles. There's a need to devise new safety procedures, laws, and regulations for hazardous conditions and in remote locations.

Manufacturing

Automation, digital twins, and the IoT are seemingly relentless in changing the manufacturing market. Made-to-order and personalized customization is increasingly becoming the norm. Metaverse technologies could help and support these efforts by interconnecting data, all the while keeping costs low.

But the rise of automation and on-demand changes both business and social needs. Robots are accelerating production lines but are bad at handling exceptions and solving errors. Keeping humans in the loop and augmenting them, both cognitively and physically, can make this transformation more sustainable in the long run.

Mark Sage, Executive Director at the Augmented Reality for Enterprise Alliance (AREA), shares that, "the most important step leaders of enterprises must take when evaluating metaverse solutions, is it must solve a business problem. I'm sure this sounds strange and obvious, but often the excitement and thrill of the immersive experience leads to poor purchasing decisions (e.g., we must buy the latest VR and/or AR hardware devices) without a clear understanding of why and what problems can be solved." He continues: "Identifying a business problem and evaluating the potential ROI is only the start. Enterprises need to consider the delivery of metaverse solutions as a 'change management' challenge and not an IT implementation project. A useful way to get started is to plan for a full metaverse implementation but start small with prototyping and end user feedback."

This transformation will impact all kinds of related organizations, including unions, government agencies, professional associations, and technical training institutes. All will need to adapt their processes and upskill in a way that positively leverages what this technological wave brings across the market.

Health

The metaverse brings a lot of opportunities to improve healthcare, including reducing mistakes, injuries, and death and improving outcomes and recovery. Doctors can make more informed decisions through biometric monitoring devices. Greater healthcare accessibility may also be possible through advanced remote solutions. Some of this may be available for the "small price" of your data through "free access" solutions. So, as with any technological advancements, we all need safeguards in place to avoid potential negative impacts. In the case of the medical field, particularly worrisome is the opportunity for the exploitation of each of our physical and mental health data, from companies within and outside of the medical fields.

Valentino Megale, CEO at Softcare Studios and expert advisor at XR Safety Initiative, shared with us that, "As a biologist familiar with how the brain works, I'd say we already live in a mix of physical-imaginative perceptual experiences, and thanks to the metaverse we'll now have new tools to experiment with our imagination, augmenting what we know about how our cognition works (and how much is often just taken for granted). I think the immediate impact could be underestimating the influence this new 'perceptual freedom' could have on our identity, behavior, and social dynamics, but if we'll promote related awareness and knowledge, the next years could open great opportunities for businesses, communities, and individuals." As to the key major challenges ahead, he points out the need to "laser focus on the development of real-world case studies, be able to solve problems that are close to our daily life, so that everyone could perceive the benefits and potential of the metaverse and its related technologies."

Education

Carla Gannis, an artist, designer and Industry Professor at New York University shared her struggles with metaverse platforms for teaching "There is still the seductive gee whiz factor that comes with 'elastic' avatar representation, augmented locomotion (flying, teleportation, spawning), and game-like graphics that can be exciting to students, but the challenge is to harness these elements for deeper level learning and retention."

Most likely avatars and digital beings shouldn't replace traditional teaching, as we still have an access issue to solve worldwide. "[The] metaverse will [not] replace in-person education any time soon, at least NOT everywhere, particularly when you take into account that only about 60% of the world currently has Internet access.[11]

Still, empowering teachers and instructors with metaverse experience enables more people to prepare for the next Industrial Revolution. This includes not just school-age and university students, but also upskilling members of the workforce to avoid any potential metaverse illiteracy. This can be addressed locally, regionally, nationally, and potentially internationally. For those looking to accelerate the adoption of the metaverse, this kind of training is essential. It will be necessary to understand how to behave and interact and work in the metaverse. Creating more responsible consumers, workers, and leaders is paramount, not only in the physical world and on the Internet, but also in the future metaverse.

Governments' Immediate Challenges

Due to the daunting volume of the impact of the metaverse, the active participation of governments will be required to bring the metaverse building blocks to the mainstream. Governments are the ones that can support the creation of a safer hybrid space that aligns with our physical world, while dealing with these new challenges:

Decentralization   A lot of promises are made about the decentralizing benefits of the blockchain. Many talk about how it brings more participation, transparency, and democratic accuracy to the processes. However, the current experiences of decentralized autonomous organizations (DAOs) show that voting rights depending exclusively on tokens will ultimately result in more plutocratic governances rather than democratic ones. Governments' role across the physical and digital worlds requires hybrid transparency. Although seemingly antithetical to the ethos of the blockchain technology, much of that can happen with regulations.

Identification   Citizens will need to be able to identify themselves universally across the metaverse. This interoperability tenet requires technological solutions (likely on blockchain) that can accomplish this in the most straightforward and transparent way, but integrated with already existing citizen ID systems. We likely will need to connect our identity to our multiple avatars and have the opportunity to attach it to the medical data from our digital twin. This would allow us to own our own identity and define what information we want to show (e.g., driver's license, passport, work details, or university diplomas) and when.

Infrastructure   Governments will need to determine their role in enabling all technological cornerstones needed for the metaverse to run. That may mean facilitating the convergence of these exponential technologies and promoting interoperable and open solutions.

Job Creation   Many metaverse-related jobs are coming, some that we don't even yet know will exist. Stimulus packages and skills-enhancing policies will help these jobs become reality in ways that make sense to existing nations.

Jurisdiction   Institutions and tools are needed for justice to be delivered. Meeting this challenge involves establishing which rules apply for every space, person, and asset. These will need to be upheld by institutions with the level of authority and international acceptance needed to effectively apply them.

Safety   Protecting consumers, ensuring child safety, safeguarding privacy, defining locations where no augmentations are allowed, and upholding human rights are just some of the safety topics that need to be directly on the radar of public officials in the metaverse. Leveraging the work already done by NGOs and integrating experts in multidisciplinary teams might be the secret sauce to build a well-knit framework that can cover all privacy and safety issues.

Worldwide Upgrade   The Internet united all of us, and the metaverse has the opportunity to bring us even closer. There is the potential to enable a new social and economic dimension, rather than a technological one. This could require a worldwide institution, either as part of an existing one like the World Economic Forum or the United Nations, which have both begun exploratory work. Or perhaps there is a need for a new institution that establishes a human-focused, global approach to govern the social and economic aspects of the metaverse to help make sure that the right kind of building blocks shape its future form.

Notes

1. Shikhar Ghosh, "Making business sense of the Internet." *Harvard Business Review*, March 1998. http://hbr.org/1998/03/making-business-sense-of-the-internet

2. Catherine Clifford, "Elon Musk: 'Mark my words—A.I. is far more dangerous than nukes.'" CNBC, March 13, 2018. www.cnbc.com/2018/03/13/elon-musk-at-sxsw-a-i-is-more-dangerous-than-nuclear-weapons.html

3. Tupac Martir, recorded voice testimony, August 2022.

4. James Watson, personal communication, 2022.

5. Alan Smithson, LinkedIn message, June 2022.

6. Vince Kadlubek, LinkedIn message on June 2022.

7. Marco Magnano, personal communication, 2022.

8. Kiira Benzing, sent an email, June 2022.

9. Emily Olman, sent mail, June 2020.

10. Angeli Gianchandani, mail sent to SGW, June 2022.

11. www.currentware.com/blog/internet-usage-statistics/#global-internet-access

Chapter 14

A Toolbox
for the Metaverse

Don't panic.
—Douglas Adams, The Hitchhiker's Guide to the Galaxy

As you finish up this book, we hope you can see into the future of the metaverse and how it applies to your company. Technology is evolving at an accelerated pace, which brings with it many new business, societal, environmental, and ethical challenges. It can feel like there is no way to keep up, because there *is* no way. You just have to understand and embrace that it's constantly changing.

Now that you know about the metaverse and its potential impact, you can make decisions to prepare for it. But it won't be easy. Not everyone will believe you. They may assume you have transformed into a video gamer as they think the metaverse is just a gaming platform. Some will dismiss the concept as they assume it's only about VR. Still others could think you have become a crypto investor.

So, be ready for the confusion and be patient with those who don't understand . . . yet. You can help them to begin to be inspired by the upcoming opportunities and to prepare for the risks. Also, remember that, most likely, you're not the first in your industry. There are examples here from over 25 markets that are already building their business processes toward the metaverse, integrating its related technologies in different ways.

Don't judge your peers and colleagues on their ignorance. Would you have listened to someone 20 years ago talking about how we'd be spending hours every day staring at rectangular black device that can fit in our pockets? Would you have believed that almost every person and every organization would have an online profile and monitor the feedback from hundreds or thousands of people? Probably not.

But those who did were able to see into the future. They could take advantage of the upcoming wave. They were willing to take a calculated risk, to become one of the first of their colleagues to evolve what was standard practice in their industry. Now you can, too, and be even more responsible in your approach than those in the Internet and social media industries as the market was just being built.

Not only may you face some skepticism from your colleagues, you will also see many articles and many pundits hype the coming of or the demise of the metaverse. This is standard with any new technology. That's why there is a Gartner Hype Cycle methodology that shows the progress of how some of the newest technologies are overly hyped while others face over-scrutiny. However, just because major publications or networks use attention-grabbing headlines, it doesn't mean it isn't coming. The metaverse isn't being built overnight. This next industrial revolution, wave of innovation, or whatever you may call it is more complex and impactful than we can even fathom yet.

The metaverse isn't a get-rich-quick, buy-my-NFT kind of situation. It's going to come slowly, and then it will just be here. There is no roadmap or treasure map into the next dimension. No one can predict exactly what will happen. (If they say they can, be very skeptical of how much they actually know.) As you venture into the domain of the metaverse, you will get a lot of conflicting information and some information will just be confusing. That said, with this book, you now can have a bit more of a critical eye about the upcoming opportunities and obstacles.

To add a bit more confusion to the months ahead, it's possible that the word "metaverse" will go away. There is still some resentment about Facebook's name change that could influence that shift. It may be spatial computing, the spatial Internet . . . there could be an expansion of the meaning of the term "Web3." But even if we call it some other name, the metaverse will happen.

There will be new metaverse behemoths, but the FAANG collective isn't going to let go of the market they've invested billions to dominate. There will be prolific new executives who will tout their world-changing businesses. A *Fast Company* headline in April 2022 said, "Tech workers are fleeing FAANG for Web3, here's why."[1] Get ready for high-profile executives to leave their cushy Internet jobs to lead metaverse companies. There will be many who will profess that they are the visionaries and the answer to the killer app of the metaverse will be whatever their company is selling. Don't let all the talk distract you. Focus on the value your company is bringing and how the metaverse can and will amplify that (for now) and will transition into something even bigger (later). Understand that the trust your company builds is going to be more important than ever. The decisions you make regarding third parties' data management can build a safer ecosystem, where privacy and the rights of all of us are tended and safeguarded.

But know that—even with potentially conflicting perspectives from your colleagues and media pundits on if, when, and how—the metaverse needs to be built the right way today in the middle of all of the disagreements—now you understand what the metaverse can do and what could go wrong.

Now it's your turn to act on those insights. That action isn't just for the CEOs and department heads. It's not just for the technologists, designers, and developers who are neck-deep in the tech platforms. Every kind of employee, every student, every executive needs to understand how the metaverse will change their jobs and how to make sure those changes are for the better. Lawyers, lawmakers, and governments don't have a choice, really—because the metaverse will affect all of us in ways we haven't yet imagined.

So, get involved in the metaverse ecosystem, outside of your professional role. This chapter has a treasure trove of information, references, and communities where metaverse builders meet. Don't be intimidated by any tech-speak or tech-bro posturing. Even if you don't understand how they are coding, those working within the space are passionate enough to talk to you about what could be possible. Use this book as an excuse to start a conversation ("Well, I was reading *Metaversed* . . . "). If you are at a trade show or at a New York or Lisbon event, you may even run into one of us.

The following is the start of what you can do and where you can go for more information after finishing this book. As technology evolves so quickly, there will be more resources and recommendations, publications, articles, and podcasts to help you on your journey. The resources in each list are in alphabetical order, not based on size or value to you. Think of the following as a toolbox to get you started.

Predictions

Trade organizations and industry experts continuously work on producing information about the metaverse. All the major consultancies have released reports on the topic and are publishing more detailed ones:

- Accenture: "Meet Me in the Metaverse"[2]
- BCG: "The Corporate Hitchhiker's Guide to the Metaverse"[3]
- Deloitte: "Exploring the Metaverse and What It Could Mean for You"[4]
- EY: "Journey to the Center of the Metaverse"[5]
- KPMG: "Go Boldly, Not Blindly, into the Metaverse"[6]
- McKinsey: "Value Creation in the Metaverse"[7]
- PwC: "Demystifying the Metaverse"[8]

Some of the banks and advertising agencies also have released their perspectives on the coming metaverse:

- JPMorgan: "Opportunities in the Metaverse"[9]
- Media.Monks: "Make Sense of the Metaverse"[10]
- Wunderman Thompson: "Into the Metaverse and Beyond"[11]

Many authors have already published on the topic, from the foundational approach given by Matthew Ball (*The Metaverse: And How It Will Revolutionize Everything,* Liveright, 2022) to the books of our colleagues at Wiley:

- *Understanding the Metaverse: A Business and Ethical Guide*, by Nicola Rosa (2022)
- *The Metaverse Handbook: Innovating for the Internet's Next Tectonic Shift*, by QuHarrison Terry and Scott Keeney (2022)
- *Navigating the Metaverse: A Guide to Limitless Possibilities in a Web 3.0 World*, by Cathy Hackl, Dirk Lueth, and Tommaso Di Bartolo (2022)
- *Step into the Metaverse: How the Immersive Internet Will Unlock a Trillion-Dollar Social Economy*, by Mark van Rijmenam (2022)

Beyond the books on the topic, many major tech news outlets now feature a section dedicated specifically to the metaverse.

Technologies

Web3 and Blockchain

Attending industry events for Web3 is a great start to immerse yourself in Web3—a faithful crowd tends to gather at these events. Here are a few to navigate through the reality and the hype:

- CryptoWorldCon (CWC, http://cryptoworldcon.com)
- Future Blockchain Summit (http://futureblockchainsummit.com)

- NFT.NYC (http://nft.nyc)
- World of Web3 (https://wowsummit.net)

Some of the largest companies within the Web3 market hold their own corporate conferences, where they announce new products and services, such as:

- ETHDenver BUIDLathon (http://ethdenver.com)
- ETHOnline (http://online.ethglobal.com)
- Polygon BUILDit (http://buidlit.polygon.technology)
- Solana Summer Camp (http://solana.com/summercamp)

There are also hundreds of meetups across the world (for instance, Ethereum community promotes meetups both in Singapore and in London, while you can attend a Bitcoin Meetup in Zurich). Some of the top people in the industry attend to mingle with their peers and bring in new converts. Many of these events also allow participants to join online.

There are also associations with memberships. Here are a few:

- ABCA (American Blockchain and Cryptocurrency Association, http://abcaonline.org)
- Blockchain Association (http://theblockchainassociation.org)
- Blockchain Alliance (http://blockchainalliance.org)
- European Blockchain Association (http://europeanblockchainassociation.org)

Several portals and directories also share a wealth of information on these topics:

Coin Telegraph (http://cointelegraph.com) Offers news and research on the cryptocurrency markets. Ideal for tracking the growth of crypto payments in both the digital and physical worlds.
Decrypt (http://decrypt.co) A portal focused on news and reviews about digital coins and digital collections.

Messari (`http://messari.io`) A research destination about all things blockchain. It boasts a number of ecosystem maps, applied to identifying key players in NFTs, decentralized finance (DeFi), and other decentralized business themes.

Milk Road (`http://milkroad.com`) A straight-to-the point newsletter about Web3 and blockchain, specially aimed at non-initiates.

You can also find new Web3 decentralized applications (dapps) at Dappradar.com or TheDapplist.com.

Spatial Web

Besides the book with this exact name, The `SpatialWebFoundation.org` is the go-to source for more in-depth knowledge about the principles, protocols, and news on the Spatial Web model.

5G, IoT, and Edge Computing

There likely are going to be many metaverse-themed talks and panels at every industry event. If you want to deep-dive into the topic of IoT, the following events can give you a deeper understanding:

- BDVA (Big Data Value Association, `http://bdva.eu`)
- euRobotics (European Robotics Association, `http://eu-robotics.net`)
- Internet of Things Directory (`http://iot-directory.com`)
- IoT Tech Expo (`http://iottechexpo.com`)
- IoT Tech News (`http://iottechnews.com`)

Regarding 5G, the news sites tag the news related to 5G and 6G in such a way that you can quickly search or enter a filtered news section dedicated to the topic. Examples are:

- Economic Times – India (`http://Economictimes.indiatimes.com/topic/5g-network`)
- Euronews (`http://euronews.com/tag/5g`)
- Wired (`http://wired.com/tag/5g`)

Following the 6G discussion is also key to getting insights into the next wave of telecommunications that will hit us around the end of this decade. To become involved, check out:

- 6G Industry Association (http://6g-ia.eu)
- One 6G Workgroups (http://One6G.org/working-groups)

Digital Twins

Big Tech is already offering several commercial solutions for digital twins technology, such as Azure Digital Twins or Amazon IoT TwinMaker. You'll find a comprehensive directory of service providers at the Digital Twin Consortium (http://digitaltwin consortium.org/dtcmembersearch) and details on workgroups focused on advancing digital twins. In addition to the companies building digital twins, many research projects are focusing on this technology. For instance, Neuro Twin (http://neurotwin.eu) is diving into the possibilities opened by digital twins of our brains. There are also public entities that operate research programs, like the DT Hub (http://DigitalTwinHub.co.uk) or the OnePlanet Research Center (http://oneplanetresearch.nl).

Cloud Computing

Beyond the Big Tech providers, a full list of cloud service companies are listed at Cloud Harmony (http://cloudharmony.com/ directory). You can also join the interoperability debate at the Open AR Cloud (http://openarcloud.org). Also, look to GeoPoses (geographically anchored poses, with location and orientation in the metaverse) to understand how to extract the full functionality of an AR cloud.

XR

The following events usually gather many of the best and brightest thinkers in the extended reality (XR) fields:

- Augmented World Expo (http://awexr.com)
- CES (Consumer Electronics Show, http://ces.tech)

- Immerse Global Summit (http://immerseglobalnetwork.com)
- La Biennale di Venezia (Venice VR Expanded; http://labiennale .org)
- Laval Virtual (http://laval-virtual.com)
- NFT.NYC (http://nft.nyc)
- Stereopsia (http://stereopsia.com)
- South by Southwest (SXSW) (http://sxsw.com)
- VR Days (http://vrdays.co)

Meetups within the emerging tech industry can be extremely high quality. For example, in New York City you can try ARKit, AWE Nite, and NYAR.

If you like art or movies, get tickets to the immersive or VR parts of film festivals (for example, Tribeca, Cannes, Venice, and Sundance). Fair warning: many pieces showcase dark and depressing themes. Still look to see if you can figure out how some innovations in the technology showcased might be able to help your business.

If there's not a festival nearby, you also might give one of the VR locations that have popped up in malls a try. Look beyond the zombie shooters, and try experimenting with various one-player and multiplayer games. Note how the experience changes.

A wide variety of media sources cover XR and headset-related news, including:

- AR Post (http://arpost.co): Zoomed in on augmented reality market players and their impact, this portal showcases not just news articles but also expert advice and insights.
- Auganix (http://auganix.org): XR news portal with a cross-Atlantic team, connecting Vancouver and Bristol. They report news and publish their own market analysis articles, with a nifty filter tool that lets you organize them by industry, market, and geography.
- Company newsletters: Depending on the topics you are interested in, you can sign up for the newsletters from some of the top companies in the space, such as HTC, Nvidia, and Unity. You'll be surprised at how much the trade publications can miss about what's happening.
- *Forbes* (http://forbes.com): Many industry leaders contribute articles to the online publication. Some are lightly disguised sales

tools, but others have some of the most updated information available.

- Immersive Wire (http://immersivewire.com): A biweekly newsletter that curates content and offers industry analysis.
- XR Today (http://xrtoday.com): Started as a portal dedicated solely to news in the virtual and AR space, XR Today slowly migrated to metaverse topics.

Blogs from industry experts like Antony Vitillo (http:// skarredghost.com) can also provide different perspectives of the industry from the consumer standpoint.

- ARtillery Intelligence: The organization publishes detailed reports on the XR field and its vertical impacts across the market. ARtillery also operates its own blog, AR Insider (http:// ARInsider.co)
- CB Insights: Known for publishing metaverse ecosystem maps that include the major players of the industry

Several XR associations showcase the breadth and depth of industry applications:

- The AREA (Augmented Reality for Enterprises Alliance; http:// thearea.org)
- Euromersive (http://euromersive.eu)
- VR/AR Association (http://thevrara.com)
- XR4Europe (http://xr4europe.eu)
- XR Association (http://xra.org)

Headsets and Glasses

The ever-increasing number of XR glasses can be found within the directory at VR Compare (http://vr-compare.com). There are some open source headset projects available as well. They are blueprints for creators to build their own head-mounted displays (HMDs), which can be useful for prototyping and educational purposes.

- OpenAR (http://openar.fi): Professor Jyrki Saarinen from the Institute of Photonics at the University of Eastern Finland, of OpenAR says, "To speed up the development of AR technology, we wanted to design affordable AR glasses that are accessible to everyone—just like was done with virtual glasses made of cardboard and a smartphone some 10 years ago. With the OpenAR glasses, anyone can explore the opportunities of augmented reality. Throughout the process, the aim has been to keep the costs very low."[12] These DIY glasses can only support simpler applications, but the open source community of tinkerers and educators building on top of the OpenAR concept will add to this inventory over time.
- OpenBCI (http://openbci.com): OpenBCI creates open source tools to interface our brains with computers, but not necessarily by implementing chips in our brains. Its latest project is called Galea. It gathers EEG, eye-tracking, and other biofeedback information that sends commands to virtual and augmented reality experiences just with the power of your thoughts.
- Relativty (www.relativty.com): Maxim Perumal and Gabriel Combe built a headset from scratch when they were 15 years old, for the simple reason that they couldn't afford to buy one. That effort became Relativty, an open source VR headset that garnered a community on its own merit and is mostly used by hackers and tinkerers.

Artificial Intelligence and Machine Learning

An increasing number of AI tools are popping up in the market. Generative AI tools like Midjourney (http://discord.com/invite/midjourney) and DALL-E (http://openai.com/dall-e-2) gives the nondeveloper the opportunity to use AI to generate new online content. Write on a prompt the details of an image and the AI generates it—hence it is called generative AI. You can even find tools to better communicate with AIs at Prompter (http://prompterguide.com) and Promptomania (http://promptomania.com).

It is set to disrupt several professions in design, sound and in the creative arts. If you're looking to generate videos from text, head out to Runway ML (http://runwayml.com). The same happens at Copy.ai or Jasper.ai when you want to generate longer texts and articles from a single sentence.

There are other kinds of AI tools available. Synthesia (Synthesia.io) is an AI-powered video creator for brands that leverages virtual beings to your benefit. Aiva (http://aiva.ai) or Soundraw (http://soundraw.io) lets AI generate music themes for your projects.

Both Big Tech like Google (http://Google.ai) and organizations like the open source Stability AI (http://stability.ai) promise to deliver even more.

AI associations can prove valuable as well to keep up to date with the trends. They not only list AI companies operating, but also keep tabs on the main opportunities and challenges within the industry:

- AAAI (Association for the Advancement of Artificial Intelligence, http://aaai.org)
- EurAI (European Association for Artificial Intelligence, http://eurai.org)
- Global Artificial Intelligence Association (http://globalai.life)

Woven Together

There are many ways that you can stay up-to-date on the constantly evolving and innovative metaverse ecosystem. Follow who is winning the awards in the space. It's an indicator of what technologies are being put to creative use and what technologies the judges have found interesting and/or innovative. Awards are given out at most of the festivals, as well as at trade events, which award the best developers in the business. Often companies host their own events to see what is possible with their new technologies. Look toward hackathons, too. Just remember that the winners aren't creating finished products but are showcasing what is possible with a few days of development.

If you would like to kick off something within your organization, there are many approaches you can take since there are many technologies that serve as entry points. You can look at some open source development consortiums and websites as a potential starting point. These can give your technical team a quick way to start experimenting:

- Ethereal Engine (http://etherealengine.org): Formerly known as XR Engine, it gathers several of the building blocks that shape the metaverse in one open source package: a blockchain ready to enable identity, currency, and ownership to every user; AR clouds that enable spaces to become filled with 3D models, videos, and animations; and tools to easily integrate your digital humans, be they assistants or avatars.
- Mozilla Hubs (http://hubs.mozilla.com): This platform is an open source, web VR world that can be interconnected and enable social VR experiences. There are several templates for your world, or choose to upload and edit elements to create a personalized experience through its content administration tool, Spoke.
- Open Geospatial Consortium (http://osgeo.org): Although this standard is already used by a number of platforms, like the Open AR Cloud, you'll find a lot of the discussion happens under the auspices of this membership-based organization.
- Vircadia (http://vircadia.com): Mainly an engine to build virtual reality worlds and connect them over the web. Its decentralized structure and the fact that it's open source allows for a quicker deployment of VR internal solutions, like corporate congresses, demonstration worlds, or even training worlds for professional teams.

The Race Has Begun

Definitely try the most diverse number of games on the most number of platforms to experience firsthand many of the terms we've described. Even if you aren't a gamer, understanding what is possible within a game will help give you a frame of reference.

Follow the gaming industry as well. Game news is updated periodically in specialized portals, like Gamespot (http://gamespot.com), IGN (http://ign.com), and PC Gamer (http://pcgamer.com). There are specific sources if you're looking for more in-depth knowledge on VR gaming (e.g., http://UploadVR.com) or on play-to-earn games (http://blockchaingamer.biz/news). Look to many industry experts as well. For gaming and the metaverse, check out Jon Radoff's Medium posts (http://jradoff.medium.com) or one of his books.

New Rules

For a comprehensive list of organizations focused on the metaverse or different parts of it, look to the Metaverse Standards Forum (http://metaverse-standards.org), where you can browse the members' directory and explore each one's causes and points of view. There's also the Open Metaverse Alliance for Web3 (http://oma3.org), which gathers the most relevant Web3 metaverse platform creators to propel interoperability of digital land, assets, and services in their platforms. Regarding creators, there are several directories of metaverse-related service providers like the Immersive Directory (http://immersivedirectory.com) and the VRARA Directory (http://thevrara.com/directory). However, if you're looking to tap into marketplaces where you can see the work and directly hire immersive tech artists, head to platforms like CatchAR (http://catchar.io) and Crosscreators (http://crosscreators.com).

On the crypto side, OpenSea (http://opensea.io) is still the largest NFT marketplace, where you can find collectibles and digital art projects minted by a vast number of artists registered on the platform. Go on and browse through the immense amount of work available.

Finally, to explore the user's interface transformation and the expansion of new design needs in our online experience, the Internet of Senses Institute (http://internetofsenses.com) can provide interesting insights. Chris Valentine, Founder and CEO of the IOSI, shared with us its main purpose: "We live our day-to-day using all five of our sense (taste, touch, smell, sight and hearing) in one form or another but currently with technology we are mostly using just two (sight and hearing). With the Internet of Senses Institute we are working toward a world where all our senses, with the enhancement of technology, will impact our daily live from work to play with the understanding we can turn off that technology when we need to. It is with this enhanced sensory experience are real world will have a greater level of engagement as it will impact every facet of our life."[13]

A Great Reset

The United Nations list of Sustainable Development Goals (http://sdgs.un.org) is available on the U.N. website. Now there's even an award called the SDG Metaverse Prize (http://sdgmetaverseprize.org) that celebrates responsible and sustainable metaverse projects. You could also consider joining the Metaverse Observatory at http://metaobs.io. The organization studies ways to navigate the climate crisis via new business models, in addition to mapping the metaverse services as a whole.

Doing Business in the Metaverse

If you haven't already, try creating your wallet: head to Metamask (http://metamask.io) or Coinbase (http://coinbase.com) and be ready within the hour. From there, log in to digital art marketplaces like Rarible or OpenSea or metaverse platforms like The Sandbox or Decentraland.

As for finding job opportunities within the metaverse, there are specific portals like Cryptocurrency Jobs (http://cryptocurrencyjobs.co) or http://web3.career, in addition to the more traditional platforms. Several professionals are creating their own resumés on the chain and issuing tokens at www.Talentprotocol.com so that everyone can literally invest in the talent of the future.

Digitalizing Humans

Most gaming and VR platforms offer avatar creation tools for their own service. But to develop an interoperable one, check out the services provided by Ready Player Me (http://readyplayer.me), Didimo (http://didimo.co), or Liquid Avatar (http://liquidavatar.com).

Regarding virtual beings, you can start by creating your own chatbots with technology like Microsoft's Power Virtual Agents (http://powervirtualagents.microsoft.com). Try generating an AI-powered version at Replika (http://replika.com) that you can use as an empathetic chat friend. But be wary of giving away your private, sometimes intimate, data to a private company. Make sure you are comfortable with the terms and conditions.

Metaverse Markets

Of course, each professional association we've listed will develop knowledge and, eventually, share the metaverse market experiences of its members in the form of workshops, events, or even reports. brainXchange (http://brainxchange.ca) has a directory of use cases in XR, and the Blockchain Council (http://blockchain-council.org) has Web3 use cases, business cases, and resources.

Interoperability

Although the metaverse technologies are still evolving, there are ways to attain this interoperability. The following are a couple of communities that support openness of the technology being built:

- Open AR Cloud (http://openarcloud.org): A global nonprofit organization with the mission to drive open technology standards in AR Clouds, enabling interoperability between virtual and augmented worlds

- Open Metaverse Interoperability Group (http://omigroup.org): A community of business professionals and individuals, ranging from artists to corporate decision-makers, working toward creating an interoperable metaverse

Privacy and Safety

Several institutions are creating the necessary guardrails for the metaverse:

- IEEE Global Initiative on Ethics of Extended Reality (http:// standards.ieee.org/industry-connections/ethics-extended-reality): The Institute of Electrical and Electronics Engineers (IEEE) describes itself as the "world's largest technical professional organization dedicated to advancing technology for the benefit of humanity." Co-chaired by North American podcaster and journalist Kent Bye, who has run his "Voices of VR" podcast since 2014, this global workgroup on ethics in XR is focused on identifying best practices and worst practices in these matters, as well as creating a standard for ethical issues related to XR technologies. It relies on volunteers from a wide spectrum of large and small corporate participants, researchers in academia, as well as government agency officers.
- MKAI (http://mkai.org): MKAI stands for Morality and Knowledge in Artificial Intelligence. Through a community of experts, the organization helps governments, universities, colleges, and corporate players identify potential risks and harms in the different applications of AI.
- XR Guild (http://xrguild.org): Founded by veteran developers, XR Guild is a community of concerned metaverse experts aiming to promote a healthy discussion of ethical practice in businesses across the metaverse marketplace.
- XRSI (http://xrsi.org): The XR Safety Initiative is a volunteer-based organization that is dedicated to creating standards to protect privacy and safety in immersive worlds. They have created several tools to adopt a safety- and privacy-oriented behavior model, both personally as well as professionally.

They have created several tools to adopt a safety- and privacy-oriented behavior, for both organizations and individuals. Kavya Pearlman, founder and CEO of XRSI, believes that safety starts with experimentation. "Don't be afraid to take a shot at new things and ask for a spot at various tables, especially if you are a minority. (. . .) While scary, the time we live in is also the most exciting one to build solutions in the cybersecurity domain and break or hack things with purpose."[14]

All of these organizations participate in specific events, like the Metaverse Safety Week (http://metaversesafetyweek.org), where new and upcoming challenges are continuously discussed. Also, you may come across internal workgroups that address child safety or medical data sharing.

Rights and Regulations

There is already a first legal directory to the metaverse: LawCity (http://lawcity.com), which gathers the references of many law firms with a metaverse practice. Of course, self-regulation and industry regulation will become equally important sources of information and engagement in this field. Professional associations, bar order websites, and the Metaverse Standards Forum (http://metaverse-standards.org) will help you explore the many layers of this topic.

New Humanity

Keeping up with the posthuman trend is important, independently of you wanting to become involved or disagreeing with the fundamental principles of it. The PostHumans (http://posthumans.org) portal can help you with news and updates on posthumanist activity, and Critical Post-Humanism (http://criticalposthumanism.net) is a peer-reviewed directory of online thought-leadership stories and articles on posthumanism.

Building the Metaverse

Creating small-scale experiences can help you to quickly educate others about your vision. Check out tools like ShapesXR (http://Shapesxr.com) or just go through the options at XR Prototyping (http://xr-prototyping.org). If you're looking to create a scan of your room, install the Matterport or RoomScan app, and you'll be able to replicate it both on screen and in VR headsets. If you own a 360 camera, editors like Cyango (https://cyango.com) or Veer Editor (http://veer.tv/veer-editor) can certainly help in setting up the experience.

Next Steps

Now, it's on you. You have the tools, the references, and the insights to start your journey. You can see past some of the hype, plan for the future possibilities, and confront and address the challenges ahead. From the moment of the publishing of this book, there is the high likelihood that new innovations will shift the market once again, so it's imperative to leverage the principles learned here and keep learning. Ask questions. Look beyond the exaggerated hyperbole and emerging tech pundits. Do your best to avoid the mistakes of the past.

Take an active stance in bringing others, everyone to build the metaverse. It isn't here (yet), but we all are responsible for what it will be, regardless of our titles or coding abilities. It will change all aspects of society and that's why we need to have everyone onboard on this one, contributing with what it can be. We need both business and social development goals. We can build something of value for investors, shareholders, but that will be meaningless without building for our family, friends, colleagues, industry and for the future of us all.

We are on the edge of a whole new way of life brought about by the metaverse. With this book, you've walked through and past some of the most difficult topics. Now, it's your time to take your own path and begin your new role as an informed, balanced future metaverse leader.

Notes

1. Danica Lo, "Here's why tech workers are fleeing FAANG for Web3." *Fast Company*, April 8, 2022. www.fastcompany.com/90739257/leaving-faang-web3-jobs.

2. Penelope Pratt, "Our latest Technology Vision invites you to meet me in the metaverse." *Accenture* (blog), May 9, 2022. www.accenture.com/us-en/blogs/how-accenture-does-it/our-latest-technology-vision-invites-you-to-meet-me-in-the-metaverse

3. Jean-François Bobier, Tibor Merey, Stephen Robnett, Michael Grebe, Jimmy Feng, Benjamin Rehberg, Kristi Woolsey, and Joel Hazan, "The corporate hitchhiker's guide to the metaverse." *BCG*, April 2022. http://web-assets.bcg.com/85/18/a876a489473c98a41f406aa5ddfb/bcg-the-corporate-hitchhikers-guide-to-the-metaverse-27-apr-2022.pdf

4. Andrew Blau, Lauren Lubetsky, Amadin J. Enobakhare, Michael W. Walker, and Aiden Shiller, "A whole new world? Exploring the meta verse and what it could mean for you." *Deloitte*, April 2022. www2.deloitte.com/content/dam/Deloitte/us/Documents/technology/us-ai-institute-what-is-the-metaverse-new.pdf

5. EY, "Journey to the center of the metaverse." *EY* (undated). https://assets.ey.com/content/dam/ey-sites/ey-com/en_gl/topics/telecommunications/ey-metaverse-for-telcos.pdf

6. KPMG, "Go boldly, not blindly, into the metaverse." *KPMG*, Spring 2022. http://advisory.kpmg.us/articles/2022/consumer-pulse-metaverse.html

7. McKinsey & Company, "Value creation in the metaverse." *McKinsey & Company*, June 2022. www.mckinsey.com/business-functions/growth-marketing-and-sales/our-insights/value-creation-in-the-metaverse

8. PwC, "Demystifying the metaverse." PWC (undated). www.pwc.com/us/en/tech-effect/emerging-tech/demystifying-the-metaverse.html

9. J. P. Morgan, "Opportunities in the metaverse." J. P. Morgan (undated). www.jpmorgan.com/content/dam/jpm/treasury-services/documents/opportunities-in-the-metaverse.pdf

10. Media.Monks, "Report: Make sense of the metaverse." *Media.Monks* (undated). https://media.monks.com/articles/report-make-sense-metaverse

11. Wunderman Thompson Intelligence, "Into the metaverse and beyond." *Wunderman Thompson*, May 4, 2022. www.wundermanthompson.com/insight/new-realities-into-the-metaverse-and-beyond

12. Jani Vallirinne, "The world's first freeware AR website introduces DIY AR glasses: The OpenAR glasses." OpenAR, January 24, 2022. https://openar.fi/the-worlds-first-freeware-ar-website-introduces-diy-ar-glasses-the-openar-glasses

13. Personal communication, September, 2022.

14. https://insightssuccess.com/kavya-pearlman-a-cyber-guardian-for-extended-reality

Index